CHARLES N. GENNO and HEINZ WETZEL are both members of the Department of German at the University of Toronto.

This collection of eight essays in honour of the distinguished Canadian Germanist G.W. Field treats themes in German narrative prose of the First World War, the pre-war era, and the earliest days of the Weimar Republic. The aim of the book is not to present a comprehensive study of the field, but rather to shed new light on specific problems.

The essays are organized in the historical sequence of the events and situations to which they are related. The topics include discussions of the concept of war as presented by Robert Musil in *Der Mann ohne Eigenschaften*; the treatment of war as a catalyst by the Expressionist writers Carl Sternheim and Leonhard Frank; the preservation of values in the face of war as dealt with in Hesse's *Demian*; and an exploration of the effects of war on individual and social values in the works of Salomo Friedländer and Alfred Döblin. An essay on H.G. Wells' *Mr Britling Sees It Through* helps to clarify the ways in which the reaction of German writers to the war may be viewed as specifically German by providing an outsider's point of view. The final chapter, a survey of the most recent literature on the topic, shows how much World War 1 lives on in the minds of German writers as the great turning point in German political and cultural history.

George Wallis Field

The First World War in German Narrative Prose

Essays in honour of George Wallis Field

Edited by Charles N. Genno and Heinz Wetzel

UNIVERSITY OF TORONTO PRESS
Toronto   Buffalo   London

© University of Toronto Press 1980
Toronto Buffalo London
Reprinted in paperback 2017
ISBN 978-0-8020-5490-6 (cloth)
ISBN 978-1-4875-9894-5 (paper)

Library of Congress Cataloging in Publication Data
Main entry under title:

The First World War in German narrative prose.

"Publications of George Wallis Field": pp. 159–61
Includes index.
Contents: Genno, C.N. The anatomy of pre-war
society in Robert Musil's *Der Mann ohne Eigenschaften*.
– Dierick, A.P. Two representative expressionist
responses to the challenge of the First World War. –
John, D. The *Sperber* in Hesse's *Demian*. – Wetzel, H.
War and the destruction of moral principles in Arnold
Zweig's *Der Streit um den Sergeanten Grischa* and
Erziehung vor Verdun. [etc.]
1. German fiction – 20th century – History and
criticism – Addresses, essays, lectures.   2. Euro-
pean War, 1914–1918 – Literature and the war – Ad-
dresses, essays, lectures.   3. Field, George Wallis –
Addresses, essays, lectures.   I. Field, George
Wallis.   II. Genno, Charles N., 1934–   III. Wet-
zel, Heinz, 1935–
PT405.F5   833'.009'3   79-26625
ISBN 978-0-8020-5490-6 (bound).   ISBN 978-1-4875-9894-5 (pbk.)

This book has been published with the help of grants from
the Canadian Federation for the Humanities, using funds provided by
the Social Sciences and Humanities Research Council of Canada, and from
Victoria College, University of Toronto, and the Publications Fund
of University of Toronto Press.

Contents

Preface

This book is dedicated to Professor George Wallis Field, who, in his long years of service to our discipline, has won the respect and admiration of his students and his colleagues for his distinguished scholarship, his inspiring teaching, and his humanitarianism. Those of us who have had the privilege of either working with him or studying under him – in some cases both – have been impressed primarily by his acute intellect, his wry humour, and his uncompromising integrity.

The contribution that Wally Field has made to the development of German studies in Ontario since he joined the Department of German at Victoria College, University of Toronto, in 1948 is incalculable. Students whom he has introduced to German language and literature have experienced his personal interest in their intellectual development. Inspired by his example, many of them have committed themselves to the study of German literature, and are now teaching at high schools, colleges, and universities throughout Canada and the United States, as well as abroad. He was a founding member of both the Canadian Association of University Teachers of German and the Ontario Association of Teachers of German, and has served on the executives of many professional organizations. From 1966 to 1974 he was the chairman of the Department of German at Victoria College. The list of his publications on various aspects of German literature from the eighteenth century to the present is, as his bibliography at the end of this volume indicates, formidable. His scholarly reputation among Germanists at home and abroad rests, however, largely on his books and articles on Hermann Hesse.

Wally Field was born in Cobourg, Ontario, in March 1914, several months before the two pistol shots signalling the onslaught of the First World War were fired at Sarajevo. His childhood years were spent in

Cobourg, close to the original site of Victoria College, which had been founded there in 1836 with Egerton Ryerson, the architect of the Ontario secondary-school system, as its first principal. After a distinguished history in Cobourg, the college moved to Toronto when federation with the University of Toronto took place in 1892. Since several members of his family had earlier been associated with Victoria College, it is not surprising that Wally Field chose to pursue his study of modern languages and literatures there. In 1935 he received his Bachelor of Arts degree, and was awarded the Regents' Gold Medal in German and French.

He was a young man of twenty-five, teaching in the Far East, when the Second World War broke out. From 1940 to 1945 he served with the British and Canadian armies. After the war he continued his association with the military and attained the rank of lieutenant-colonel.

Most of the literature discussed in the present volume was written during Wally Field's formative years. His valuable contributions to Hesse scholarship bear witness to the interest that he took in contemporary literature, an interest that he never abandoned, as students whom he has taught in recent years well know. It is on these two counts that it seems appropriate to dedicate to him a book that is devoted to studies on the reflection of the First World War in German narrative prose.

Our aim has been to shed some new light on specific problems rather than to give a comprehensive and systematic account of German prose fiction on the First World War. We could have organized the volume around the most prominent names of the period, such as Joseph Roth, Ernst Jünger, and Thomas Mann with his *Zauberberg*, but in many cases the most pertinent aspect of their works have already been subjected to detailed investigation. We chose instead to ask friends and colleagues of Wally Field to contribute essays on topics of interest and significance to them that would make a fresh contribution to scholarship on the theme of this volume.

We have arranged the individual articles roughly in the historical sequence of events and situations to which the works they discuss are related. Thus, an inquiry into the concept of war, into its causes and origins as they appear in Robert Musil's *Der Mann ohne Eigenschaften*, is the topic of the first essay in the volume. It shows the extent to which Musil considered war to be a result of the moral, spiritual, social, and political decay of Austria during the decades preceding Sarajevo. Attempts to hold on to mere conventions, while the substance of life within the empire was eroded, appeared more and more grotesque, and the empire itself seemed doomed to destruction.

The second paper, by A.P. Dierick, concentrates on two authors who are generally associated with the expressionist movement, Carl Sternheim and Leonhard Frank, and on their treatment of war as something like a catalyst that helps to intensify and make visible conflicts that these authors also found rooted in pre-war German society. However, instead of presenting an extensive panorama containing the various facets of such conflicts, Sternheim and Frank concentrate on the fates of individuals who are confronted with the demands of social norms and ideals that have become as excessive and intolerable as they are obsolete. The protagonists in these stories can conform to them only by relinquishing their individuality; as an alternative they can rebel and risk being crushed. Here war and the perversion of the collective consciousness are presented as threats to values that, although they are never identified in the stories, seem to be embodied in the very principle of individuality. The intensity of the threat to the individual by a society preparing for and waging war was felt to be extreme by Sternheim and Frank. This is evident in the exalted style and the sometimes unlikely plots of their stories.

David John, in his essay on the enigmatic *Sperber*, the central symbol of Hesse's novel *Demian*, addresses himself to the question of possible values that the individual may preserve intact in the face of war. Hesse's novel very strongly implies the existence of such values, and the development of Sinclair and of Demian seems to be geared to the recognition and acceptance of them. However, since these values remain quite obscure, a close examination of the *Sperber* symbol yields some much-needed enlightenment. The conclusions that David John draws in his very careful examination cannot easily be put in a nutshell; one may still ask whether the fascination of the book, which generations of adolescents have felt, is due to the fact that these values can only be partly discerned and that, to a large extent, they remain enigmatic.

The novels by Arnold Zweig that are the topic of the next article are concerned with active service in the First World War, and its effects on individuals. Since these novels are largely autobiographical, Zweig's perspective differs from that of the other authors. To them war was an abstract phenomenon, a decisive event in the political and spiritual development of Europe. Zweig felt its brutal reality more immediately. He concluded that this war ended the development of European civilization, and that it destroyed the moral tenets on which that civilization was based. In his novels he attempts to find, through his main characters, a suitable reaction to this experience. One of his most impressive characters resigns; another commits suicide; a third tries to adapt in a Nietzschean manner to the laws of the jungle that prevail in wartime. But Zweig increasingly comes to accept the spontaneous solidarity and the kindness of the common people as the only values that can withstand the general destruction of morality. On this basis, he finally comes to embrace socialism as the theory that, in his view, is built on these values.

Salomo Friedlaender, the critic and satirist whose reaction to the general disillusionment and disorientation of the post-war period Manfred Kuxdorf examines, sought refuge from the catastrophe of the First World War by clinging to the eighteenth-century ethic of reason, more particularly to Kant's categorical imperative, and by denouncing any attempt to make the present chaos appear tolerable, which, to his mind, Remarque had done in his sentimental account of trench warfare.

Alfred Döblin, deeply marked by the experience of the war and by the general destruction of humane values, found a new orientation in 1941, after his conversion to Catholicism. Anthony W. Riley shows in his article on *Karl und Rosa*, which is the final volume of Döblin's trilogy *November 1918*, that the author came to see the chaotic events of 1918 from his newly gained Christian perspective. The very fact that he felt the need to explain those past events, the end of the First World War, in terms of his new faith bears witness to the deep and lasting impact that this final breakdown of the old order must have had on Döblin at the time. From the harmony that prevails, as Anthony Riley points out, in the aesthetic arrangement of *Karl und Rosa*, it may be concluded that it was only after his conversion that he came to terms with his direct experience of war as a young medical officer from 1915 to 1918.

When Colin Butler suggested that he might contribute an article on a subject outside the area on which we had decided to concentrate, we first hesitated, but we soon became aware of the possibility that the resulting juxtaposition might help to clarify the ways in which the reaction of German writers to the war may be viewed as specifically or typically German. Butler's discussion of H.G. Wells's *Mr Britling Sees It Through*, and especially the biographical information on Wells that he provides, bring out a reaction to the war by this English writer that differs considerably from what we have been able to observe in German writers. In Wells's England, social tensions that had existed since the nineteenth century had intensified by 1914, as they had in Germany, and, like the Germans, the British, according to Wells, no longer felt secure within their long-established political, economic, and social system; traditional religious convictions no longer went unquestioned as they had in the past. And yet, while Wells carefully notes this development, his world is not shattered. Tradition still holds; adjustments can and must be made, and rather than seeking a radically new order, all efforts seem directed at reforming the old order. Where German authors reflect a complete breakdown of tradition and hence tend to feel a need for something radically new, not really knowing what this might be, there is no such complete loss of orientation in the world of H.G. Wells. The general conclusion that suggests itself can hardly be drawn on such a narrow basis, but the indications are most interesting.

It was our good fortune that Hermann Boeschenstein, Wally Field's teacher and truly a father-figure in Canadian *Germanistik*, provided a survey of the most recent literature on our topic. Certainly, his article shows how much the First World War lives on in the minds of German writers as the great turning-point in German political and cultural history. But perhaps even more important is the fact that none of us could have a better knowledge of this than Hermann Boeschenstein, who was himself a young man at the time. His stimulating discussion of the books and memoirs on the First World War that appeared after 1945 is not only borne up by his subtle humour, but is also leavened by his deep humanity and by his empathy for the literature and authors of the period.

The index to this volume was compiled by Barry W.K. Joe.

We trust that this collective effort will contribute to knowledge of the literature of this period, and will bring Wally Field some small pleasure.

C.N.G.

H.W.

THE FIRST WORLD WAR
IN GERMAN NARRATIVE PROSE

CHARLES N. GENNO

The Anatomy of Pre-War Society in Robert Musil's *Der Mann ohne Eigenschaften*

Since Adolf Frisé's first edition of Musil's masterpiece *Der Mann ohne Eigenschaften* appeared in 1952, ten years after the author's untimely death, it has been widely criticized. Most of the controversy has centred on Frisé's assumptions about Musil's intention for the conclusion. Book one of the novel, consisting of 123 chapters, was published in 1930. The opening section of book two, comprising an additional thirty-eight chapters, appeared three years later. From then until Musil's death no new material was published. The voluminous *Nachlass*, embracing copious notes, withdrawn proof-sheets, fair copies, and sketches, has proved to be a rich source for scholarly investigation.

How did Musil intend to end his novel, according to the critics? A cursory survey brings one to the conclusion *quot homines tot sententiae*; nevertheless, two larger factions are discernible. In the one camp are Frisé and his supporters (including Wolfdietrich Rasch, Dieter Kühn, and Helmut Arntzen); in the other, Ernst Kaiser and Eithne Wilkins and theirs (among them, Wilhelm Bausinger, Cesare Cases, and Wilhelm Braun). In their book *Robert Musil. Eine Einführung in das Werk* Kaiser and Wilkins maintain that Musil in the last few years of his life had lost interest in and sympathy with a number of the earlier themes of the novel. They argue, 'Der gealterte Musil dieser Jahre hatte innerlich nur mehr wenig mit dem noch jungen ungeduldigen Mann zu tun, der 1930 den ersten Band des *Mann ohne Eigenschaften* veröffentlicht hatte.'[1] In particular they dispute the importance of the Collateral Campaign in the overall concept of the novel, and the inclusion by Frisé of the chapter 'Reise ins Paradies,' which marks both the culmination of and the turning-point in Ulrich's relationship with his sister Agathe. The *Geschwisterliebe* theme, they believe, was gradually to become the focal point in the novel as the theme of the

Collateral Campaign diminished in importance. They claim, 'In jedem Falle kommt der Geschichte von der "Parallelaktion" nicht die zentrale Bedeutung zu, die ihr oft beigemessen wird, was übrigens aus dem Roman selbst hervorgeht, in welchem diese österreichische Geschichte im gleichen Masse in den Hintergrund rückt, in welchem die Geschichte Ulrichs und Agathes an Bedeutung zunimmt.'[2]

Although their hypothesis has generated much dialogue about Musil's ultimate design for the novel, it is another rather startling statement in their book that has provided the impetus for this paper. Not only do Kaiser and Wilkins minimize the importance of the Collateral Campaign, but they also question whether Musil intended to adhere to his original plan to have the novel end with the outbreak of the First World War. They claim, 'Der Roman endet *nicht* in Unheil und Katastrophe, und, wie sich in späteren Notizen andeutet, möglicherweise auch nicht mit dem ersten Weltkrieg.'[3]

Nowhere in Musil's later notes is there convincing evidence to support their assertion that he considered abandoning his earlier intention to conclude the novel with the advent of war. His major problem was not whether to incorporate the theme of war into the novel, but rather how to relate it in a meaningful way to the fate of his young protagonist, Ulrich. As late as 1926 he spoke of having Ulrich become a spy as a protest against a society that allowed the intellectually weakest to enjoy the greatest opportunities.[4] By 1932, however, as his note 'Zum Aufbau des zweiten Teils von Band II im Groben' indicates, he had already scrapped this idea in favour of a less radical solution.[5]

Although Musil did, of course, make various minor thematic changes in the novel as it slowly evolved in the 1920s and 1930s, he never lost sight of his major themes: the disintegration of the Austro-Hungarian Empire, the outbreak of the First World War, and Ulrich's efforts to find 'das rechte Leben' in the midst of these momentous historical developments (255). While he was still in the employ of the Austrian Ministry of War in 1920, Musil expressed in a diary entry his determination to comprehend the holocaust that he and millions of other Europeans had just experienced: 'Man darf auch der Frage nicht aus dem Weg gehen, was dieser Krieg eigentlich war. Man kann nicht weggehen, wie wenn man von einem Rausch eben aufgestanden wäre, wo Millionen Menschen ihre Nächsten verloren haben oder ihre Existenz.'[6] The essays that he wrote in the early 1920s were almost exclusively devoted to an analysis of the war, its causes, and its effects. Much of the spadework for *Der Mann ohne Eigenschaften* was done in these essays.

Although Musil had initially shown some enthusiasm for the war and had publicly endorsed it in his essay 'Europäertum, Krieg, Deutschtum,' published in *Die Neue Rundschau* in September 1914, he came out of it a well-decorated hero, but a confirmed pacifist.[6] In 'Der Anschluss an Deutschland,' which appeared in the same journal five years later, he openly criticized the earlier growth of anti-Semitism and nationalism among German-speaking Austrians as powerful determinants of the war.

Musil's three essays 'Der Anschluss an Deutschland,' 'Die Nation als Ideal und Wirklichkeit,' and, in particular, 'Das hilflose Europa' contain *in nucleo* the basic social, political, historical, and philosophical ideas later expounded by him and his characters in *Der Mann ohne Eigenschaften*. In 'Der Anschluss an Deutschland' he also assailed the notion of 'Austrian culture' in pre-war society as a myth, invented by German-speaking Austrians who did not want to identify themselves with 'German culture.' He described the Austrian state as a disunified and spiritless corpse that was unwilling to accept its own demise.

In 'Die Nation als Ideal und Wirklichkeit,' written in 1921, Musil attacked the emergence of 'Volksidealismus' as an insidious racist threat, and condemned war as a specious means of creating a mystical sense of communion among people. In 'Das hilflose Europa,' written the following year, he attempted to diagnose the cause of the war by first placing it in a larger, teleological framework. After explaining his own philosophy of history and progress, he concluded that his own era could best be described as 'ein babylonisches Narrenhaus.'[7] As a possible remedy for its lunacy he proposed the same exactitude-soul synthesis that Ulrich later recommends to Graf Leinsdorf in *Der Mann ohne Eigenschaften*.

Musil viewed history as essentially static. For his theories on progress he found support in the writings of one of his favourite authors, Ralph Waldo Emerson. In his essay on 'Self-reliance,' written in 1841, Emerson writes: 'Society never advances. It recedes as fast on the one side as it gains on the other. It undergoes continual changes; it is barbarous, it is civilized, it is christianized, it is rich, it is scientific; but this change is not amelioration. For everything that is given something is taken. Society acquires new arts and loses old instincts.'[8]

In *Der Mann ohne Eigenschaften* Ulrich expresses the same belief in a conversation with the bank director, Leo Fischel, and the young fascist, Hans Sepp. He tells them, 'Ich denke, jeder Fortschritt ist zugleich ein Rückschritt. Es gibt Fortschritt immer nur in einem bestimmten Sinn. Und da unser Leben im Ganzen keinen Sinn hat, hat es im Ganzen auch keinen Fortschritt' (484). The law governing world history, he believes, is reflected in the fundamental principle of government operative in old Austria, namely, that of *Fortwursteln,* 'muddling through.' He describes history as a pendulum, swinging first in one direction, then in the opposite. Since history is a series of accidental occurrences, everything could just as easily have happened in a different way. Ulrich's so-called essayistic approach to life derives largely from this conviction. Ulrich serves as Musil's mouthpiece in the chapter 'Seinesgleichen geschieht oder warum erfindet man nicht Geschichte' when he remarks to himself:

Grösstenteils entsteht Geschichte aber ohne Autoren. Sie entsteht nicht von einem Zentrum her, sondern von der Peripherie. Aus kleinen Ursachen. Wahrscheinlich gehört gar nicht so viel dazu, wie man glaubt, um aus dem gotischen Menschen oder dem antiken Griechen den modernen Zivilisationsmenschen zu machen. Denn das menschliche Wesen ist ebenso leicht der Menschenfresserei fähig wie der Kritik der reinen Vernunft; es kann mit den gleichen Überzeugungen und Eigenschaften beides schaffen, wenn die Umstände danach sind, und sehr grossen äusseren Unterschieden entsprechen dabei sehr kleine innere (360–1).

Musil had expressed exactly the same idea almost verbatim in 'Das hilflose Europa,' as can be seen in the following extract:

Es gehört gar nicht so viel dazu, um aus dem gotischen Menschen oder dem antiken Griechen den modernen Zivilisationsmenschen zu machen. Ein kleines, dauernd in einer bestimmten Richtung wirkendes Übergewicht von Umständen, von Ausserseelischem, von Zufälligkeiten, Hinzugefallenem genügt dafür. *Dieses Wesen ist ebenso leicht fähig der Menschenfresserei wie der Kritik der reinen Vernunft.*[9]

According to Wolfdietrich Rasch, who became a close friend of the author in Berlin in 1932, 'Robert Musil sah im Ersten Weltkrieg das schicksal-bestimmende Ereignis des Jahrhunderts.'[10] Applying his philosophy of history to the First World War, Musil concluded that it need never have happened. While the focus in the novel is on the nexus between the decline and fall of the Austro-Hungarian Empire and the outbreak of war, his criticism extends far beyond the Austrian border. The collapse of the Hapsburg monarchy was, he believed, symptomatic of the universal disintegration of contemporary culture. For him this always remained the central problem in the novel, as the following note, written in the late 1930s, verifies: 'Nochmals oberstes Problem: – Zusammenbruch der Kultur (und des Kulturgedankens). Das ist in der Tat das, was der Sommer 1914 eingeleitet hat ... Österreich also besonders deutlicher Fall der modernen Welt' (1577).

Throughout the novel Musil intersperses a number of miniature essays dealing with various aspects of the war – for example, the chapter 'Eine Einschaltung über Kakanien. Der Herd des Weltkriegs ist auch der Geburtsort des Dichters Feuermaul.' In it he argues that the catchword 'der Herd des Weltkriegs' is often used with a certain imprecision concerning its actual meaning. While the older generation tends, he states, to identify 'der Herd' with Sarajevo, others, depending mainly on their degree of education, associate the phrase with international political intrigues or the centres of big business interests, such as Essen or Pilsen. From these conflicting interpretations Musil deduces that the 'seat of the war' was actually to be found in many places simultaneously. Rejecting the usual simplistic explanations, based on theories of cause and effect, he advocates a more up-to-date, scientific approach, namely, a functional method of considering relationships:

Mit anderen Worten: die Ursachenkette ist eine Weberkette, es gehört ein Einschlag zu ihr und alsbald lösen sich die Ursachen in ein Gewirk auf. Längst hat man die Ursachenforschung in der Wissenschaft aufgegeben oder wenigstens stark zurückgedrängt und durch eine funktionale Betrachtungsweise der Zusammenhänge ersetzt. Die Suche nach der Ursache gehört dem Hausgebrauch an, wie die Verliebtheit der Köchin die Ursache davon ist, dass die Suppe versalzen wurde. Auf den Weltkrieg angewendet, hat dieses Forschen nach einer Ursache und einem Verursacher das höchst positive negative Resultat gehabt, dass die Ursache überall und bei jedem war. Es zeigt sich damit, dass man wahrhaftig ebenso gut Herd wie Ursache oder Schuld des Krieges sagen kann; dann aber muss man wohl die ganze Betrachtungsweise durch eine andere ergänzen (1568–9).

Applying the principle of 'funktionale Betrachtungsweise der Zusammenhänge' to the plot, Musil sets out to demonstrate that the causes of the First World War were, indeed, to be found in everyone and everywhere.

Several chapters in the novel are devoted to a general sociological and historical account of the Austro-Hungarian Empire from 1867 on, in order to explain the cultural schizophrenia rampant on the eve of the war. In the chapter 'Geistiger Umsturz' (Bk. 1, chap. 15), he describes the disquieting incongruity developing in the second half of the nineteenth century between commercial and technological advances on the one hand, and cultural and moral tastes on the other. He defines it as an eclectic era, in which painters and writers imitated the old masters rather than develop their own style, and architects slavishly copied Gothic or

Renaissance designs. By the last two decades of the century, Musil notes, change for the better seemed imminent with the arrival of Nietzsche and the Naturalists, men with new vitality, promising a new art, a new morality, and a new society. The dream was short-lived, he claims, as a new cultural lull set in after the turn of the century. Austrian society on the eve of the First World War was, according to Musil, characterized by its propensity to exalt the weak at the expense of the strong, and by its vain effort to reconcile rapid industrialization with outmoded moral values, in which no one believed anyway.

To compound the problem of cultural schizophrenia, inhabitants of the Austro-Hungarian Empire were required to feel themselves to be, at one and the same time, Imperial and Royal Austro-Hungarian patriots and Royal Hungarian or Imperial-Royal Austrian patriots. The full irony of their situation was evident in their slogan *viribus unitis*: 'united we stand.' Musil argues that the Hungarians were first and last Hungarians with their own language, while the Austrians were essentially nothing at all, since there was really no such entity as Austria in any case. If an Austrian in the pre-war period were asked what he was, he would reply that he was a Pole, a Czech, a Croat, or a Serb, but not an Austrian. According to Musil, the Austrian and Hungarian Austro-Hungarian Dual Monarchy perished in 1918 primarily for want of a name.

To depict the social, political, and spiritual bankruptcy of his nation on the threshold of the First World War, Musil introduces approximately twenty major characters, representing a cross-section of society. A number of them are modelled on historical figures of the period.[11] The characters can be divided into four general groupings, with Ulrich providing the link joining them together. The Clarisse-Walter-Moosbrugger-Meingast cluster serves mainly as a means of introducing the themes of insanity and salvation and various Nietzschean ideas into the plot. The characters who come and go in the Fischel household reflect current views on nationalism and anti-Semitism, while the third group, revolving around Ulrich's sister Agathe, engages in discussions about modern pedagogy and contemporary morality. The fourth and largest of the groupings comprises the characters who frequent Diotima's salon, either as participants in or as observers of the frantic activities of the Collateral Campaign.

Musil mixes some historical facts with a considerable amount of fiction in *Der Mann ohne Eigenschaften*. His professed aim is to capture the spiritual climate of the era, not to present an accurate historical account of events. As he explained to Oskar Maurus Fontana in 1926, 'Die reale

Erklärung des realen Geschehens interessiert mich nicht ... Mich interesssiert das geistig Typische, ich möchte geradezu sagen: das Gespenstische des Geschehens.'[12] The Collateral Campaign epitomizes a crumbling society, unwittingly charting its own course of destruction. Contrary to Kaiser and Wilkins's assertion that it does not merit the central importance usually attributed to it, it is the backbone of the novel. Of the material published during Musil's life, more than one-half deals directly with the campaign or with characters closely identified with it. Musil's mastery of irony is best seen in those chapters dealing with the three major sessions of the campaign (bk. 1, chaps. 42–4 and 116; bk. 2, chaps. 34–8). It is, for instance, ironic that the Collateral Campaign is founded as a scheme to outwit the troublesome Prussians, who are already busily planning a major celebration in honour of the thirtieth anniversary of Wilhelm II's accession to the throne. It seems that the only way the Austrians can demonstrate their superiority over the Prussians is to imitate them, to outdo them at their own game. Since Wilhelm II's anniversary falls on 15 June 1918, some six months before the seventieth jubilee of Franz Josef's coronation, the Collateral Campaign is forced to organize a whole year's festivities.

It is, of course, also highly ironic that Ulrich, of all people, should be appointed honorary secretary of this patriotic endeavour. As a schoolboy he had almost been expelled for expressing in an essay the opinion that anyone who really loved his country should never think it the best, and that probably even God preferred to speak of His world in the *conjunctivus potentialis* – 'the subjunctive of potentiality.' As the novel opens, Ulrich, who at the age of thirty-two has experimented with careers in the military, civil engineering, and mathematics, has decided to take a year's vacation from life, in order to find a purposeful channel for his considerable talents. His involvement with the campaign serves only to reinforce his cynical conviction that participation in contemporary society is an exercise in futility.

Graf Leinsdorf's opening address at the first meeting of the Collateral Campaign sets the tone for all future dialogue concerning the search for a crowning idea for the jubilee. He states that the purpose of the campaign is to demonstrate to the world that the Austro-Hungarian monarchy stands united around its great ruler. Each of his four suggestions reveals how he and his enthusiastic supporters have lost touch with reality. By the end of their deliberations the 'Emperor of Peace' will have led his people into war. He will die half-way through the war, leaving others to clean up the mess. 'True Austria' will disintegrate by 1918; Austria as a 'European

Landmark' will lose most of its influence, and 'Culture and Capital' will all but disappear.

Diotima's proposal to make 'ein Grösser-Österreich' and 'ein Weltösterreich' the slogans of the campaign, in order to show the feuding nations of the world how to live in a higher harmony with each other as do the Austrian peoples in their fatherland, further demonstrates the naïveté of many of Musil's compatriots regarding social and political reality (174). In one chapter the author compares the world towards the end of 1913 to a seething volcano that no one believed would ever erupt (381). The deliberations of the members of the campaign confirm his cynical view of the situation. Ulrich's files are replete with proposals advocating a return to the past or a leap forward into the future, but no one is willing or able to come to grips with the reality of the present. Musil's idealism is rooted in the reality of the present. He equates Utopianism with possibilities: 'Utopien bedeuten ungefähr so viel wie Möglichkeiten; darin, dass eine Möglichkeit nicht Wirklichkeit ist, drückt sich nichts anderes aus, als dass die Umstände, mit denen sie gegenwärtig verflochten ist, sie daran hindern, denn andernfalls wäre sie ja nur eine Unmöglichkeit' (246). Significantly, the only two members of the Collateral Campaign to attain their goal are the two intruders: the Prussian tycoon-cum-littérateur Arnheim and General Stumm von Bordwehr. Both are very much in touch with present reality. Arnheim ultimately acquires the Galician oilfields necessary for the expansion of his munitions empire; and Stumm's request for funds to strengthen the military is granted in spite of the pacifist poet Feuermaul and the machinations of the World Peace Congress. Paradoxically, the Collateral Campaign, established to promote peace and unity, leads directly to war.

The main characteristics of the period immediately preceding the First World War, according to Musil, were the espousal of dozens of conflicting ideologies and the effort to impose a strong feeling of solidarity on individuals and nations. In practice, every idea generated a counter-idea, resulting in a society where people acted differently than they thought and thought differently than they acted. As a result of his exhaustive research into the great works of the era, General Stumm von Bordwehr arrives at a very disconcerting conclusion:

Er hatte nach vollzogener Bestandaufnahme des mitteleuropäischen Ideenvorrats nicht nur zu seinem Bedauern festgestellt, dass er aus lauter Gegensätzen bestehe, sondern auch zu seinem Erstaunen gefunden, dass diese Gegensätze bei genauerer Beschäftigung mit ihnen ineinander überzugehen anfangen ... Dem gegenwärtigen Zeitalter sind eine Anzahl grosser Ideen geschenkt worden und zu jeder Idee durch eine besondere Güte des Schicksals gleich auch ihre Gegenidee, so dass Individualismus und Kollektivismus, Nationalismus und Internationalismus, Sozialismus und Kapitalismus, Imperialismus und Pazifismus, Rationalismus und Aberglaube gleich gut darin zu Hause sind, wozu sich noch die unverbrauchten Reste unzähliger anderer Gegensätze von gleichem oder geringerem Gegenwartswert gesellen (373).

Stumm describes his era with a phrase lifted from 'Das hilflose Europa' as 'ein babylonisches Narrenhaus.'[7] Madness and salvation are major motifs throughout the novel. Symptoms of insanity are evident in every corner of society. The most obvious examples are the murderer Moosbrugger and Ulrich's friend Clarisse. At one point Ulrich says, 'Wenn die Menschheit als Ganzes träumen könnte, müsste Moosbrugger entstehn' (76). Moosbrugger, with his vacillations between periods of sanity and of insanity, personifies the spirit of the times. His psychiatrist, Dr Friedenthal, describes him as a borderline case. Ulrich's interest in him is sparked initially by his beatific countenance. Indeed, Musil invites the reader to draw a number of parallels between this murderer of prostitutes and Christ. Moosbrugger, whose given name is Christian, is thirty-four years old, supposedly Christ's age when he was crucified, and is a carpenter by trade. Clarisse, his female counterpart, comes to regard him as the new Messiah and is obsessed with the idea of liberating him from prison.

Moosbrugger's trial makes a latter-day martyr of him by demonstrating the pathetic inadequacies of the legal system. Musil devotes several chapters to this theme. While Ulrich's father and a rival colleague, Professor Stumm, engage in a petty academic dispute over the use of the co-ordinate conjunctions 'und' and 'oder' in a planned revision of paragraph 318 of the Penal Code, concerning borderline mental cases, society itself totters on the brink of dementia. In a note dealing with the proposed conclusion of his novel, Musil wrote, 'Nationen haben einen unzurechnungsfähigen Geist. Richtiger: Sie haben überhaupt keinen Geist. Vergleich mit Irrsinnigen' (1577).

In the period immediately before the First World War, the period in which literary expressionism was born, the word *Erlösung*, 'salvation,' was on everyone's lips. In the chapter 'Die unerlösten Nationen und General Stumms Gedanken über die Wortgruppe Erlösen' Musil describes the era as 'eine recht messianische Zeit' (520). While whole nations within the Austro-Hungarian Empire ('die unerlösten Nationen') struggled for redemption from the crown, the conviction arose that all problems would be resolved if a Messiah were to appear. The character Meingast, a devastating caricature of the writer Ludwig Klages, is introduced as an indictment of all such prophets and would-be saviours of the *Abendland*. Meingast, a disciple of Nietzsche, preaches the gospel of salvation through brute force, anti-intellectualism, and male supremacy. While members of the Collateral Campaign seek the redeeming idea in such diverse proposals as a Greater Austrian Franz Josef Soup Kitchen for the poor or an Austrian Nietzsche Year, the world moves closer and closer to war. Ulrich, frustrated by the inanity of the campaign's activities, decides finally to withdraw from it and seek his own salvation outside society in a mystical union with his sister Agathe. His Utopian experiment with 'the other state' fails, however, when Ulrich comes to the realization that withdrawal from society resolves nothing. Love cannot survive in a state of isolation: 'Sie kann nur eingefügt in eine Gesellschaft bestehen' (1425). All attempts to find salvation in *Der Mann ohne Eigenschaften* end in failure. Ulrich rejects 'the other state' as a solution; Clarisse goes mad in her quest for redemption, and the efforts of the Collateral Campaign end disastrously.

In Musil's novel Ulrich serves as the conscience of modern man. In book one he is essentially a passive character, observing and analysing events without committing himself to anyone or anything. The question with which he is preoccupied at all times is 'die [Frage] des rechten Lebens.' His favourite topic of conversation is contemporary morality. Agathe is not far off target when she remarks to General Stumm von Bordwehr at one of Diotima's gatherings, 'Mein Bruder spricht überhaupt nur von Moral' (1030).

In the realm of morality Ulrich is far in advance of his time. Unlike the other characters, he recognizes that science has developed a conception of hard, sober intellectual strength that renders mankind's traditional moral and metaphysical notions untenable. He is an adherent of the so-called cultural-lag theory, which argues that modern man has for the last one hundred and fifty years been developing his intellect at the expense of emotion, thereby disrupting the balance upon which a good life and real culture depend. Ulrich finds support for his theory in the writings of Nietzsche, the most oft-quoted author in the novel. In *Freud: The Mind of the Moralist*, Philip Rieff writes: 'The evolutionist vision of rational development drove Nietzsche to his deepest nightmare, of the last man, the mass man, whose posture is reclining, whose feeling is ennui, bored in a world in which intelligence has made of passion a routine.'[13]

The imbalance between intellect and emotion, which led to a deterioration of morality, was, according to Musil, one of the prime causes of the war. In one of his notes dealing with the novel's structure, he wrote: 'Das Aufbauprinzip der moralischen Probleme bildet doch eigentlich die Moral des Kriegs! Kriege treten nicht wie Epidemien durch äussere Einflüsse auf, sondern von innen!' (1590).

Ulrich is an outspoken adversary of all moral absolutes. Throughout the novel he campaigns for a new definition of good and evil. Early in book two he explains to his sister his theory about the interdependence of good and evil. He tells her, 'In jedem Minus steckt ein Plus ... In allem Schlechten etwas Gutes ... Gewöhnlich steckt in einer menschlichen Minusvariante eine nicht erkannte Plusvariante' (735). Anyone familiar with Goethe's *Faust* will recognize the striking similarity between Ulrich's views on this subject and those expressed by God in 'Prolog im Himmel.' Musil acknowledged the affinity in a diary entry from 1934: '"Von Zeit zu Zeit seh ich den Alten gern" d.i. feudal gesprochen, aus dem Verwandtschaftsverhältnis ... Aber der Teufel hat etwas von Gott in sich. So spricht der aus dem Haus gegangene Engel. Zwischen Gott und Teufel besteht auch nicht der krasse Gegensatz (des Orients) zwischen Licht und Finsternis als Prinzipien; der Teufel ist ein Bestandteil von Gottes Weltordnung usw.'[14]

Ulrich believes that the world cannot exist without evil, since evil in fact promotes good. Paradoxically, Ulrich claims that everything is moral, yet morality itself is immoral. By morality here he means conventional social morality. He devises a new definition to supplant the defunct one. Morality, he believes, is 'das unendliche Ganze der Möglichkeiten zu leben' (1028). Man in his highest state knows no good and evil, just faith and doubt. All hard and fast precepts contradict the nature of reality. Morals, to be meaningful, must be regarded as variable functions. Ulrich's 'Moral des nächsten Schrittes' postulates that man can do no evil; he can only launch it. Recognition of this truth, he maintains, would lead to a new, meaningful system of social morality.

The 'crowning idea' that Ulrich proposes to Graf Leinsdorf for the big celebration in 1918 is the establishment of a General Secretariat for Precision and the Spirit, with a mandate to undertake a spiritual inventory of the era. The ultimate goal would be a synthesis between the rational, scientific, and logical on the one hand, and the emotional, spiritual, and metaphorical on the other. Ulrich is convinced that such a synthesis, if realizable, would provide a panacea for the spiritual sickness prevalent everywhere. Ulrich's advice goes unheeded.

In one of the key speeches in the novel Ulrich expresses his dissatisfaction with the present and his faith in the future to Agathe, who has asked him to explain his beliefs to her:

Du hast mich gefragt, was ich glaube! Ich glaube, man kann mir tausendmal aus den geltenden Gründen beweisen, etwas sei gut oder schön, es wird mir gleichgültig bleiben, und ich werde mich einzig und allein nach dem Zeichen richten, ob mich seine Nähe steigen oder sinken macht ... Ich glaube aber vor allem nicht an die Bindung von Bös durch Gut, die unser Kulturgemisch darstellt: das ist mir widerwärtig! Ich glaube also und glaube nicht! Aber ich glaube vielleicht, dass die Menschen in einiger Zeit einesteils sehr intelligent, anderenteils Mystiker sein werden. Vielleicht geschieht es, dass sich unsere Moral schon heute in diese zwei Bestandteile zerlegt. Ich könnte auch sagen: in Mathematik und Mystik. In praktische Melioration und unbekanntes Abenteuer! (770).

In the interview with Oskar Maurus Fontana cited earlier, Musil, discussing the historical background of *Der Mann ohne Eigenschaften*, insisted that his novel was not restricted to events occurring between August 1913 and August 1914. There was nothing in it that was not still relevant at the time of writing. He was very conscious that the problems that had led to the war had not vanished with the signing of the Treaty of Versailles.

Soon after book two was published, Hitler came to power. It is, no doubt, significant that Musil's progress on the novel diminished considerably just at this time. Five years later his books were banned in Germany and Austria. Suddenly deprived of a reading public, Musil felt little encouragement to continue his work. The abject poverty that he endured during the last years of his life also contributed to his difficulties in finishing the novel.

Several months before his death Musil expressed in one of his diary entries his frustration at not being able to move ahead more quickly with the book: 'Meine geistige Ausrüstung für den Roman war dichterisch, psychologisch, und z. T. philosophisch. In meiner jetzigen Lage bedarf es aber des Soziologischen und wessen dazugehört. Darum verlaufe ich mich immer hilflos in Nebenprobleme, die auseinander-, statt zusammengehn. Oft habe ich den Eindruck, dass meine geistige Kraft nachlässt; aber eher ist es wahr, dass die Problemstellung über sie hinausgeht.'[15]

It is fruitless to speculate how Musil would have responded to this dilemma had he lived long enough to complete the novel. That it would have ended with the onslaught of The First World War seems certain. What Musil planned to do with Ulrich, however, must remain a mystery.

In the chapter 'Seinesgleichen geschieht oder warum erfindet man nicht Geschichte?' Ulrich compares life to a mathematical problem that does not admit of any general solution. Perhaps, in view of this philosophy, it is not altogether surprising nor inappropriate that the novel was never completed.

NOTES

1 Ernst Kaiser and Eithne Wilkins, *Robert Musil. Eine Einführung in das Werk* (Stuttgart: Kohlhammer 1962) 19.
2 Ibid. 142.
3 Ibid. 20.
4 Robert Musil, *Tagebücher, Aphorismen, Essays und Reden*, ed. Adolf Frisé (Hamburg: Rowohlt 1955) 787.
5 Robert Musil, *Der Mann ohne Eigenschaften*, ed. Adolf Frisé, 5th ed. (1952); reprint ed., Hamburg: Rowohlt 1960) 1587. Further references to this work appear in the text.
6 Musil, *Tagebücher* 216.
7 Ibid. 634.
8 Ralph Waldo Emerson, *Selections from Ralph Waldo Emerson: An Organic Anthology*, ed. Stephen E. Whicher (Boston: Houghton Mifflin 1957) 165.
9 Musil, *Tagebücher* 627. Musil incorporated the section that I have italicized into his novel.
10 Wolfdietrich Rasch, *Über Robert Musils Roman 'Der Mann ohne Eigenschaften'* (Göttingen: Vandenhoeck & Ruprecht 1967) 30.
11 See Eithne Wilkins, 'Gestalten und ihre Namen im Werk Robert Musils,' *Text + Kritik*, nos. 21–2 (1968) 48–58.
12 Musil, *Tagebücher* 785.
13 Philip Rieff, *Freud: The Mind of the Moralist* (New York: Viking 1959) 184.
14 Musil, *Tagebücher* 377.
15 Ibid. 491.

AUGUSTINUS P. DIERICK

Two Representative Expressionist Responses to the Challenge of the First World War: Carl Sternheim's *eigene Nuance* and Leonhard Frank's Utopia

Anyone attempting to assess the character and value of expressionist prose that discusses the First World War is quickly confronted by the peculiar nature of the discussion. One finds here a singular lack of detail, of chronology, of factual information. Instead, the discussion inevitably turns to a much larger issue, the meaning of war in the progress of mankind. The novellas of Leonhard Frank and Carl Sternheim are representative. They not only discuss the war, but attempt to come to terms with the more central theme of the relationship between the individual and society, since they view the problematic nature of this relationship as a major cause of the war. They also attempt to understand the lessons provided by the war that relate to this problem. But, though both authors sense that the war is a watershed, a cataclysmic event, there is a striking difference of opinion as to the message that war conveys, and the attitude to be adopted towards it.

To understand the divergence in attitudes among expressionists towards war, one must refer to the character of the whole movement. Expressionism is a profoundly contradictory movement, characterized by extremes that seemingly exclude each other. Formally, expressionism embraces the unbounded, ecstatic outpourings of J.R. Becher and Franz Werfel as well as the careful compositions of Georg Heym's sonnets and the poetry of the *Sturm*-group; it includes Georg Kaiser's strictly logical constructions (*Denkspiele*) as well as works such as Oskar Kokoschka's *Mörder Hoffnung der Frauen* and Wassily Kandinsky's *Der gelbe Klang* ('eine Bühnenkomposition'). The extreme range of forms is paralleled by equally striking differences in expressionist *Weltanschauung*. Many expressionists so despair over the human condition that they tend towards nihilism. In prose works such as Max Herrmann-Neisse's *Hilflose Augen* or

Paul Zech's *Der schwarze Baal*, in Georg Heym's 'Der Irre' and 'Die Sektion,' the human condition is viewed as one of suffering and inevitable defeat. The tone of the writing is one of pathos, a pathos of such intensity that it easily tips over into either bathos or the grotesque. In Albert Ehrenstein's 'Tubutsch' the borderline between maudlin sentimentality and uncompromising nihilism is constantly being crossed. At the other extreme, an equally excessive optimism preaches imminent change and the advent of Utopia – witness Leonhard Frank's collection of novellas, *Der Mensch ist gut*, or Paul Kornfeld's 'Legende.' The concept of Utopia exists side by side with the idea of a *Weltende*; in some cases these opposing tendencies even go hand in hand in the works of one author, as in Alfred Wolfenstein, whose Utopian vision in his collection *Der Lebendige* results precisely from an excessive, intolerable degree of suffering.

The antithetical statements about the human condition in expressionist writings can, however, be shown to have a common inspiration in the awareness of a crisis, which some critics have claimed was responsible for the first manifestations of the movement. Provided that it is understood in a very wide sense, this idea of an awareness of a coming crisis appears indeed to be valuable for a discussion of the common expressionist *Lebensgefühl*. The crisis alluded to is, for the expressionist, one in which mankind might soon be forced to choose between annihilation or regeneration. Ultimately, therefore, not a merely political or social concept is involved, but a more metaphysical one, man's fate: 'die Entwicklung des Menschen war das Hauptthema des expressionistischen Schriftstellers.'[1] Only when we formulate the crisis in this way can we understand why expressionists present their views in terms of extremes, and why both optimistic and pessimistic assessments of man's situation and of the possibility of regeneration into a 'new man' are usually absolute, all-embracing, and unremitting.

The question of survival or obliteration, of *Weltende* or Utopia, is of course linked with the question of the causes for the actual state of decay of the 'old world.' This decay appears in literary works, on the one hand, as a justification for a sense of despair, and on the other as a contrast to the brave new world to come. Leonhard Frank's novel *Die Ursache* and dramas such as Bronnen's *Vatermord* and Hasenclever's *Der Sohn* 'propagieren die Notwendigkeit des neuen Menschen, indem sie die Verdorbenheit des alten schildern.'[2] In these works the destruction of the old world is interpreted as a new beginning. War itself may be welcome. J.R. Becher writes: 'Ekstatisch wurde Weltbrand verkündet und Massensterben, daraus die Geburt einer neuen Menschheit erfolgen sollte.'[3] The glaring differences in attitudes towards war, a feature of expressionism (at least in its initial stages),[4] can indeed be understood only when we keep in mind the idea of a much more general crisis.

The actual coming of the war, of course, lent new urgency to the already existing question of survival. War had long been expected; Erich Kahler claims that 'das wachsende Gefühl einer herannahenden ungeheuren Krise' could be detected well before 1914, 'von 1911 an.'[5] Max Brod, in his autobiography, *Streitbares Leben*, writes that he could feel, in the mass of literature submitted to him for his *Arkadia Jahrbuch* of 1913, a sense of impending disaster: 'Es war wie ein Wetterleuchten. Das furchtbare Gewitter des Jahres 1914 kündigte sich unter fernen dunklen Wolken an.'[6] War, the inevitable outcome of all the questionable aspects of the old world, already figures to some extent in most expressionist writings *before* 1914.

A new task presents itself in 1914, however. The discussion must now shift from theory to reality, from abstract ideas to concrete phenomena, from the timeless to the timely. This paper examines how two authors met this challenge, or rather, how they failed to meet it. Time and the horrendous changes it has wrought have rendered most expressionist writings dealing with the First World War obsolete, unpalatable, and irrelevant. If the novellas of Leonhard Frank and Carl Sternheim still hold interest for us today, it is not because of their artistic achievement but rather because of their failure, for in their failure they are representative of most expressionist prose that deals with political and social phenomena. Moreover, because these authors formulated the problems and solutions more clearly than most other expressionists, their novellas may serve to illustrate the ultimate *reasons* for the expressionist failure.

Between 1912 and 1923 Carl Sternheim wrote nineteen short stories. Fourteen of these he collected in 1918 under the title *Chronik von des zwanzigsten Jahrhunderts Beginn*.[7] Several of these novellas deal with the First World War. As the title suggests, Sternheim's intention was to write a chronicle of the progress of the German society as a whole. But the word *Chronik* has also a more specific meaning for Sternheim because, in choosing this title, he wished to convey his ambition to write a quasi-scientific, objective work in which the author would disappear behind his material. The ideal of objectivity is related to Sternheim's cultural philosophy. Sternheim maintains that the German bourgeoisie has adopted a vision of the world that no longer corresponds to reality but is intended to perpetuate the position of the bourgeoisie itself. This vision of the world Sternheim calls 'metaphorical.' In the bourgeoisie's tendency constantly to relate empirical reality to some 'higher reality' or some transcendental realm, Sternheim sees an attempt by the bourgeoisie to mythicize its own existence. The factual pre-eminence of this social class is explained in terms of logical as well as historical necessity. Without such 'mythical' references the bourgeoisie's position of predominance could not be maintained, since it draws its legitimacy solely from them.

The upshot of this metaphorical vision of the world is that the bourgeoisie is constantly being subjected to a barrage of metaphors, clichés, and slogans of its own making. One of the most interesting aspects of Sternheim's work is precisely his attempt to 'report' objectively on the manipulation of language and to reveal how linguistic corruptions lead to corruption of truth in general. In doing battle with metaphorical language, by reinstating language as an instrument of revelation and cognition rather than as an allusive and myth-making device, Sternheim tries to re-create the world 'as it is.' In his essay 'Das Arbeiter-ABC' he claims, therefore, that art itself must neither mythicize nor satirize, but must be 'einfache Spiegelung des irgendwie Hervorragenden.' It must concentrate on essentials, on the representative, but only as a mirror, 'ohne die Spur bewusster sittlicher Predigt.'[8] This, then, is the reason behind the title *Chronik*.

Sternheim's battle against the metaphor is only one aspect of a much larger and more profound cultural and social criticism levelled at the destruction of the bourgeois's individuality and uniqueness. The trend towards greater individualism and autonomy, which dates from the Renaissance, has been reversed in bourgeois society for the last two hundred years, and particularly since the French Revolution, according to Sternheim. The idea of self-sacrifice for the benefit of the common goal has restricted the individual's freedom of action precisely in the area where man *is* free, namely, in the social sphere. With the rise of the bourgeoisie, freedom has been eroded by such notions as Kant's categorical imperative, Hegel's doctrine of historical inevitability, Marx's economic determinism, and Darwin's theory of natural selection – all theories eagerly accepted and fused into a morality of *juste milieu*. Since conformity to the collective is henceforth *de rigeur* in bourgeois society, only he who revolts against this principle can now attain his own individuality. Sternheim calls this individuality the 'eigene Nuance.'

The theory of the *eigene Nuance* is amply illustrated in the novellas of the *Chronik*. In fact, the collection may well be called a catalogue of various ways in which the individual may reach his *eigene Nuance*. With few exceptions the protagonist of each novella goes the road from conformity to self-fulfilment. Often Sternheim gives a picture of his hero from birth to death, a kind of miniature biography. The hero's inner development is accompanied by external *Wendepunkte* and, though these are intended to be of less importance than the intellectual and emotional development of the protagonist, they are often crucial. This is particularly the case with the First World War. In many stories one is tempted to consider the war as *the* catalyst in the struggle of the individual towards self-fulfilment.

For Sternheim, a typical expressionist, war is a philosophical rather than a political and social problem. War holds a particular fascination for him since, in war, the conflict between the individual's claims and those of the society in which he lives is most clearly formulated. Sternheim sees in the First World War a situation that triggers a kind of *Denkspiel* in the manner of some of the plays of Georg Kaiser. In war society's true face is revealed. War claims self-sacrifice; patriotism plays the role of a collectivity myth, stifling the aspirations of the individual. In 'Meta,' one of the novellas dealing with the war, Sternheim writes of the outbreak of the war, 'Vom eigenen Schicksal war täglich weniger die Rede' (89).

Of course the war also dramatically increases the use of metaphorical language. Clichés, slogans, whitewashing, and euphemistic phrases forge the war into an instrument for the achievement of collective glory. In 'Meta,' language and its corruption are as much part of war as the actual physical phenomenon itself; this is illustrated through the effect the war has on the conversation of the heroine and her fiancé. Meta and her fiancé 'sprachen von geschlagener Schlacht Gefahr Verwundung der Freunde und Verwandten, lernten Artillerie und Infanterie, spickten Sätze mit kriegerischem Begriff, unterlagen dem Eindruck von Sieg und Niederlage. Zeitungen bestätigten der Gegner märchenhafte Niedertracht, bravouröse Tapferkeit der eigenen Truppen stets von neuem' (88–9).

The new vocabulary indicates that a new world has opened up for Meta's fiancé Franz. Although he had found an almost religious ecstasy in his idolizing love for Meta (another myth-making process was at work here!), he now comes under the influence of an even more powerful force: 'Religion war das Vaterland, Vorbild der tapfere Soldat. Ein anderer Gott stand kriegerisch geschient in einem Himmel geschwungener Fahnen und Lanzen' (89). The young man unhesitatingly discards his erotic experience as no longer appropriate; Meta is 'als Ideal unbrauchbar ... Er stellte sie der mit Standarten stürmenden Angriffslust des männlichen Prinzips, das aus allen Kulissen der Welt blies, richtig als ein anderes, das ruhend ergriffen sein wollte, gegenüber' (89), and he abandons her for the greater activity at the front.

Franz soon reaps the harvest of war, though not in a heroic death, but in death through dysentery: '[er] fällt nach Monaten treuer Pflichterfüllung in ein hastiges Leiden, das ihm die Därme immer von neuem entleert, bis seine gemarterte Seele aus kaum angebrochenem Leben entweicht. Mit rühmlicher Gefallenen verschwindet sein Kadaver ohne Sang und Klang in fremde Erde' (92). Meta, however, goes on to reach her *eigene Nuance* via a number of 'Irrwege,' among which is the cult of the memory of Franz, and via a period in which she blackmails a family into satisfying her selfish goals. In the end she discovers that her true mission is to show others the road to self-realization: 'In Menschen, die nach Schema und Klischee ein nutzloses Sein hinbrachten, war sie als Flamme gefahren, hatte sie zu eigener Äusserung gebracht' (110). In making others aware of their *eigene Nuance* lies Meta's own *eigene Nuance*: 'Schönste irdische Wirklichkeit bin ich mir selbst' (112). The cult of the self, praised at the end of the novella, is clearly intended to contrast with the collective ecstasy that had accompanied the outbreak of the war.

Meta's *eigene Nuance* is realized only after several *Irrwege*. In 'Ulrike' the war acts much more directly upon the title heroine, in that it destroys the beliefs by which this daughter of a Prussian nobleman has lived so far. Sternheim shows how religion and patriotism had served to provide the family with its necessary ideological stability: 'Aller Mahlzeit Beginn und Schluss hiess Gebet. Brot, Schwein und Kartoffel lagen inmitten. Das und die Familie war protestantisch. Preusse der liebe Gott' (141).

The illusory nature of this dual faith is revealed when the war breaks out. Ulrike is at first able to function within the new circumstances as a nurse at the front, and is able to retain her principles with such success that her qualities as a Christian, virgin, and martyr lead her to triumph over the 'liebeshungrige Herzen' (149) of the soldiers at the front. Ultimately, however, she comes up against one of those truly Sternheimian creatures, the pure egoist August Bäslack, 'nur noch Rumpf mit einem Arm' (150). The discussions between these diametrically opposed characters furnish us with a sharply focused paradigmatic situation. Bäslack 'verteidigte begeistert sein feindliches Verhältnis zur Menschheit, das er mit Moralbegriffen nicht zu messen doch natürlich fand; das er politisch nannte. Wie sie Christentum den Greueln verbinde, mit denen ein Erdteil gerade kreise? Ob es nicht peinlicher sei, in des Erlösers Namen unter besiegten Völkern brennen und sengen zu müssen als nach eigenem oder der Obrigkeit Willen?' (150-1).

Ulrike is soon forced to seek support from the other soldiers, and from a companion of her youth, Kittel, 'der als Feldgeistlicher das eiserne Kreuz erworben hatte' (152). Kittel lives by the very ideas that Bäslack is trying to destroy. His letter to Ulrike is 'Begeisterungsschrei'; it is in fact a metaphor on war: 'Mannschaft, untere obere Führung – prachtvoll. Schlacht und Sieg folgten sich wie in Bilderbüchern. Der Soldat rief Halleluja und Hurra, fiel angemessen schlicht' (152).

Unfortunately, Kittel's enthusiastic endorsement of war comes too late; the poison planted by Bäslack has penetrated too deeply. Ulrike realizes that the philosophy of her class is obsolete: 'Ulrike sah ihr Leben in Schläuchen, die nicht mehr dicht waren, sickern' (152). The madness of war causes her to adopt substitute myths: 'Sie ging geköpft durch tolle Zeit. Und als in Reden und Schriften der Unsinn krass wurde, groteske Ereignisse lärmender prasselten, rettete sie sich vor der Not in äussere Zerstreuung. Fand Licht vor europäischer Nacht bei exotischen Kinobildern' (153). Reality is replaced by cinema, a reality twice removed, because the 'zu Brei gewälzte Phrasen' (154) of press and government no longer fill her need.

Finally, in the figure of the painter Posinsky, she encounters the 'männliche Bestie' (155) who helps her to find a suitable answer to her existential doubts, and her true *eigene Nuance*. Under the influence of Posinsky, to whom she is both 'Modell und Geliebte' (157), Ulrike sinks further and further into a realm of animalistic eroticism and irrationalistic primitivism: 'Da er sie afrikanisch wollte, schickte sie sich an, Trope schwarzer Beischlaf, halbtierische Schwellung und Geruch von Negerbeize zu sein. Alles Wirkliche war so von ihr gespült, dass Geschosse, die oft genug noch in die Stadt fielen, ihr von draussen schreckliche Gegenwart nicht mehr vermittelten' (157).

In Ulrike's conversion to barbarism the novella reaches a problematic climax. Ulrike escapes into a world of 'Rausch' that is the opposite of the arid rationalism of her original Prussian background. Sternheim glorifies this ecstatic life Ulrike shares with Posinsky as a means of achieving the true self, 'ihr dichtestes Ich' (158). Yet in both 'Meta' and 'Ulrike,' war, also called *Rausch*, is clearly rejected. How are we to explain this apparent contradiction?

Helmut Liede[9] comes to the conclusion that criticism of both is implied, and one might at first sight agree, for Ulrike's reverting to an animalistic level shocks our sensibilities. But Sternheim's intentions are different. Sternheim states that the individual must find his *eigene Nuance* regardless of society's norms or morals. We must therefore be prepared to be confronted by protagonists that cannot be measured by conventional standards and values. As Wolfgang Wendler claims, there are no vices for Sternheim, 'er billigt jede Handlung, wenn sie nur der wirkliche

Ausdruck der Person ist.'[10] It is understandable that Sternheim's graphic treatment of lust for power, uncommonly strong sexual drives, unscrupulous pursuit of wealth, and lawless manipulation of others has led critics to see in him a moralist and critic of bourgeois vice. But in 'Meta' and 'Ulrike' the message is clear: collective ecstasy (such as patriotism, nationalism, and war) is to be rejected, but personal ecstasy is acceptable as a possible true expression of the self.

This does mean, however, that judgments are made exclusively from a subjective point of view. Hence, for Sternheim, war itself is not intrinsically good or bad; its evil stems from the fact that war represents an obstacle in the path towards self-fulfilment, and must be overcome through adoption of a suitable attitude, no matter how outrageous this adopted solution may seem.

The whole problem of collective versus personal *Rausch* is in fact reiterated in 'Heidenstam.' Heidenstam, a bourgeois whose enormous wealth, acquired through shrewd investments, allows him to lead a life away from sordid reality (Sternheim calls this life-style 'impressionistisch'), believes he is out of reach of harmful circumstances. His capital is well distributed over large segments of the economy, from municipal bonds to munitions and arms factories. Heidenstam's sense of security stems not only from the fact that the German national character promotes his interests, 'da Aufschwung Gelassenheit Friedensliebe wie forscher Chauvinismus in seine Pläne passten' (163), but that God himself is a kind of 'Präsident der Gesellschaft "Deutschland"' (164).

Even the outbreak of the war initially only strengthens Heidenstam's position, since the exploitation of patriotism causes his coffers to swell: 'Im Ausgleich für geringe Verluste, die sich nicht vermeiden liessen, stürmten Rüstungsaktien in die Höhe' (166). In the long run, however, war becomes an increasingly incalculable phenomenon, threatening to destroy Heidenstam's invulnerability. The egocentric capitalist, who looks upon the world as his private property, ultimately comes up against 'das eiserne Zeitalter,' a seemingly insurmountable obstacle.

Yet even now Heidenstam is triumphant, for he becomes a 'Kenner auf dem Kriegsmarkt' (176). So successful is he, in fact, that, after a short second period of feverish activity as a speculator, he can afford to retire, to devote himself exclusively to the new philosophy he has adopted. His previously sheltered, impressionistic existence no longer suffices in view of the excitement sparked by the war: 'Das Ganze gab sich bunt und grell' (176). The spectacle of war seems to Heidenstam to externalize the boundless inner excitement and feverish energy that has now taken hold of him: 'Europa schien ihm zu seinem Vergnügen moussierend gequirlt.' The new life-style is conveniently channelled into the ecstasy of war: 'Bis in die Nacht liess er den Phonographen die Nationalhymne spielen, trank Punsch dazu' (179).

Heidenstam's mistake, unfortunately, is to cultivate his private madness without regard for the external world's madness. Even though he praises the war as 'Erwecker zu tätigem Leben' (177) and idolizes even the greatest excesses, he still places himself outside society, because Heidenstam's notion of war does not entail patriotism, but self-indulgence. In bourgeois society, Sternheim argues, violence is strictly reserved for collective goals.

Heidenstam's career ends in an insane asylum. Nevertheless, individual madness triumphs over collective madness, since Heidenstam now rules over a reality of his own making. This solution, though it might appear strange to the reader, is again intended seriously. Madness overcomes the obstacles of reality, and Heidenstam is perfectly correct in considering himself a new man, at last able to direct his own destiny. The subjective viewpoint is all that matters, for Sternheim as well as for many other expressionists, even though this extreme subjectivism poses enormous problems of intelligibility and evaluation from a critical point of view.

Unrestrained subjectivism must lead to ever-increasing extremes, as in 'Posinsky,' a novella that continues the story of the painter after the death of his mistress Ulrike. Sternheim opens this story with a reference to his theory of the artist as chronicler, and he also hints at the representative character of the various episodes of the *Chronik*: 'Da durch der Gräfin Bolz Tod Posinsky im Leben alleinsteht, bleibt für den gründlichen Chronisten manches von ihm zu sagen, das späteren Geschlechtern Wesentliches von den im Weltkrieg zu Hause Gebliebenen an einem üppigen Exemplar der Gattung zu zeigen vermag' (217). The 'zu Hause Gebliebenen,' then, form yet another group within society to be dealt with in the *Chronik*.

Posinsky has opted for an exclusive cult of the body, and he pursues the search for food and drink fanatically. His efforts are made well-nigh impossible by the war: 'Ihm gegenüber stand im grossen und ganzen hungrig die Welt' (218). Against a background of unprecedented suffering Posinsky practises a materialism that has grotesque overtones. His hoarding of supplies, his constant and absolute rejection of all things spiritual, appear as instances of black humour. Posinsky has decided: 'Nur Materie sei unvergänglich' (224); the cultural and social advantages of the upper classes, he asserts cynically, can be attributed to their having more and better things to eat. In view of the pressing need for food, Posinsky feels justified in claiming: 'Wichtiger als "Rätsel der Weltenseele", "Kritik aller Offenbarung", blieb ein Rezept, schmackhaftes Gemüse aus Brennesseln und Unkräutern zu machen' (227). The bankruptcy of the bourgeois philosophy has hardly ever been formulated more sharply and jarringly.

Posinsky's preoccupations stand in strong contrast to those of a young actor-couple living next door, whose experiences are drawn, according to Posinsky, from illusion and myth. The contrast is calculated and slightly strained. Sternheim is once again doing battle with the metaphorical view of reality. In the face of war and the destruction of bourgeois mythology, art as it has been practised hitherto can have no more meaning; it must be discarded, for it stands in the way of a true understanding of the functioning of society. Schiller's plays, which the young couple rehearse, illustrate particularly well the obscuring function of the metaphor and of poetry in general: 'Seit Jahrhunderten wurden so Völker verblödet. Vor grösstem Nonsens stand dem Pöbel, wurde er gereimt, gebundener Sprache vorgetragen, die Schnauze still. Gierig, diesen Gallimathias zu schlucken, wissenschaftliches historisches Blech, Entstelltes Erlogenes Hypothetisches aus tausend Vorstellungsgebieten zu schlürfen, übersah er seine körperliche Aufzucht' (236). According to Sternheim, poets have become collaborators in the process of obscuring reality; they have become clerks in the pay of the bourgeoisie.

So strong is Posinsky's aversion to these 'tin' myths that he cannot believe in the sincerity of even the last words of the dying girl: 'Der Kleinen letzter Seufzer war Klischee nach Shakespeare' (239). Posinsky eventually kills the young widowed actor when he returns to his flat to mourn his wife, in an almost Gidean *acte gratuite*.

From the novellas analysed it becomes clear that in Sternheim's writings the First World War is used as an expedient for the exposition of his more general ideas about civilization, the bourgeoisie, and the *eigene Nuance*. Sternheim's fundamental attitude towards war remains problematic. The final paragraph of 'Heidenstam' suggests that war can function as a liberator in the capitalist's life: 'Dazu sei nicht der Weltkrieg gekommen, dass nur ein Mensch noch länger Rücksicht nähme. Ausleben sollte nach des Schöpfers bewiesenem Willen sich alle Kreatur. Ihm wenigstens – Heidenstam – stünden ab neunzehnhundertachtzehn die Augen auf. Er bestimmt wollte nicht zu sogenannter Moral, geschminkten Vorbehalten zurückkehren. Für ihn sei jenseits von Gut und Böse Morgenrot!' (184). The parallel with the ending of 'Meta' is obvious; moreover, the references to the terminology of Nietzsche seem to suggest that Heidenstam, in his madness as well as his amorality, aspires to the status of *Übermensch*. War, then, might be beneficial as well as destructive; it might illustrate folly, but it might also act as a catalyst allowing one to reach the *eigene Nuance*.

Can we speak of reformatory tendencies in Sternheim? Is the glorification of the self a solution to the problems posed by the war? The greatest obstacle to an acceptance of Sternheim's doctrine clearly lies in the fact that the very excesses the individual protagonists cultivate with zeal are those that have caused the war and the collapse of society in the first place. Bestiality, self-indulgent barbarism, eroticism of a grotesque nature, violence, and madness constitute the climax of these stories. The absence of moral categories prevents us from interpreting these works as satire; Sternheim's omnidirectional attacks on society, combined with a universal acceptance of the characteristics described above, provided that they are the expression of true individuality, must result in a loss of meaning.

In Sternheim's prose the triumph of irrationalism seems complete because all social concepts are ridiculed. All norms by which society lives are demolished *because* they are social norms. Yet the individual seems to lack a norm within himself. When the affirmation of the self reaches its highest intensity and goes unchecked by outside reality, it finally results in escape and madness. One of the basic tenets of the expressionist movement, the superiority of the subjective viewpoint, seems to lead directly to the affirmation of all that is vile in the real world, a paradoxical conclusion tragically underscoring the weakness of expressionism's philosophical foundations. This very problem of subjectivity without reference to the outside world will again preoccupy us when we turn to the writings of Leonhard Frank.

For Sternheim war is a *Wendepunkt* in an ever-present conflict between the self and the collective. By eliminating one pole of this opposition, the collective, man can achieve complete self-fulfilment. Leonhard Frank's efforts go in the opposite direction: he attempts to fuse the two poles, to make them coincide in the idea of Utopia. To him war is also a *Wendepunkt*, the catastrophe that anticipates the conversion to man's innate goodness.

Expressionist prose deals relatively infrequently with the phenomenon of *Wandlung*, so familiar from expressionist drama, and there are only very few examples of the other common theme, the *Aufbruch der Massen*, the ultimate social consequence of the individual *Wandlung*. A combination of these is evoked, however, in Leonhard Frank's *Der Mensch ist gut*.[11] These novellas are Utopian, since they anticipate a state of affairs beyond the events at the time of writing (1917–18), beyond the Great War and the subsequent revolution, in a period which is as yet only a subject of speculation. The events of 1917–18 are given exemplary and universal significance; they anticipate what the author considers necessary, namely, a revolution of the heart. This explains the great role assigned to rhetoric and its devices: these stories reach out to the larger audience of mankind.

Like Sternheim's *Chronik*, Frank's collection might be seen as presenting a theme with variations. Frank describes a single process that leads from the discovery of the evils of society as they appear epitomized in the First World War to the collective awareness of the need to return to man's goodness. This pattern, introduced in the first novella, 'Der Vater,' is the basic structure of all of his subsequent novellas.

Robert, the main protagonist of 'Der Vater,' achieves his transformation with exemplary, paradigmatic swiftness and completeness, and goes to work on society in a quasi-missionary capacity. Before the war he is a waiter who attempts to compensate for the frustrations resulting from his humiliating position by looking forward to a brighter future for his son, whom he adores and spoils. But Robert's dreams are shattered when his son dies on the battlefield, or, as the authorities prefer to call it, the 'Feld der Ehre' (9).

Like Sternheim, Frank is concerned with the corruption of language and thought that has occurred in pre-war society, and that is intensified during the war. The analysis of the word *Ehre* leads Robert to realize that he, like millions of other Germans, has been living with a deliberate lie: 'Ehre. Das war ein Wort und bestand aus vier Buchstaben. Vier Buchstaben, die zusammen eine Lüge bildeten von solch höllischer Macht, dass ein ganzes Volk an diese vier Buchstaben angespannt und von sich selbst in ungeheuerlichstes Leid hineingezogen hatte werden können' (9). Enlightened, Robert intervenes in a children's game involving a toy gun, and then goes on to address the bystanders as murderers for having forgotten the command of love. In a vision he evokes the dead on both sides of the conflict and pleads for an abandonment of the folly of war. The speech is highly rhetorical, employing questions, paradoxes, and striking images, as is characteristic also of expressionist drama. The speech is punctuated only by emotional exclamations of the bystanders. The subsequent mass scenes, too, are reminiscent of dramas by Toller and Kaiser. The protest march against the continuation of the war, which results from Robert's speech, is clearly intended to counterbalance the scenes of exuberance at the outbreak of the war. The ending, an echo of Georg Heym's story 'Der fünfte Oktober' and of many expressionist dramas, symbolically provides the story with an expanding context, from city to country to continent, with bells pealing and 'vieltausendstimmigem, gewaltigem Gesange' (22).

The novella is typical of Frank's view of the world as a theatre of the conflict between good and evil. War is raised to the level of an apocalyptic cataclysm. It is not explained in terms of political, social, economic, or even psychological conditions; instead, it becomes the symbol of moral guilt, and a solution is hence sought in quasi-religious terms, in atonement, in the doctrine of love. The *Wandlung* is not only based on intellectual enlightenment; it has the character of a miracle.

Compared to 'Der Vater,' the second novella, 'Die Kriegswitwe,' is far less typical. It shows a greater awareness of politics, and its organization follows that of a learning process. At first this process is very slow. The shock caused by the husband's death in battle does not immediately trigger the widow's revolt; she resorts instead to an 'Abzementierung des Gefühls' (27). It is only through her struggle for survival that her husband's death appears in its proper context. The power of money and the economic implications of war are revealed to her in a grocery store, in which she is refused credit. Again Frank focuses on the use of clichés and slogans as devices for obscuring truth. The defence of the 'heiligste Güter' is meaningless to a person who has been deprived of all means to survive. The alleged 'community of the afflicted,' too, proves illusory when the widow receives a harsh letter urging her to pay her debts. Through suffering, particularly at night, when her powers of rationalization are low, she arrives at a correct interpretation of war. At this point, Robert is reintroduced into the story as one who has already reached true understanding. Entirely by accident, the widow one day hears Robert speak in public, and she is immediately drawn towards him.

In her anguish the widow publicly calls for the destruction of all institutions of government as sources of man's inhumanity to man. This call to violent action is immediately neutralized by Robert's contention that individual rather than collective, 'institutionalized' guilt is involved. The waiter's plea is for passive resistance, not violence. However, the attempt by a wealthy businessman to interfere with the demonstration ends in his carriage being overturned and set on fire. For the time being, the question of violence remains unresolved. The progression of the argument shows that Frank's own viewpoint is being voiced by Robert, in which case Frank himself appears to be caught in the dilemma of wishing for change, while rejecting the violence needed to achieve it. The problem of the role of institutions in the process of change is side-stepped, because Frank's revolution is 'die Revolution der Liebe' (71). This, too, is part of the expressionist creed. By the sheer power of words, by evocation, by example, it is felt, the world can be changed. The faith of the expressionist in the power of rhetoric and emotion is enormous.

The next novella, 'Die Mutter,' shows a decline in political awareness. This time Frank operates with a heavy-handed religious symbolism. Since in the official churches the doctrine of love has lost its vital position, the son, fallen in battle, becomes a Christ-like figure. His mother is likened to the Virgin Mary ('die Verklärte,' 101). Yet another protest march ends with the opening up of space, but the Utopia remains conveniently vague: 'Die Wahrheit braucht nicht den Ton. Die Wahrheit ist still' (110).

From 'Die Kriegswitwe' on, Frank more and more abandons the pretext of fiction in favour of polemics. Whereas 'Der Vater' had a well-structured plot and well-defined characters, the last novellas are almost formless; they have become mere vehicles of argumentation and discussion. Unfortunately, this discussion becomes more and more dubious because of its rather simplistic antitheses and abstractions, which reach a climax in 'Das Liebespaar.' This story consists of a series of loosely connected discussions between a doctor who is to identify a suicide in a morgue, and the resurrected suicide. The latter is a philosopher who has written a book protesting the 'Ungeist' of the German state, which is apparent in the state's fanatical insistence on technology, geared, it seems, only to provide the machinery of war and equipment for the disposal of corpses.

In 'Die Kriegswitwe' the problem of violence had remained unsolved. In 1916 and 1917 this was no longer a purely theoretical problem. Opposition to the war had surfaced openly, and the leadership of the Left in a possible revolution is under discussion in 'Das Liebespaar.'

The open display of malcontentedness by the Social Democrats might have suggested to the pacifist philosopher, who is a protagonist in this novella, that here was a force emerging that might legitimately aspire to the leadership of the nation. But the philosopher rejects the Left on two accounts. First, its past is tainted, for initially it did not oppose the war. The explanation for this lack of protest provides the second reason for the philosopher's rejection. The working classes did not oppose the war because they owed their allegiance to an organization 'die ihre Mitglieder nur für den Klassenkampf um materielle Vorteile drillt' (131).

Here Frank echoes Heinrich Mann, who claimed that the materialistic, comfort-oriented working classes facilitated the continuation of the oppressive system: 'Sie [die Arbeiter] verstrickten sich täglich tiefer in die Sorge, Gewinn zu ziehen äus der Welt, wie sie ist. Ihr Denken war zuletzt kapitalistisch – mit Vorbehalt oder wissentlich oder in der Färbung der

Heuchelei; aber kapitalistisch.'[12] In other words, the working classes have become collaborators because of their concern for progress in material terms only. According to Frank, the scramble for wealth is one of the causes of the war: 'Dieses rapid ins Geldverdienen hineingeratene Volk hat, aus einem öden Materialismus heraus, vor dem Kriege "Hoch" geschrien, bei Kriegsausbruch nichts als "Hoch" geschrien. Und jetzt schreit es nur deshalb nicht mehr "Hoch", weil der Magen schreit' (131).

Robert, the hero of 'Der Vater,' claims: 'Die Kultur eines Volkes ist unabhängig von der Besitzanhäufung' (57). Against materialism, which disguises itself as 'Impressionismus' in Sternheim's 'Heidenstam' and as the accumulation of 'heiligste Güter' in Frank's 'Die Kriegswitwe,' the expressionist proclaims the crucial importance of *Geist*. Even a working-class poet such as Gerrit Engelke claimed: 'Die neue Weltdichtung kann uns vom starren, unfruchtbaren Materialismus, zu dem unsre Zeit in ihrem gesteigerten Aussenleben natürlicherweise neigt ... erlösen.'[13] But Frank's attacks are much sharper than those of most other expressionists, because Frank sees materialism as the direct cause of the war: 'Materialismus: angefangen beim entseelten, maschinierten Fabrikarbeiter, über den vor Bequemlichkeit stinkenden Kanapeebürger und über den Kapitalisten, den modernen Philosophen und Dichter weg, bis hinunter zum ersten Diener des Staates. Hier haben Sie die Ursache des Krieges.' (132). Such passages reveal Frank's distance from the proletarian masses. No attempts by post-war critics (primarily East German) to claim Frank for the communist cause can hide the fact that, in 1918, Frank was not at all convinced that a *social* revolution would bring about the Utopia he had in mind. If the philosopher of 'Das Liebespaar' is indeed a mouthpiece for the author, it is clear that, at the time of writing, Frank had not only retained the vocabulary of German idealism, but that he was still dominated by the dualism of self and world inherent in this philosophy. In defending 'das reine Ich' against 'das korrumpierte, krummgenagelte Weltgeschehen' (134), Frank sets up a dichotomy that precludes the kind of harmony between the individual and his society that the *Aktivisten* sought to realize through political action within the historical process.

'Das Liebespaar' is no longer a serious attempt to integrate the political discussions into a plot. It lacks the interest of earlier stories because its very abstractness renders it more vulnerable to argumentation that starts from different premises. The formal weaknesses of Frank's art also show more clearly. The protagonists are little more than voices carrying the ideas of the author; psychology is lacking, and repetition turns the story into a pedantic and tedious exercise.

The final story of the collection, 'Die Kriegskrüppel,' shows very much the same weaknesses, though the opening scenes, with their descriptions of a hospital tent near the front, are powerful enough. Frank presents an almost grotesque vision of the terrible waste caused by the war. Compared with this evocative presentation, the reintroduction of tedious argumentation about the war is a stylistic mistake. But the return of the war-wounded, which leads to a genuine 'Gefühlssturm,' provides Frank with a last chance to convince by the sheer power of words. Here a truly expressionist language is employed to convey the gestures of those caught in this outburst of emotions: 'Ekstase flammt. Schreie steigen. Die Wahrheit gerät in Fluss. Die Seele tagt' (201). At the height of the 'march of the crippled,' reactions surface that reduce the spectators to animals: 'Menschen, die ihn [den Krüppel] erblicken, brüllen auf und brechen brüllend in die Knie. Elegante Damen brechen im Weinen zusammen und erheben sich als Magdalenen' (203).

These exaggerations, painful if not ludicrous, seem to constitute a last desperate attempt to bring about Utopia by the magic of language, by a form of incantation. But the wish to outdo the closing sections of the other novellas is doomed by force of its very repetitiveness.

In the last novellas there is a complete lack of interest in action; these stories are practically without plot. We are left with a series of dialogues and with descriptions of mass movements. There is, moreover, a mixture of styles that cannot be reconciled. On the one hand, the style is theoretical, didactic and pedantic; on the other, an ecstatic, visionary, and exaggerated expressionistic style, associated with *Wandlung* and *Aufbruch*, prevails. This mixture of styles must be considered a failure. More importantly, however, the aesthetic failure is paralleled by a failure in the enunciation of political ideals and ideas. Neither the abstract speculations nor the uncontrolled outbursts of emotion in these stories indicate how the concept of the new man is to be realized in the realms that Frank is consciously avoiding, those of economics, of political activity, of history. Frank's solution of a brotherhood of mankind is not rooted in the realities of history and, like Sternheim's solution, must be relegated to the domain of mere subjective phantasmagoria. Thus, while the conflict between the individual and the self is solved in radically different ways in Sternheim and Frank, the solutions break down at the same point: in their removal from reality, in their abstractness, which ultimately reduces these writings to speculations without any practical significance.

Frank's failure indicates yet another weakness in expressionism. Despite the importance attached to the notion of community by almost every expressionist writer, it is primarily because of a very private need of the author to re-establish contact with society that he reaches out to his public. Even those poets who celebrate the brotherhood of man do not express a social goal, but an individual desire to break out of their isolation. The writings of Heym, Ehrenstein, Loerke and many others are replete with this problem. The hysterical forms taken by the projected integration of the subject into a transformed society (Frank is representative of all such writings) can only be understood against this background of *Weltfremdheit* and isolation.

Frank and Sternheim tell us a great deal about the reasons for the failure of expressionism to come to terms with the First World War. It is clear that, while seeking to break away from a multiplicity of doctrines in a relativistic bourgeois society, expressionism in turn became the victim of a multiplicity of doctrines. Where the subject is the only guide to the formulation of theory, no norm can be established. Though private Utopia remains possible, if only in a madhouse, as Sternheim argues, the social Utopia, when it is not based on objective and universally valid principles, cannot be achieved. The revolution after the catastrophe of war envisioned by Frank must fail, because Frank does not even grasp the nature of war.

Eva Kolinsky's admirable investigation of expressionism as a concrete, historical phenomenon[14] confirms on a general level what this paper has tried to establish by examining the prose writings of two representative writers: expressionism could not but fail in its attempt to deal with war and its aftermath, because of the many misconceptions held by expressionist writers about social reality. Thus, expressionism ends in contradictions and despair, in a mood of resignation and bitterness, paradoxically mirroring the initial despair that gave rise to it.

NOTES

1 Armin Arnold, *Die Literatur des Expressionismus: Sprachliche und thematische Quellen*, 2nd ed. (Stuttgart: Kohlhammer 1971) 58.
2 Ibid. 59.
3 Quoted in Hans-Jürgen Schmitt (ed.), *Die Expressionismusdebatte: Materialien zu einer marxistischen Realismuskonzeption* (Stuttgart: Suhrkamp 1973) 18.
4 A particularly striking case of pro-war feeling is Fritz von Unruh; his 'conversion' to pacifism, after the outbreak of the war, is discussed in Walter H. Sokel, *The Writer in Extremis: Expressionism in Twentieth-Century Literature* (Stanford,

Calif.: Stanford University Press 1959), chap. 7, 'The Revolt.'

5 Erich Kahler, 'Die Prosa des Expressionismus,' in *Der deutsche Expressionismus: Formen und Gestalten*, ed. Hans Steffen, 2nd ed. (Göttingen: Vandenhoeck & Ruprecht 1970) 164.

6 Max Brod, *Streitbares Leben (1884–1968)* (Munich: S.A. Herbig 1969) 82.

7 Now in Carl Sternheim, *Gesamtwerk*, ed. Wilhelm Emrich (Neuwied: Luchterhand 1964). Further references to Sternheim in the text are to this edition, vol. 4, 'Prosa.'

8 Ibid., vol. 6, 482.

9 Helmut Liede, *Stiltendenzen expressionistischer Prosa* (Dissertation, Freiburg 1960), chap. 2, 'Sternheim und die Kritik der Ekstase,' 3.

10 Wolfgang Wendler, *Carl Sternheim: Weltvorstellungen und Kunstprinzipien* (Frankfurt: Athenäum 1966) 45.

11 Leonard Frank, *Der Mensch ist gut* (Zurich: Max Rascher 1918). Further references to Frank in the text are to this edition.

12 Quoted in P.E. Boonstra, *Heinrich Mann als politischer Schriftsteller* (Utrecht: Kamink en Zoon – Over den Dom 1945) 84.

13 Gerrit Engelke, *Das Gesamtwerk: Rhythmus des neuen Europa*, ed. Dr H. Blume (Munich: Paul List 1960) 227.

14 Eva Kolinsky, *Engagierter Expressionismus: Politik und Literatur zwischen Weltkrieg und Weimarer Republik. Eine Analyse expressionistischer Zeitschriften* (Stuttgart: J.B. Metzler 1970).

DAVID JOHN

The *Sperber* in Hesse's *Demian*

'Unvergesslich ist die elektrisierende Wirkung, welche gleich nach dem ersten Weltkrieg der *Demian* eines gewissen mysteriösen Sinclair hervorrief, eine Dichtung, die mit unheimlicher Genauigkeit den Nerv der Zeit traf und eine ganze Jugend, die wähnte, aus ihrer Mitte sei ihr ein Künder ihres tiefsten Lebens entstanden, – zu dankbarem Entzücken hinriss.'[1] Thomas Mann's introduction to a new edition of *Demian* in 1947 is separated from Hesse's manuscript by three decades, yet his description of the novel's impact on German youth recalls at once the immediate public reaction to it in 1919. 'Auf so bedeutende Art hat noch keiner eine Erzählung in den Krieg einmünden lassen,' exclaimed a review in the *Neue Rundschau* of October 1919,[2] and when Hesse was discovered to be its anonymous author, he was inundated with letters from admiring and grateful young readers. His initial anonymity at the novel's publication had soon to be lifted, but its expressed purpose, to signify in his work a complete break with an age past, had been fulfilled.

Demian touched the hearts of the generation of German youth who had survived the First World War. It was conceived entirely during the conflict and soon signalled for thousands the beginning of a new era. This was Hesse's intention, and this indeed the immediate result. The unmistakable link between *Demian* and the First World War has not gone neglected by scholars in our own day.[3] Moreover, it is rare that a comprehensive study of the work does not attempt to elucidate the central symbol of the bird, and especially the striking image of this bird as a harbinger of war, with which the novel draws to a close. There has been no lack of attention here, and yet it is surprising that, beyond the obvious fact that the bird in *Demian* is a creature of prey, no study of the work has asked specifically why Hesse selected the precise genus *Sperber*. He certainly draws attention to this generic term throughout the work. There is no accurate English translation for it. Since my argument attempts to establish the importance of this specific genus for Hesse, *Demian*, and the period of the war, the fact that the *Sperber* is essentially a European bird should be made clear.

Demian is the first to allude to the *Sperber* escutcheon over the Sinclair doorway, and observes not just the creature's species, but also its exact genus, despite repeated painting and wear.[4] Looking into Pistorius's fire, Sinclair sees not just a bird but a 'Sperberkopf' (103). At the end of the novel the picture of the bird in Frau Eva's house is again a 'Sperberkopf' (137), and she points to the 'Sperberbild' (139). The generic emphasis could be no more forceful than in the climactic vision of the soaring bird as a harbinger of war – 'der Sperber ... mein Sperber' it is called by Sinclair (152). Is it an accident that Hesse insists repeatedly that the bird is a *Sperber* and no other? Why not an *Adler* or *Falke*, far more representative birds of prey in literary tradition and by far more common as heraldic symbols? It is primarily to this question that the following essay is addressed. By answering it, new insights into Hesse's novel of war can perhaps be gained.

Our investigation of the significance of the *Sperber* must begin with some general discussion of the bird and its egg, which together form the central symbol in *Demian*. Appreciation of these two elements is predicated by an awareness of the importance of Johann Jakob Bachofen's *Versuch über die Gräbersymbolik der Alten* and *Das Mutterrecht*, both of which undoubtedly influenced Hesse,[5] and of Carl Gustav Jung's *Symbole der Wandlung* and psychoanalytical techniques, to which Hesse was exposed intensively as he was writing *Demian* in the autumn of 1917.[6] Bachofen's interpretation of the black and white symbolic eggs in the Villa Pamfili in Rome as 'die Muttermaterie, das ursprünglich Gegebene, aus dessen dunklem chaotischen Schosse die Schöpfung an's Licht des Tages heraustritt,' and their dichotomous association with life and death,[7] lead directly to the symbol of the mother, the god Abraxas, and the key polarities of dark and light worlds in *Demian*.[8] Just as clearly, Jung's record of the frequent use of birds as soul images directs us towards understanding Hesse's bird as a representation of Sinclair's symbolic rebirth.[9] At the same time it is generally agreed that at the end of *Demian* the bird points to a process of destruction in society – on a wholly realistic level, that of the First World War – during which the old world is physically and spiritually destroyed so that the new may emerge: 'Sinclair's most private symbol is projected, at the end of the book, on to a universal screen as a harbinger of war,' and becomes a symbol of 'humanity striving to break out of the bonds of tradition,' writes Theodore Ziolkowski.[10] In sum, then, the bird and its egg in *Demian* are generally understood to represent a rebirth and overcoming of the dichotomy of good and evil in the past, in a personal sense for Sinclair and on a universal plane for humanity. On these basic interpretations of the bird and egg, undoubtedly a free syncretic blending by Hesse of elements from Roman antiquity, Gnostic cultism, and Jungian psychology, almost all scholars are in accord.[11]

Questions arise when we re-examine some of the ingredients of this syncretic blending. Hesse's appropriation of Jung's explanation of birds as soul images could be called the borrowing of an entirely positive symbol – at least this is the way that scholarship has tended to see it. Certainly such a view seems well founded on the basis of Jung's work. He writes of the world-wide heroic myths in which the hero is saved from impending doom by a helpful bird;[12] the Jewish legend of Adam's first wife, Lilith, whom Adam forces to return to him with the help of bird-angels (248 and n. 85); the singing swan as a sun symbol, signifying 'rebirth, the bringing forth of life from the mother, and the ultimate conquest of death' (348); the Maori myth of Maui, who is helped by the birds (348); the Siegfried legend, in which the hero learns to understand the language of birds, leading to a particular relationship with nature, which he then dominates by knowledge (364); and in more recent literature, Hölderlin's 'Patmos,' which includes images of eagles as sun birds (409).[13] The most striking example of bird imagery in Jung is his picture of the mountain as a symbol of emerging consciousness. Rising from blue waters, a green mountain is crowned by the golden sun, from which appears a gigantic bird of prey with wings outstretched.[14]

Two further references to Jung's bird symbolism require re-evaluation. The first has not gone unnoticed by critics, but at the same time has not been adequately explained. This core reference in Jung to birds as soul images deals with the apocalyptic vision in Revelation (18:2 ff.) of the whore of Babylon, whom Jung describes as 'not only the mother of all abominations, but the receptacle of all that is wicked and unclean. The birds are soul-images, by which are meant the souls of the damned and evil spirits' (214-15). The second reference to my knowledge has gone completely unnoticed by Hesse scholarship to date. It concerns the Roman legend of king Picus, who was changed by Circe to a soul-bird in the form of a *Picus martius* (woodpecker). Jung explains that the father of Picus was Sterculus or Sterculius, a name derived from *stercus*, 'excrement.' Sterculus is said to have invented manure, and in alchemy excrement signifies the *prima materia* (352 and n. 93). In other words, this legend lends distinctly tellurian associations to a myth of spiritual rebirth. A bird contains the soul of a man, but a man physically born through the rejuvenating powers of excrement, here synonymous with the earth. From the apocalyptic bird symbolism and the legend of Picus, there results an entirely different dimension to the bird in Jung's work. Here, at least, the bird as soul image is linked not only with the apparently positive process of spiritual rebirth, but also with the most negative tellurian abominations of the whore of Babylon and with the fecal allusions in the Picus legend. The apparently negative dimensions arising from the Biblical myth and the scatological imagery of the Roman legend will prove important for our understanding of *Demian* and the *Sperber*.

On the question of the egg, a fresh look at Jung also proves valuable. For the most part, interpretations of *Demian* refer largely to the bird but not to the egg symbolism in Jung. Without denying the importance of Bachofen we should note that Jung deals extensively with egg symbolism as well. He refers repeatedly to the cosmic egg that in essence is the shell of the world. The legend of Hiawatha, for example, tells of the world enclosed in the egg that surround it on all sides; it is the cosmic birth-giver (354). Connections to Hesse's bird, breaking through the egg of the world, are of course self-evident and have been duly noted by numerous critics. But it should be added that a constant for much of Jung's egg symbolism is the idea of the egg as self-perpetuated life. Prajapati, Lord of Creation in the Rig-Veda, is 'the self-begotten egg, the cosmic egg from which he hatches himself' (380 and fig. 36);[15] and in the Egyptian Book of the Dead, Khnum 'shapes his egg on the potter's wheel, for he is "immortal growth, his own generation and his own self-birth, the creator of the egg that came out of the primeval waters"' (256). In this same regard, Jung refers to Nietzsche's poem 'Ruhm und Ewigkeit' from the 'Dionysos Dithyramben' (382), in which the bird alludes to the self-rejuvenating egg as he exhorts Zarathustra: 'du brütest mir noch /ein Ei/ ein Basilisken-Ei/ aus deinem langen Jammer aus.'[16] Beyond the idea of self-perpetuation, Jung also associates the entire process of egg-laying with the Picus legend. He connects this excremental myth to the story of the Creator who 'laid an egg, his mother, from which he hatched himself out' (352 and n. 93). The laying of an egg is described as a parallel activity to the dropping of fecal matter, a comparison not contrary to biological fact, both synonymous for the initiation of the self-bearing process. Hence life is self-perpetuating through an excremental act.

Now zoological facts tell us that the eggs of the *Sperber* (*Accipiter nisus*) are unusual and distinctive. Almost round, they have a bluish white background with large blotches of dark reddish brown.[17] In conjunction we might add that for centuries in folk medicine it was thought that the *Sperber*'s feces contained life-giving potential: 'Sperberkot galt ehedem als geburtfördernd,' we read in records of folk beliefs.[18] This information on *Sperber* eggs and feces, along with Jung's references to the egg and the Picus legend, immediately suggest Hesse's treatment of the bird and egg symbols in *Demian*. Unlike most birds' eggs, the almost-round *Sperber* egg approximates the shape of the earth ('Das Ei ist die Welt,' 91). Beyond the shape, its reddish brown dark areas and blue background reflect the colouring of the *prima materia* against the blue of earth's oceans. In addition, this distinctive light and dark dichotomy points to the key polarity of the novel and completes a trio of associations – the earth, Bachofen's mystery eggs, and the polarity of good and evil.[19]

Through the folk medical belief in the power of *Sperber* excrement and the Roman legend of Picus, who was born of both egg and excrement in one, it would seem that Hesse's *Sperber* also connects the process of birth to the idea of self-perpetuation, and once again to the *prima materia*. Sinclair's entire journey is of course an inward one, and from within himself he gains new spiritual life. But in doing so he always retains his connection to the earth and to humanity. The tellurian link is never broken. We may add a further association at this point. According to biblical tradition, the *Sperber* genus is one forbidden for human consumption. Twice in the Old Testament, man is warned, 'Und dies sollt ihr scheuen unter den Vögeln, dass ihr's nicht esset: ... den Sperber mit seiner Art' (3 Mos. 11:16, 5 Mos. 14:15).[20] This biblical prohibition to mankind points clearly to Sinclair's dream, in which he is forced by Demian to consume the bird (88). In doing so he commits a cardinal sin in biblical terms, but at the same time demonstrates a dramatic rejection of the fundamental moral code of his childhood that had long prevented his development.

By Hesse's time, the *Sperber* had occupied an important place in German culture for centuries. First recorded as the genus *speruarius* in the Lex Salica,[21] the *sperbaere, sparwaere, sparwer,* or *sperwer* achieved its greatest importance in the medieval period, when killing it often led to severe penalties.[22] We can read in Konrad von Megenberg's *Buch der Natur* (1482) that, unlike the hawk and the falcon, 'des adels hât der spärwaer niht' (2159). Hence it enjoyed the distinction afforded birds of nobility while belonging in fact to a lower class. Of the bird's character, Megenberg relates that 'der sparwer fleuget mit den falken, ... wan er ist ain häzziger hôchvertiger vogel, und dar umb versmaeht er seineu geleichen und sein aigen gesläht durchaehlt er reht sam ainen fremden vogel, und daz ist wider aller anderr vogel siten' (2159). Unlike all other birds, then, the arrogant and hostile *Sperber* rejects his genus entirely. Proceeding with this exclusivity, Konrad Gesner writes in his *Tierbuch* (1563) that 'darumb ist allein der sperber desz adels unwüssend, als auch der mensch, der under andern irrdischen thieren nit aufhört seyn geschlächt zu neyden und zu hassen' (2159). Yet Megenberg adds an interesting incongruity to this unfavourable image: 'iedoch hât der spärwaer ain tugent an im, daz er winterzeiten ainen lebentigen vogel, den er gevangen hât, die ganze naht helt under seinen klâen, daz im dester wärmer sei, und laezt in des morgens fliegen. alsô gedenkt er der guottaet' (2159). It seems that on the one hand the medieval *Sperber* is the embodiment of enmity, hatred, and social exclusivity, but on the other capable of acts of profound generosity. In sum, the medieval image of the *Sperber* is one based upon his apparent nobility and consequent exclusivity from his genus, his arrogant and aggressive nature, compared by Gesner to human envy and hatred, and his enigmatic capacity for benevolence towards those weaker than himself.

This medieval picture underscores Hesse's use of the *Sperber* in *Demian*. In the case of both Emil Sinclair and his bird, we are dealing with the question of social legitimacy. Like the *Sperber*, Sinclair's role throughout the novel points to an increasing social exclusivity despite his bourgeois background. His family even has a coat of arms over its door – an emblem normally associated with aristocratic lines. From the beginning a conflict develops between Sinclair and the society in which he lives, stressed in the early chapters by his relationship with Kromer. Sinclair is the 'Herrensöhnchen' (14) who attends the *Lateinschule*, Kromer the working-class boy from the *Volksschule*.[23] An almost complete social rift is demonstrated at the end by his acceptance into the élite circle at Frau Eva's home. Moreover, Sinclair's uniqueness is linked repeatedly with the possibility of aggression against his fellow man, if this be necessary to maintain his select position. His mentors, Demian and Pistorius, both advocate murder in certain circumstances (43, 111) and the Nietzschean attitude towards the 'Herdenmenschen' has long been recognized as a continuing motif in the work. The final image of the *Sperber* as a harbinger of war is thus a natural conclusion to the motif of aggression for both the *Sperber* and Sinclair, and a parallel in the novel to Gesner's equation of the *Sperber*'s intrinsic belligerence with human bellicosity. Still, it is at this point, too, that the obverse side of both personalities is emphasized. Just as the aggressive impulse is at its height, both Sinclair and his medieval counterpart demonstrate their deepest capacity for benevolence. The *Sperber* unexpectedly releases his fallen prey and grants it new life; Sinclair's vision of combat clearly represents a necessary stage towards a new phase of humanity. It is the culmination of that latent sense of compassion demonstrated in the mysterious Knauer episode earlier.

What should be stressed above all in the nature of the *Sperber* is the tension between aggression and benevolence. Just as the real genus *Sperber* embodies this curious dichotomy, so does the bird throughout the novel. We should remember that the first reference to the *Sperber* by Demian is juxtaposed to his explanation to Sinclair of the story of Cain, an account of primal conflict and fratricide (30), and one that for Demian demonstrates the role – even the necessity – of physical violence for the development of the individual. Added to this is the repeated cryptic message: 'Der Vogel kämpft sich aus dem Ei. Das Ei ist die Welt. Wer geboren werden will, muss eine Welt zerstören' (91). Violence is a necessary component of this birth and it should not be seen only in its purely symbolic form, but also in certain circumstances as a truly physical struggle.

All the evidence of the *Sperber*'s warlike nature corroborates this argument. What is more, it can readily be shown that the association of the bird with physical violence was a theme alive in other Hesse works at the time he wrote *Demian*.[24] In 'Merkwürdige Nachricht von einem anderen Stern' (1915), we are told of a messenger sent to find flowers for the grave of a friend. 'Ein grosser dunkler Vogel, wie er noch keinen gesehen hatte, flog ihm voraus, und er folgte ihm.'[25] Not just the creature's size, but also his 'gebogener Schnabel' (55) tells us that he is a bird of prey. The messenger rides this bird to a distant land that has been reduced to ruins by a war caused by 'Hass,' 'Mord,' and 'Eifersucht' (54). Upon arriving, the bird is seen sitting alone and 'schlug von Zeit zu Zeit gewaltig mit seinen ungeheuren Flügeln, dass es rauschte wie ein Sturm in den Bäumen' (53), an image remarkably similar to the final bird allusion in *Demian*. Moreover, the conclusion of the tale again brings *Demian* to mind: 'Wir ahnen Glück,' says the king, 'wir ahnen Freiheit, wir ahnen Götter. Wir haben eine Sage von einem Weisen der Vorzeit, er habe die Einheit der Welt als einen harmonischen Zusammenklang der Himmelsräume vernommen' (63). Here the bird is linked directly to the physical destruction of war as well as to the vision of a future liberation of the spirit. We can add to this example the story 'Vogel' (1932), which, despite its chronological distance from *Demian*, bears a striking parallel. The mythical *Vogel*, it is told, is 'so alt wie die Welt, er sei einstmals dabeigewesen, als Abel von seinem Bruder Kain erschlagen wurde, und habe einen Tropfen von Abels Blut getrunken, dann sei er mit der Botschaft von Abels Tod davon geflogen und teile sie heute noch den Leuten mit, damit man die Geschichte nicht vergesse und sich von ihr mahnen lasse, das Menschenleben heiligzuhalten und brüderlich miteinander zu leben' (*GW*, vol. 6, 464). At the end of the tale, the *Vogel* disappears, 'zurück entflohen ... zu Kain und Abel, ins Paradies' (478). Is this not in a nutshell the same function as that of the *Sperber* in *Demian*? In both, the bird points to the same myth of primal human aggression and, within constant memory of this beginning, moves towards a higher humanistic plane.

At the outset we noted that the bird symbol in *Demian* has gained general acceptance as a harbinger of war at the end of the novel and that the symbol of the bird is entirely personal for Sinclair in the early chapters, while it assumes the broadest connotations for humanity towards the end. In keeping with this view we may now cite the description of the *Sperber* in the Beatrice chapter, at the centre of the work, from which a striking turning-point is evident. At what must be seen as a critical time in Sinclair's development, he recounts as follows: 'In der Nacht träumte ich von Demian und von dem Wappen. Es verwandelte sich beständig. Demian hielt es in Händen, oft war es klein und grau, oft mächtig gross und vielfarbig, aber er erklärte mir, dass es doch immer ein und dasselbe sei' (88). Now the *Accipiter nisus* is described by zoological encylopaedias as eleven to fifteen inches long with slate grey or grey (male) or grey brown (female) colouring, a lighter underside, and touches of yellow and blue in the eyes, legs, and beak.[26] We should remember too that Jung's famous picture of the bird of emerging consciousness is based upon the primary colours of yellow and blue. Before Sinclair's eyes, the bird shows two dimensions: once it is small and grey – the actual size and basic colouring of a real *Sperber*, and then large and colourful – the golden sun bird that flies into the blue heavens with Sinclair's soul at the end. The same bird contains at once two facets of reality, always maintaining both, but reflecting different aspects at different times. Sinclair immediately afterwards speaks of 'meiner inneren Umwandlung' (90) and attempts to paint what he has seen, adding colours 'je nach Laune' (89). The yellow and blue he selects are suggested by the *Sperber*'s natural colouring on the one hand, but on the other are plainly an unconscious expression of his inner consciousness, and foreshadow the conclusion of the novel.

G.W. Field has asserted that *Demian* 'illustrates strikingly the shift from fictional realism to the plane of surrealism' and that a key distinction in the work is the level of 'sogenannte Wirklichkeit' as opposed to Hesse's idea of 'echte Wirklichkeit.'[27] Surely this important distinction is illustrated no more forcefully than in the passage above. And indeed, from this point on, the novel does move from the plane of *sogenannte Wirklichkeit* towards the realm of *echte Wirklichkeit*, Sinclair's goal.[28]

This key distinction requires that we now define as precisely as possible how the second realm of reality differs from the first. The first half of the novel contains few, but nevertheless unmistakable references to the realm of *sogenannte Wirklichkeit*. These include above all indications of deep social change. The image of girls streaming from the factories in the evening heralds the power of a new class of workers (10), and the struggle reflected in the Kromer episode the necessary dissolution of an outdated hierarchy. Yet it would be a mistake to divorce entirely this realm of *sogenannte Wirklichkeit* from that of *echte Wirklichkeit*, for the latter in fact should be seen to absorb reality of all kinds, just as the *Sperber* contained two facets at once. 'Draussen war die "Wirklichkeit,"' says Sinclair from within Frau Eva's élite circle, 'draussen waren Strassen und Häuser, Menschen und Einrichtungen, Bibliotheken und Lehrsäle – hier drinnen aber war Liebe und Seele, hier lebte das Märchen und der Traum. Und doch lebten wir keineswegs von der Welt abgeschlossen, wir lebten in Gedanken oft mitten in ihr, nur auf einem anderen Felde, wir waren von der Mehrzahl der Menschen nicht durch Grenzen getrennt, sondern nur durch eine andere Art des Sehens' (142).

As final proof of the inextricability of the two realms, we need only turn to the conclusion of the novel. Here there is direct discussion of the state of European politics (143–5), consideration of the impending war (156-7), and then upon its outbreak the immediate enlisting of Demian and Sinclair soon after. Here again, late in the work, concrete references to the world of *sogenannte Wirklichkeit* come to the fore. The difference from the early chapters lies in the possibility now of a higher aim for the individual and society. When injected with this aspiration, the *sogenannte Wirklichkeit* becomes transformed, not forgotten or annulled. The transformation is punctuated at the end of the work as Sinclair frequents Frau Eva's home, passing regularly beneath the *Sperber* 'wie ein Sohn und Bruder' (142) just as he had done in his own home for years, but now it is 'auch wie ein Liebender,' with that greater dimension of humanity just at his grasp.[29]

The realm of *echte Wirklichkeit* thus encompasses *sogenannte Wirklichkeit* and adds to it unheard-of dimensions. Every facet of its conflict and struggle is incorporated into the vision, but now with a sublime objective for those involved. One of these facets, the most immediate in the novel, is the reality of the First World War. When we understand that this too contributes to Hesse's *echte Wirklichkeit*, then it is not surprising that his young men are both among the earliest to enlist for action. The war, too, is part of their vision.

The linking of *Demian* to Hesse's actual experience of the First World War should be the final step. Two primary sources provide information here, his political essays written during the war and the letters of the same period.[30] Like the young men of his novel, Hesse was one of the first to enlist when war was declared in the summer of 1914. His volunteering for service in August 1914 is particularly well recorded by a legal declaration from the hands of a lawyer, Conrad Haussmann, on 2 November 1915,[31] and through a missive from the Kaiserlich Deutsche Gesandtschaft in Bern on the following day (*GB* 545). This unusual documentation was necessitated by anonymous and unjust accusations of cowardice against Hesse, published on the front page of the *Kölner Tageblatt* of 24 October 1915 (*GB* 537–9). Despite his willingness to join the ranks, Hesse was refused for active service on medical grounds (his poor vision), but from that time on assumed a leading role in war-related activities through the publication of two journals for German prisoners of war (*Sonntagsboten für die deutschen Kriegsgefangenen*, 1916–19; *Deutsche Interniertenzeitung*, 1916–17), as well as the collection and distribution of thousands of works of literature to these men. Hesse devoted himself totally to these activities – he often complained in his letters that he had no time for his own work. For this, it should be added, he received no remuneration.

Hesse's letters reflect a consistent attitude towards the physical brutality of war and its consequences. 'Am Krieg plagt mich zur Zeit am meisten die Brutalität,' he writes in October 1914 (*GB* 247), 'mit der über alles Politische und Soldatische hinaus allgemeine Geisteswerte verachtet und bespuckt werden.' He recognized and accepted the inevitable brutality of war, yet he worked every day to offset its spiritual consequences. Almost a year later, in September 1915, we see that this impression is even more deeply ingrained, so that his work now seems a desperate daily struggle to counteract it: 'Und das Elend, das einen jetzt aus der ganzen Welt her anruft, ist so ungeheuer, dass ich in meiner kleinen Ecke alles tun will, was ich dabei helfen kann' (*GB* 284).

Some impressions left by his writings during the early years of the war must be carefully weighed against later statements. At times, Hesse seemed intensely nationalistic. In reply to his fervently patriotic critics, he wrote in 'O Freunde, nicht diese Töne' (September 1914), 'Ich bin Deutscher, und meine Sympathien und Wünsche gehören Deutschland.'[32] A year later he was to write a highly enthusiastic review of Max Scheler's *Der Genius des Krieges und der deutsche Krieg* (Sept. 1915, *GB* 525–6), a fervour much tempered fifteen months later (30 Dec. 1916, *GB* 342). Yet the same enthusiasm shown for Scheler's book can be read in letters as well. 'Deutschland wird sich in der Welt durchsetzen, mit seinen Waffen und seiner Wirtschaft,' he says in December 1915, 'wie es sich ehemals mit seiner Musik, seiner Dichtung und seiner Philosophie durchgesetzt hat. Und es wird, dessen ist mein Gefühl sicher, über den Waffen und der Wirtschaft die Künste und alle andern Gebiete seelischer Kultur nicht vernachlässigen' (*GB* 309–10). There is no abrupt change in Hesse's apparent nationalism in the later war years. In an open letter published in the *Frankfurter Zeitung* (2 Aug. 1917), he shows a continuing sense of service and duty to his country: 'Wenn ich es als Dichter ablehne, mich den Forderungen einer geistig nicht hochstehenden Zeit zu unterwerfen, so kann ich trotzdem als Mensch, als Nummer und Soldat meine Arbeit tun' (*GB* 356). And finally, just three weeks before armistice, Hesse still states: 'Mein Glaube an jenes Deutschtum, dem mein Herz gehört und das seit Jahrzehnten fast unsichtbar geworden war, ist jetzt stärker als je' (19 Oct. 1918, *GB* 380).

We must immediately add some amplification and interpretation to these statements. In all of them lies a hint of Hesse's own particular idea of what national duty and responsibility should mean. 'O Freunde, nicht diese Töne' goes on to say, 'Da man jetzt einmal am Schiessen ist, soll geschossen werden – aber nicht des Schiessens und der verabscheuungswürdigen Feinde wegen, sondern um so bald wie möglich eine höhere und bessere Arbeit wieder aufzunehmen!' (*PB* 11). His enthusiasm for Max Scheler's book resulted from the detection of a European, if not an international standpoint beneath the nationalism, and his confidence in Germany's success emphasizes not the military prowess but the cultural leadership. Hesse's nationalism was essentially a sense of loyalty to his homeland and a feeling of duty towards it, but contained none of the 'Hurrapatriotismus' that he repeatedly denounced. For Hesse, war was part of life. To deny it would be to deny reality. His open letter to the pacifists makes this abundantly clear: 'Aber der Krieg, seine Greuel und Erhebungen, mein Schmerz über ihn und alle meine Sorgen, all dies war Leben, all dies war Wirklichkeit, war greifbare, strotzende Welt, durchflossen vom Strom des Lebens, oft schön, oft furchtbar hässlich, aber glaubhaft, wirklich, real. Dagegen waren die Worte der Friedensleute zwar gut, zwar edel, zwar einwandfrei, aber es floss nicht der Strom des Lebens in ihnen, es sprang mir aus ihnen nicht

Wirklichkeit entgegen wie rotes Blut' (*GB* 550). Hesse found himself in an impossible situation. He accepted the reality of war and became an active part of it as a loyal and conscientious citizen, and yet he despised the short-sighted goals it assumed. His aims were different and his idea of the potential of war was directly opposed to that of most of his countrymen.

Hesse speaks of the positive role of war for human development as early as 1914, just months after the outbreak of fighting: 'Und manchmal wird der ganze Krieg mir für Momente ganz nah und verständlich und fast schön, obwohl es an Gegengewichten nicht fehlt. Es muss jetzt einmal sein, und eine gute Zukunftsahnung ist doch dabei' (4 Dec. 1914, *GB* 253). His optimism heightened as time passed. A year later he called the war 'nur ein Mittel, und dass er nicht nur ein Mittel zum Entsetzlichen sein kann, sondern auch eines zum Guten, zu neuem Leben, zu Vertiefung und Besinnung, das haben wir in dieser Zeit oft genug erlebt' ('Den Pazifisten,' *GB* 550). As the conflict neared its end, and the bloodshed coincided with the emergence of *Demian*, Hesse's premonition of the positive function of war had reached its zenith. 'Dass der Krieg als Ganzes beitragen wird, das Gesicht der Welt zu ändern und der Befreiung der Seele in Europa zu dienen, ist mir gewiss,' he wrote in June 1917 (*GB* 350). This vision includes the notion of a unified Europe, with Germany as either 'Führer oder doch starker Mitführer eines einiger werdenden Europa' (*GB* 269). With *Demian* it became clear that even Hesse's vision of a unified Europe was only a forerunner of a broader unity. The final stage would see the liberation of all humanity from national, political, and even earthly bonds.

Demian could well be called a lyrical summary of Hesse's insights into the First World War and its significance for mankind. Still today, it reflects what the public and reviewers immediately recognized, the struggle of an entire generation to break through the limitations of a dying political and social order, and the period of conflict in Europe that acted as a catalyst. Just as important is its exploration of the soul of man, a soul yearning for freedom and humanity while tethered inextricably to the dark currents of human frailty – envy, hatred, and aggression. As the central symbol of the novel, the *Sperber* is a constant reminder that the human spirit encompasses both extremes. When this symbol is properly understood within biblical, medieval, mythological, and zoological terms, the complexity of *Demian* can be fully appreciated. In July 1917, just weeks before beginning the story of Emil Sinclair, Hesse complained, 'Ich habe ein Loch im Flügel und muss darum auf der Erde gehen, solang das dauert' (*GB* 353). Four months later *Demian* was finished, and Hesse again aloft.

NOTES

1 Thomas Mann, 'Hermann Hesse: Einleitung zu einer amerikanischen *Demian*-Ausgabe,' *Neue Rundschau* 58 (1947) 248.
2 *Neue Rundschau*, Heft 10 (October 1919), quoted from Adrian Hsia (ed.), *Hermann Hesse im Spiegel der zeitgenössischen Kritik* (Bern and Munich: Francke 1975) 174.
3 For an up-to-date critical summary of scholarship on *Demian*, see G.W. Field, *Hermann Hesse. Kommentar zu sämtlichen Werken*, Stuttgarter Arbeiten zur Germanistik, no. 24 (Stuttgart: Akademischer Verlag Hans-Dieter Heinz 1977) 85–92.
4 Hesse, *Gesammelte Werke* (Frankfurt: Suhrkamp 1970), vol. 5, 30. Further references to this edition of *Demian* are included in the text.
5 Reference to Hesse's studies of Bachofen can be found in 'Aus einem Tagebuch des Jahres 1920,' *Corona* 3 (1932–3) 204. For further connections, see Theodore Ziolkowski, *The Novels of Hermann Hesse* (Princeton, NJ: Princeton University Press 1965) 112.
6 We know that Hesse had read Jung's *Symbole der Wandlung* by the time he wrote *Demian*, and possibly some of Jung's earlier writings as well. See the correspondence between E. Maier, Jung, and Hesse, *Psychoanalytic Review* 50 (1963) 15–16 (365–6). There is no doubt, too, that the more than sixty analytical sessions Hesse had with Jung's disciple, Dr J.B. Lang, in Sonnmatt from June 1916 to November 1917 heightened the impressions made by his own reading. The most exhaustive studies on the influence of Jung on Hesse are by Emanuel Maier, 'The Psychology of C.G. Jung in the Works of Hermann Hesse' (Dissertation, New York University 1952), esp. 66–111, and Malte Dahrendorff, 'Hermann Hesse's *Demian* and C.G. Jung,' *GRM*, N.F. 8 (1958) 1, 81–97. For the most recent concise study in this regard, see Joseph Mileck, 'Freud and Jung, Psychoanalysis and Literature, Art and Disease,' *Seminar* 14, no. 2 (1978) 107–8.
7 Johann Jakob Bachofen, *Das Mutterrecht. Eine Untersuchung über die Gynaikokratie der alten Welt nach ihrer religiösen und rechtlichen Natur*, 2. unveränderte Aufl. (1897; reprint ed., Brussels: Culture et Civilisation 1969) 70b with Tafel 4, and 135b.
8 On this point, see Ziolkowski, *Novels* 114–15.
9 See ibid. 117–18, and G.W. Field, *Hermann Hesse* (New York: Twayne 1970) 56.
10 *Novels* 116–17.
11 The term 'free syncretic blending,' so appropriate in this context, has been borrowed from Ziolkowski, *Novels* 111.

12 *Symbols of Transformation.* 2nd ed., 2nd printing with corrections, trans. R.F.C. Hull, Bollingen Series 20 (Princeton, NJ.: Princeton University Press 1967) 347–8. Unless noted otherwise, further references to Jung appearing in the text are to this edition.

13 Hesse's interest in Hölderlin and the name Isaak von Sinclair, Hölderlin's friend, underscore the relevance of this reference to Jung. See John Christopher Middleton, 'Hermann Hesse as Humanist' (Dissertation, Oxford 1954) 172.

14 A full-colour reproduction can be found in Jolande Jacobi's *The Psychology of C.G. Jung* (New Haven: Yale University Press 1973) 96, plate 4.

15 We should remember that Pistorius introduces Sinclair to the Rig-Veda among other works of Eastern religion (120–1).

16 Friedrich Nietzsche, *Werke* (Leipzig: Kröner 1919); vol. 8, 463. Hesse's well-known fascination with Nietzsche is evident repeatedly throughout his personal correspondence and works. In this regard, see Herbert W. Reichert, *Friedrich Nietzsche's Impact on Modern German Literature: Five Essays* (Chapel Hill: University of North Carolina Press 1975). The fifth essay, 'The Impact of Nietzsche on Hermann Hesse,' deals specifically with *Demian* (97–100).

17 See A. Rutgers and K.A. Norris (eds.), *Encyclopaedia of Aviculture* (London: Blandford Press 1970–7), vol. 1, 167, for a description of the *Sperber* egg. A picture is accessible in the Brockhaus, listed under 'Ei.' A word of caution regarding the genus *Sperber* should be injected at this point. In English translations of *Demian*, *Sperber* appears usually as 'sparrow-hawk.' This is imprecise. Hesse's *Sperber* (*Accipiter nisus*) is a small hawk of Europe, northwest Africa, and Asia. It differs from the North American sparrow-hawk, or kestrel (*Falco sparverius*), in size and, to some extent, colouring. In this regard, see in addition to Rutgers and Norris, Roger Tory Peterson, *A Field Guide to the Birds of Britain and Europe* (Boston: Houghton Mifflin, n.d.) 76, and Peterson, *A Field Guide to the Birds* [*of America*], 2nd ed. (Boston: Houghton Mifflin 1934) 52. These reference works not only show that we are dealing with two different species here, but they also illustrate the confusion arising from the English word 'sparrow-hawk,' for Rutgers and Norris use that word when really describing the *Sperber* – they identify the bird by its German name as well.

18 *Handwörterbuch des deutschen Aberglaubens* (Berlin: De Gruyter 1936–7), vol. 8, 234.

19 We may add that because of its colouring the egg of the *Accipiter nisus* could well be likened to the Taoist Yin Yang circle. For a revealing study of the influence of oriental religion on Hesse, which includes reference to this circle in connection with *Demian*, see Adrian Hsia, *Hermann Hesse und China* (Frankfurt: Suhrkamp 1974), esp. 214.

48 David John

20 My attention was drawn to the Old Testament prohibition by Grimm's *Deutsches Wörterbuch*, 9. Aufl. (Leipzig: Hirzel 1965), vol. 22, 2159. In addition, with regard to the confusion surrounding translations of *Sperber* into English, we can add that the Revised Standard Version of the Old Testament in English renders the same portion of the Scripture simply as 'the hawk according to its kind' (Lev. 11: 16; Deut. 14:15).

21 Friedrich Kluge, *Etymologisches Wörterbuch der deutschen Sprache*, 20. Aufl. (Berlin: De Gruyter 1967) 723.

22 This and subsequent references to the *Sperber* in medieval times are quoted from Grimm's *Deutsches Wörterbuch*, vol. 22, 2158–61.

23 The social implications of the conflict between Sinclair and Kromer are well argued by Fritz Böttger, *Hermann Hesse. Leben. Werk. Zeit.* (Berlin: Verlag der Nation, n.d.) 248–9, although the Marxist tenor of his interpretation goes beyond the limits acceptable to most Hesse readers. A similar argument is presented by Erwin Neumann, 'Hermann Hesses Roman "Demian" (1917) – eine Analyse,' *Wiss. Zeitschrift der Pädagogischen Hochschule Potsdam* 12, Heft 4 (1968) 677, 682.

24 Mark Boulby alludes to the possibility of a connection here. See *Hermann Hesse: His Mind and Art* (Ithaca, NY: Cornell University Press 1967) 110, n. 62.

25 *GW*, vol. 6, 52. Further references to Hesse's tales appear in the text.

26 Rutgers and Norris, *Encyclopaedia*, vol. 1, 167.

27 'Hermann Hesse: Polarities and Symbols of Synthesis,' *Q.Q.* 81 (1974) 87–101, esp. 88–9.

28 In conjunction with the present discussion of levels of reality in *Demian*, the question of autobiographical connections between Hesse's childhood and the novel becomes relevant. There are some obvious confluent motifs, and many have been documented. But on the subject of the *Sperber*, the question naturally arises as to whether or not Hesse's childhood house in Calw did in fact have an escutcheon over the doorway. Hesse was born in a house on Calw's central square. Numerous Hesse studies contain pictures of this house: for example, Bernhard Zeller, *Hermann Hesse in Selbstzeugnissen und Bilddokumenten* (Hamburg: Rowohlt 1963) 8; Volker Michels, *Hermann Hesse. Leben und Werk im Bild* (Frankfurt: Insel 1973) 37; and Eike Middell, *Hermann Hesse. Die Bilderwelt seines Lebens* (Frankfurt: Röderberg 1975) 23. From none of these pictures is the detail over the doorway clear enough to determine the presence or absence of an escutcheon. In addition, this house has been renovated and for years has sèrved as a clothing store. Anyone who visits the structure today will find no trace of an escutcheon, if indeed it ever existed. The construction firm of Jakob Alber KG in Althengstett, near Calw, which performed the latest renovation in the mid-sixties, has no recollection of any marking over the doorway. It seems

safe to assume that none in fact ever existed, on that plane of reality at least. Finally, the other building in which Hesse lived in Calw, Bischofstrasse 4, still stands but has no bird escutcheon.

29 J.C. Middleton, 'Hermann Hesse as Humanist' (161–2), adds an intriguing note to this reversal. When Sinclair enters Frau Eva's home, he notices not only the *Sperber*, but draws attention to the colours blue and yellow. Says Middleton, 'The colours blue and yellow are opposites in the spectrum, and his going into the house thence expresses Sinclair's desire to get "behind the opposites."'

30 Virtually every book on Hesse devotes a chapter to his activities in the war. In most cases, however, authors tend to create a picture of Hesse's attitudes to the war by citing source material from the war years as well as the following decades. This retrospective view could well be very different from the immediate one formed entirely during the conflict. Because of this, my discussion of Hesse's attitudes towards the war is carried out solely on the basis of material written between 1914 and 1918.

31 *Gesammelte Briefe*, ed. Ursula and Volker Michels (Frankfurt: Suhrkamp 1973), vol. 1, 556. Further references to letters in this volume will appear in the text with the prefix *GB*.

32 *Politische Betrachtungen* (Frankfurt: Suhrkamp 1970) 9. Further references to political essays in this volume will appear in the text with the prefix *PB*.

HEINZ WETZEL

War and the Destruction of Moral Principles in Arnold Zweig's *Der Streit um den Sergeanten Grischa* and *Erziehung vor Verdun*

I

Arnold Zweig has become an embarrassment to literary historians and critics. From the appearance of his first novel, *Der Streit um den Sergeanten Grischa*, in 1927, his art seemed to decline until it reached its lowest point in his last novel, *Traum ist teuer* (1963), where the theme of the *Grischa* novel is taken up again merely in order to serve as a narrative scaffolding for political propaganda. Since his works are generally considered to form a homogeneous sequence, this decline had a profoundly negative effect on their overall appreciation. But to what extent does this homogeneity really exist?

Assuredly, most of Zweig's important works have a common theme: the causes and effects of injustice in times of war. In addition, socialist values were emphasized even in Zweig's earliest novels, so that his works seem to be linked to each other by an ever-increasing stress on these values. Thus the first and the last novel seem to mark the beginning and the end of an ideological development from which none of the works is excluded. Among other integrating elements are the interrelation of subject matter and the reappearance of some characters in several of the six novels about the First World War. It seems therefore impossible to concentrate on any one novel in particular without considering its position in the sequence. The war novels are usually considered to form a cycle; Zweig himself called the first four of them a tetralogy. Hence the embarrassment: *Der Streit um den Sergeanten Grischa* and *Erziehung vor Verdun*, the two novels that deserve more serious attention than they have received, seem inseparably linked to the weaker ones.

Why these two novels should be considered superior to the others is as difficult to explain as it seems obvious. A number of plausible reasons have been put forward, but there will be no methodologically clear solution to the problem as long as the more general question of how works of art can be evaluated remains unsolved. This, however, is not sufficient justification for scholars to neglect these two novels along with the others, nor can such justification be derived from the relationship between the war novels, since this has been over-emphasized. There are several good reasons for taking the individual novels as works in their own right rather than considering them to be parts of a greater whole.

In each novel of the 'tetralogy' the plot is entirely self-contained, as the respective endings indicate. In *Der Streit um den Sergeanten Grischa*, one of the protagonists, Grischa, is killed, while the other, General von Lychow, is defeated and resigns. Although he is still mentioned in subsequent novels, mainly in *Einsetzung eines Königs*, he never actually reappears as a character. *Junge Frau von 1914* ends in the marriage of Leonore Wahl to Werner Bertin and in the striking change in Bertin's character that solves the conflict formulated in the novel. At the end of *Erziehung vor Verdun* the major figure, Eberhard Kroysing, is killed, while Bertin, who is transferred to the eastern front, leaves the place of the action for good. *Einsetzung eines Königs* culminates in Captain Paul Winfried's spectacular conversion to democracy and in the symbolical death of the conservative General Wilhelm Clauss.

Nor was the series of war novels conceived as a cycle. They all owe their origins to different impulses. In the earlier play on which he based *Der Streit um den Sergeanten Grischa*, Zweig had formulated his moral indignation at the execution of a Russian sergeant, the scandalous circumstances of which had been brought to his attention. The story then challenged Zweig's narrative talent; in the novel he could incorporate actual details from routine military life behind the front, which he knew so well. In *Junge Frau von 1914*, the action of which is set in a period prior to that of the first novel, Zweig's primary motivation was autobiographical. He describes Bertin's inner brutalization, resulting from his enthusiasm for warfare, and his subsequent disillusionment, brought about by his actual experience of the war. Zweig, like many of his contemporaries, had gone through this process himself; by describing it he dissociated himself from an earlier phase of his development. In his third novel he intended to formulate a young man's growing awareness of social, economic, and political conditions. In 1934, four years after he had written the first version, he felt the need to rewrite this novel, introducing the story of

Lieutenant Eberhard Kroysing. It thus became *Erziehung vor Verdun*. In this second version his original intention to use Bertin, the main character, to epitomize the growing political awareness to which he meant to contribute through the novel, faded in the face of his strongly unfolding narrative talent. Kroysing became the central figure; in telling *his* story Zweig provided his novel with a homogeneous plot through which he could again interrelate many significant details from his own experience of military life.[1]

In *Einsetzung eines Königs* Zweig's specific aim was to illustrate the close relationship between war and both political and economic interests. This time the development of a young and naïve soldier's political consciousness remains in the foreground. The novel does not have a plot as tightly woven as those of the preceding ones. Given Zweig's highly conventional, realistic narrative method, this is an obvious disadvantage. In addition, he made a greater effort to record actual historical events and developments. As a result, the historical details that Zweig read and heard about tended to dominate the novel at the expense of those he knew from experience – a change that affected the artistic merits of the novel, too. In *Die Zeit ist reif* (1957) he couched his by-now unequivocally ideological interpretation of the pre-war situation in autobiographical images. Here the integrating force of a plot is lacking to an even greater extent; the figures are above all mouthpieces of ideological positions. They put forward their opinions in endless discussions, while the reader is denied not only the aesthetic pleasure of fascinating action but also the enticement to critical reflection, for light and darkness are clearly distributed by the narrator.

Consequently, Zweig's commitment to socialism, as it is reflected in his novels, does not merely grow stronger from one work to the next. There is also a decisive difference in the quality of his attitude: the open-minded sympathy that is apparent in his early novels is replaced by an uncritical acceptance even of the perversion of socialism during the Stalin era. This marks a broken rather than a consistent development.

It is then only in his first and third novel that Zweig invented an intriguing and centralized plot, into which he integrated the strongly realistic, concrete details of military life and through which he expressed his indignation at the injustice characteristic of the military environment during the war, an indignation that was still spontaneous rather than the result of an ideologically determined perspective. When, with *Einsetzung eines Königs*, he started to work consciously on a comprehensive presentation of the more hidden causes and effects of the First World War, and when he finally devised this panorama from a more and more ideologically determined perspective, he so obviously departed from his earlier approach that the resulting difference among his novels justifies the view that each of them should be seen as a work of art in its own right. We would have to consider Zweig's early novels from the point of view of his later intention if we were to agree with Hans-Albert Walter that, in his war novels, Zweig revealed the political and economic conditions of this decisive period in German history, and that he therefore came close to what Walter calls a *Staatsroman*.[2] Nor do these novels primarily serve the purpose of political enlightenment, for the optimism, the absence of which renders any such purpose meaningless, is largely, though not altogether missing from both *Der Streit um den Sergeanten Grischa* and *Erziehung vor Verdun*. These novels deal rather with moral and existential problems that the individual faces as a result of the destructive forces of the war. Solutions to these problems are not offered; they are at best hinted at.

By examining two major figures from these novels, I shall attempt to identify the problems referred to. I hope that this will at the same time help to shed some light on Zweig's ideological development; for the direction of this development, assessed by means of a comparison of the two novels, is certainly indicative of the reasons for his later political attitude.

II

In each of the two novels Werner Bertin, who reflects many of the characteristics of his creator, is a close ally and admirer of a central figure, who is more self-assured, more firmly rooted in his beliefs and principles, and at the same time more powerful than Bertin himself. Bertin is fascinated by these men, and he shares many, though not all, of their convictions. They are General von Lychow in *Der Streit um den Sergeanten Grischa* and Lieutenant Eberhard Kroysing in *Erziehung vor Verdun*, both of them officers in the German army and both of them, for different reasons, opposed to the abuse of military power; eventually they are defeated by the brutal mechanism of a war fought out of greed and without regard to moral justification. As officers in this war, they are in part responsible for their own downfall. This responsibility has a tragic dimension to it. Given their dedication to certain values – justice as the basis of a long-established social order in the case of the Prussian nobleman von Lychow, and unbroken vitality and prowess in the case of Kroysing – they support the machinery of war without realizing that those responsible for the war exploit them for their own material benefit, causing them to help in the destruction of the values they embody.

While the two officers lose their battles, Bertin, their temporary, unassuming ally, is spared this fate and is left to reflect on the course of events. Being less involved in the feuds in which the two officers are engaged, he is much less colourful a figure than they are. Through Bertin, Zweig has provided himself with the opportunity to consider the actions and opinions of the main protagonists from a critical perspective whenever this seems to be called for. But, at the same time, Bertin's general fascination with von Lychow and Kroysing obviously reflects that of Zweig himself. While these two figures bear witness to his narrative potential, Bertin is the embodiment of his compulsion towards theoretical reflection. In order to assess this constellation and to understand the development that is apparent in the transition from von Lychow to Kroysing, one must examine these two German officers, who, along with Grischa, must be considered the most impressive figures Zweig ever created.

General von Lychow, a seventy-year-old commander of a German division on the eastern front, is portrayed as demanding but fair and concerned for the welfare of his troops. He is, even in his physical appearance, a true representative of 'old Prussia.' He fights to uphold the principles on which his life and that of the country with which he identifies himself are based, but he is not a stoic who would accept destruction in order not to compromise his principles; in fact, von Lychow is quite capable of giving in and of resigning. However, if his principles cannot prevail in a given situation, he nevertheless remains true to them.

When von Lychow first appears in the novel, Zweig characterizes him by his reactions to problems that arise in the routine life of the headquarters of his division. Made aware by the regular morning report that the officer in charge of railway services has protested against the practice that officers have made of transporting pianos to Germany as part of their personal luggage when they go on leave, von Lychow is indignant at what he takes to be the practice of some officers of the occupation forces. He reveals an astonishing degree of correctness and naïveté when it does not even occur to him that officers from his own combat division might be the culprits, and when he wonders whether the complaint is justified, since he simply doubts that pianos are for sale anywhere in occupied Russian territory.

Another side of his character becomes apparent when he learns that His Royal Highness the Grand Duke of Sachsen-Eilenburg intends to come and 'shoot Russians' for entertainment, by waiting in a trench in a quiet section of the front for an unsuspecting enemy soldier to expose himself. Von

Lychow's hot-tempered reaction as well as his resolution to prevent such senseless killing testify to his secure sense of fairness and humaneness. His priorities are clearly set: much as he believes in the necessity to support the order of the state, especially in times of war, by strictly obeying those who represent it, he is far from adhering to this principle mechanically. In a case such as this he does not hesitate for a moment. He compromises yet another principle: by informing His Royal Highness that his safety cannot be guaranteed anywhere in the district of his division because of shrapnel and typhus, he departs from the truth without even being aware of it. He is so firmly entrenched in his system of values that he makes his decisions without experiencing any moral dilemma. Practical considerations play an important part; if they can be reconciled with humanitarian ones, the decision is easily made. Von Lychow opposes plans to cut the number of furlough trains for his division, which would deprive his soldiers of part of the leave to which they are entitled. The proposed cut seems to be dictated by economic necessity. His reason for opposing it is that fairness to his troops is essential, and that without such fairness the morale of his soldiers would decline, which in turn would affect their combat potential.

He does hesitate, however, when he is asked to perform the painful duty of signing Grischa's death sentence, not because he is faced with an inner conflict but because he takes this matter as seriously as such a case deserves. Out of a sense of duty, he asks to see the judge advocate of his division who conducted the investigation. The case proves to be clear. The high command of the German army in the East has decreed that Russian deserters who do not report to a German military unit within three days after having crossed the German lines must be considered spies and sentenced to be shot. Grischa, who is not a deserter but a prisoner of war who defected from a German camp in order to return to his young wife in Russia and therefore intended to cross the front from west to east, is ignorant of this ordinance. He claims to be a deserter in order not to be returned to his camp and punished.

Confronted with what seem to be the facts, but very much aware of, and sympathetic to the deep longing of his own soldiers to return home, von Lychow finds the measures decreed by the high command harsh, but recognizes that in time of war, when discipline, Prussia, and the German Empire are at stake, sacrifices must be made. In spite of the wrong statements Grischa has made with regard to his identity, the origin and direction of his flight, and the geographical location of his home, von Lychow understands quite well that this soldier is not a spy but simply wants to return home. On the other hand, he also appreciates the reason of Quartermaster General Schieffenzahn for issuing the decree: germs of insubordination, revolt, and disintegration, which have paralysed the Russian army before and after the Russian Revolution of 1917, must be prevented from infecting the German army as well. The mere notions of 'revolution' and 'insubordination' are repulsive to a conservative such as von Lychow, and so he utters a popular saying – 'wat sien möt, möt sien' – the archaic, low-German form of which suggests that the unquestioned acceptance of duty is a principle made sacred by time and rooted in the people, and that duty therefore assumes the quality of necessity. However, when Grischa reveals his true identity in order to escape execution, von Lychow feels relieved, since he is now able to reconcile his humanitarianism with his sense of duty. To his surprise, Schieffenzahn now demands that the sentence that von Lychow has signed be executed merely for the sake of political expediency: Grischa is to die in order to serve as an example to German soldiers.

It is at this point that von Lychow balks. He had been willing to sacrifice the spirit of the law when he sentenced Grischa, knowing full well that he was not a spy. This he had done for the sake of 'discipline, Prussia, the Empire.' But he is not prepared to sacrifice the letter of the law as well. For he believes that in doing so he would, like Schieffenzahn, rebel against the foundations on which the order for which he believes himself to be fighting is based. Such a measure would, in his opinion, defeat its purpose; it would open the door to chaos and arbitrariness. But his is a lost cause. In departing from the spirit of the law, he had allowed Schieffenzahn's principle of expediency to replace that of justice. He had done so in order to avoid the alternative, which would have been to challenge the moral legitimacy of war. This is von Lychow's dilemma. Because of the war situation, he can no longer reconcile the social and ethical principles in accordance with which he has developed into a fair-minded, humane, and cultivated person, with the actions that are apparently required for their own defence.

Now that Schieffenzahn manifestly intends to violate the law, von Lychow becomes aware of this dilemma. He is left with two possibilities. He can give in to the man whose duty it is to co-ordinate the German war effort on the eastern front and who, because of his enormous organizational talent, his supreme intelligence, and superior information, is in the best position to judge the extent to which the psychological effect of Grischa's death will serve the German war effort. In doing so, von Lychow would lend his hand to the destruction of a fundamental principle on which the order that even Schieffenzahn claims to protect is based. This he firmly rejects. The other line of action would be to resist Schieffenzahn and to insist on the autonomy of his divisional jurisdiction. This he does, with the active and enthusiastic support of his staff, of his judge advocate, and of Werner Bertin, a clerk in the judge advocate's office. The confrontation between the 'old Prussian' von Lychow and the 'new Prussian' Schieffenzahn[3] culminates in a situation in which, in theory, von Lychow would have to resist Grischa's execution by ordering soldiers of his division to use force against a detachment acting under orders of Schieffenzahn. Both men know that von Lychow's profound aversion to revolution and anarchy will make this impossible for him, and Schieffenzahn takes advantage of it. All that is left for von Lychow to do is to send a letter of protest to the Emperor, which results in a mild reprimand for Schieffenzahn. It is a bad omen for the future of the German Empire that no one in the entourage of the Emperor realizes that von Lychow's complaint is about more than a mere conflict over jurisdiction.

Thus, in one of the last scenes of the novel, von Lychow, who is forced to take leave because of exhaustion, sits in his study at his modest Prussian country estate, old and resigned. He is witnessing the disintegration of an order on which his material as well as his spiritual existence has been based, and the weakness of which is apparent in his very resignation. This order does not permit the flexibility required for its defence against those who unscrupulously misuse it to satisfy their lust for power.

There is one other aspect to be kept in mind: Arnold Zweig later on pointed out that his war novels present social conflicts rendered acute by the war but not actually resulting from it. In *Der Streit um den Sergeanten Grischa* he introduces representatives of big business, who discuss with Schieffenzahn the means by which the natural wealth of the occupied territories may best be made available to Germany. These discussions suggest indeed that the lingering conflict between old-fashioned aristocratic conservatism, which is primarily interested in preserving the old order, and the *bourgeois parvenu*, who is guided by expediency and motivated by his longing for power and wealth, and who acts unscrupulously and pragmatically, is brought to its culmination by a war that demands efficiency and promotes brutality. Undoubtedly, von Lychow is reminiscent of certain characters in Fontane's novels, such as Briest or Stechlin, and of the social conflict presented in these novels. But whereas Fontane in his time could present this conflict with a high degree of nuance, keeping the outcome of the process of social change in abeyance, the brutality engendered by the war determines the result in Zweig's novel: Von Lychow's humanitarianism, his sense of justice, have lost out; Grischa must die; Schieffenzahn has only experienced a slight setback. He has not fallen from grace because the Emperor himself no longer acts in accordance with the principles on which his state was built. At war with his neighbours, he needs Schieffenzahn and what he stands for.

Indeed, from the perspective that Zweig's novel opens up, one may argue that war was the logical result of the process that was set in motion in Germany when greed and a conqueror's mentality patently began to outbalance the principles of justice and humanitarianism during the last third of the nineteenth century. From this point of view, the First World War appears as the last and inevitable phase of a development brought about by this shift in values. Therefore, the novel does not merely suggest an analogy between war and social struggle. War rather appears as the climax of the social-political conflicts of the Second Empire. It finally destroyed this empire, along with the ethical principles that presumably had prevailed in a more distant past, but had been undermined during the period leading up to the First World War.

III

In *Erziehung vor Verdun*, written in 1933–4, Zweig draws the consequences from Grischa's fate and von Lychow's resignation. The action is set in the second half of 1916 and the beginning of 1917, a period which immediately precedes that of *Der Streit um den Sergeanten Grischa*, so that the author's development is reflected in the order in which the novels were written rather than in the chronological order of the events they relate. A legal controversy is at the centre of the plot of *Erziehung vor Verdun* just as it was in the first novel. The logical connection is established by having the injustice, which this time involves the death of a German sergeant, occur at the beginning of the novel, and by devoting the main action to the reactions of the victim's brother, Lieutenant Eberhard Kroysing.

This time the principle of justice is not violated by a social group that confuses its own interests with those of the nation, but rather by the overtly petty group egotism of the officers and sergeants of a German battalion stationed near Verdun who rob the common soldiers of the more valuable part of their rations. Christoph Kroysing, a young sergeant with a sense of justice, complains about these practices. But the offenders, naturally enough, consider the embezzlement a mere peccadillo, while regarding its disclosure as a grave crime against the *esprit de corps*. Kroysing is punished shrewdly and covertly by Captain Niggl, his superior, who sends him to a post that is exposed to French artillery fire. Niggl keeps him in this forlorn position much longer than is fair and necessary, while he has, at the same time, a file of fabricated accusations against Kroysing sent to the regiment's home base in Germany, implying by this 'harmless mistake' that he is unaware of Kroysing's present whereabouts. In Germany no one can even suspect that Niggl is keeping Kroysing isolated from his battalion in the front line and, while the file is passed from one office to another, Kroysing is finally killed by a French grenade. This is a solution Niggl had hoped for, as Sergeant Kroysing himself had rightly suspected. Alerted by Bertin, a common pioneer entrusted with the most menial tasks (*Armierungssoldat*) who befriended the victim during his last days in his advanced position, Lieutenant Eberhard Kroysing, the victim's brother, enters the scene.

While von Lychow's eventual defeat served to epitomize the decline of moral principles in a continuing social conflict that culminated in the war, the story of Eberhard Kroysing deals with an individual's reaction to this state of affairs. Kroysing has no illusions about it. He no longer demands justice since he knows, in contrast to von Lychow, that the very notion of justice has become meaningless. After all, his brother has died because of his 'Beschwerden über die Ungerechtigkeit der Welt' (80). Since his death seemed to prove not only the existence but also the preponderance of injustice, Eberhard Kroysing quite openly seeks revenge rather than justice. His social status and his personality help to explain this attitude. Rather than a Prussian nobleman with a commitment to both a traditional moral code and a long-established social order, he is a member of the middle class, like Schieffenzahn. A pragmatic young man, he is intent on the efficiency of everything he does. He is an engineer and a graduate of the Technical University of Berlin. Appropriately, he serves as a first lieutenant in a battalion of engineers. He uses his sharp intelligence in warfare as well as in the way in which he tries to avenge the death of his brother, but he does not use it to probe the justification of the one or the other. He is motivated by an unreflected will to live, most apparent in moments of danger, when Kroysing either attacks or when he defends himself. Danger is the element in which he thrives. For this reason he identifies himself completely with his role as a front-line officer and as the commander of a pioneer unit that occupies the notorious Fort Douaumont, which is constantly exposed to heavy French shell-fire. As a portrait of the typical front-line soldier, Kroysing is unrivalled in the entire *œuvre* of Zweig.

His shabby appearance testifies to his inner aloofness from the neatly dressed officers of the communication zone; his personality is marked by his sense of responsibility rather than his sense of his social status as an officer. The uniform of the tall, haggard man is threadbare; the silver of his shoulder straps and his sword-knot has faded into a dull grey, so that he is not easily identified as an officer. He does without nailed boots, which were common in the German army, constantly helping to boost the soldiers' self-confidence. He despises the mere formalities of military life, such as salutes and titles; he expresses himself in a matter-of-fact way or he chooses a casual, nonchalant tone in which he ostensibly uses conventional phrases for ironic effect in order to demonstrate the pretentiousness of commonly accepted euphemisms. Given both the conditions in which he finds himself in Fort Douaumont and his discovery of the crime committed against his brother, it turns out that most of the conventional phrases available to express his feelings and convictions must of necessity appear euphemistic. As a result, Kroysing's irony does not only seem inevitable but often enough turns into sarcasm.

Thus his appearance, his habits, and his language reflect his disillusionment with the lofty aims of the war as they were officially proclaimed. From the atrocities he has witnessed he concludes that no moral principles are respected, least of all Christian ones. In his discussion with Father Lochner, the army chaplain, he claims that the notions of Christian nations and a Christian morality are fictitious: 'wir leben in schönen sauberen heidnischen Zeiten. Wir schlagen tot, und zwar mit allen Mitteln. Wir lassen uns nicht lumpen, Herr, wir benutzen die Elemente, wir beuten die Gesetze der Physik und der Chemie aus, wir berechnen erhabene Parabeln, damit sie Granaten beschreiben. Wir untersuchen wissenschaftlich die Windrichtung, um unser giftiges Gas abzublasen. Wir haben die Luft bezwungen, um Bomben herunterzuregnen' (188). To him the combat zone is 'das fröhliche Reich der illusionslosen Wirklichkeit und der europäischen Gesittung,' where the sentence 'nichts ist wahr, und alles ist erlaubt' is true, while the command 'Liebet eure Feinde, segnet die euch fluchen' has lost its meaning. He therefore concludes: 'Im unversöhnlichen Widerspruch von Wahrhaftigkeit und Christlichkeit 1916 wähle ich die Wahrhaftigkeit' (188). A conclusion of this kind would have been beyond von Lychow's imagination, even after his depressing experience.

Kroysing is not the only one to arrive at this point in *Erziehung vor Verdun*. Judge Advocate Mertens draws a similar conclusion. By contrasting him with Kroysing, Zweig points to two extreme ways of reacting to the awareness that both officers have gained. Because of this relationship, we can more readily understand the position of Kroysing if we first examine that of his opposite, which is more immediately understandable.

Mertens commits suicide. This cultured professor of law is so sensitive that he cannot endure the atrocities committed by the army in which it is his responsibility to sustain a sense of justice. He is helpless and at the same time so nauseated by the mere sight of those responsible for the crimes committed against civilians that he cannot continue to live, for there is nobody he can turn to; in his opinion it is mankind in general that has failed. As he contemplates the historical development of Western culture, it appears to him 'dass in diesem Kriege die Höhe unserer Entwicklung grellbunt angeleuchtet wurde: der Geist Europas prunkte in Uniformen ... und die Gesittung diente bestenfalls als Technik zum Töten, als Tünche zur Beschönigung ... [einer] unersättlichen Eroberungsgier' (289). He can no longer bear the lies of the 'Dichter, Denker, Schreiber'; 'sie drängten sich herzu, zu sagen, was nicht war, und abzustreiten, was war, unschuldig und unwissend, aufgewühlt vor Überzeugtheit, ohne den leisesten Versuch, wirklich festzustellen, bevor sie bezeugten' (290). Earlier, when he heard secret reports about the atrocities, he decided to verify them and was shocked to find them to be true. As he is in charge of the case of Sergeant Christoph Kroysing, Captain Niggl serves him as an example of the moral decay of the human race caused by the war. He realizes that justice could neither be restored in the case of Kroysing, nor in that of the burnt-down villages and of the civilians who had been either murdered or deported. To him, the destruction of justice means the irrevocable loss of 'alles Liebenswerte, die Heimat, das Land der Geburt, das Vaterland, Deutschland' (293).

Mertens is as unable to deceive himself in these matters as is Kroysing, but the conclusions they draw from what they know to be true differ widely. Mertens clings to the values of the past: 'Anständig war es, für die grosse Gesittung, die man liebte, zu stehen und zu fallen, stillschweigend, ohne Nachdruck und Getue' (298), and so he takes an overdose of sleeping pills, rejecting the socially appropriate but violent suicide of shooting himself. This is his last and only chance to resist the pressures of the environment from which he has become alienated. Until he feels the effect of the poison, he plays the piano in order to prepare himself for the transition into the pure, uncorrupted world of harmonies that he hopes prevail in the universe. Knowing perfectly well that he has overcome the world of injustice and brutality only for himself, he would have been neither surprised nor angered had he known that the high command of the German army was to confirm this personal conviction in a macabre way. In order to check the spirit of defeatism by which Mertens was motivated, he is listed as a casualty of a French air attack.

Kroysing reacts quite differently to his discoveries, which, in principle, are identical with those of Mertens: he disregards the discrepancy between appearance and reality by dismissing the first and by facing the latter. He expressly foregoes any attempt to provide a moral justification for his actions, claiming that in a barbaric age one must behave barbarously. Since he does not believe in the possibility of restoring justice, and given his pragmatic attitude, one may well ask why he conducts his private war against Niggl and his subordinates. He himself comments: 'Ich bin gar nicht rachsüchtig. Aber wenn die Herrschaften wirklich meiner Mutter den kleinen Christoph weggezaubert haben, damit er hier in der dritten Etage dieses ehrwürdigen Grabes die Auferstehung erwarte [Christoph Kroysing was buried in the same grave with two other soldiers, his coffin being the uppermost], dann sollen die mich kennenlernen' (60). In a similar statement Eberhard Kroysing claims that his father must be spared the shame that would result from the unchallenged rumour that it was only through death that his son Christoph had avoided conviction and punishment by court-martial.

The tenor of these and similar statements suggests that Kroysing's concern for his parents satisfies a spontaneous urge he feels, rather than that it results from any awareness of a duty on his part. Obviously, the grief caused his parents impairs his own happiness. In a Nietzschean sense, he tries to compensate for this impairment by seeking the joy of hurting those in turn who are responsible for it. This would offset their advantage the more effectively, the better they 'got to know' the person who caused them harm, for their consciousness of their own superiority is part of their increased happiness; therefore, any future awareness of their inferiority to their erstwhile victim must of necessity be painful to them. In pursuing his goal, Kroysing shares one highly important characteristic with his opponents. Instead of being motivated by a moral impulse, he acts for the mere purpose of advancing his own happiness. However, there remains one important difference between Kroysing and Niggl: the latter is not aware of this state of affairs. He only realizes eventually that, as an individual, he is the weaker of the two, and therefore he lives in fear after he has recognized his adversary. Kroysing, on the other hand, is confident of his superior strength and courage; he enjoys his unscrupulous hunt, frankly admitting his Nietzschean attitude.

He succeeds in having the pioneer battalion of Captain Niggl attached to his forces at Fort Douaumont. While he is used to the frequent shelling of the fort's concrete roof, Niggl finds it impossible to live under this strain. His desire to return to the quiet life behind the front line becomes his obsession. This is Kroysing's chance. Since he has the power to have Niggl and his battalion withdrawn from the Douaumont, he hopes to have his enemy demoralized to the point where he would agree to sign a confession of his guilt in the death of Christoph, in return for permission to leave the fort.

Eberhard Kroysing knows that such a written confession, which he has already drafted, would enable him to destroy Niggl's military as well as his civilian existence, and that Niggl would be quite unable to start a new life in a new environment. The complete destruction of Niggl is precisely what he is aiming at. Thus Kroysing intends to take his revenge in the same way in which Niggl has destroyed his brother: 'Hatten die Erfordernisse des Dienstes in der Hand der Schipperhäuptlinge ausgereicht, den Unteroffizier Kroysing zur Strecke zu bringen, so reichten sie in der Hand des Leutnants Kroysing hin, ein Geständnis zu erzwingen' (85). George Salamon rightly claims that, in attributing this attitude to Kroysing, Zweig shows that there is no difference between the motives of Kroysing and Niggl.[4] Neither of them is driven by moral principles; they both try to further their personal welfare. The reader is naturally inclined to take Kroysing's side; not only does his revenge *seem* to be morally justified, but Kroysing is indeed more likeable because of those characteristics that Niggl does not possess – his honesty, his courage, and his vitality. With regard to his motivation in his fight with Niggl, however, both he and Father Lochner make it abundantly clear that he has placed himself outside the law of his country, and also outside the unwritten moral code of the society to which he belongs.

Where these restraints are abandoned, humans behave like beasts, as Nietzsche's well-known metaphors suggest.[5] Mertens the refined humanist had been unable to accept this law of the jungle that prevails in war, but Kroysing is so fascinating a figure precisely because Zweig subtly and convincingly emphasizes his vitality, courage, and determination, which, in conjunction with his sharp intelligence and the clarity and elegance of his moves and actions, give him the appearance of a beast of prey. This is most obvious in traits such as his close familiarity with the conditions of trench warfare, the pleasure he derives from a game of chess, and his fast and decisive victory when he woos a nurse, Kläre, shrewdly driving two rivals from the field. These traits are also emphasized by Zweig's frequent use of suitable metaphors. When Kroysing draws Mertens's attention to the case of his brother, he 'breaks into' Mertens's idyll. Occasionally he is called a 'wolf' (145); he smiles 'angenehm und mit Wolfsaugen' (184) or, even more dangerously, he laughs silently, baring his 'Wolfszähne' (225). At times Kroysing, too, speaks of himself as a beast of prey, as for instance after the French have driven him from Fort Douaumont. On this occasion, Niggl has managed to get away, back to his easy life in the communications zone. But Kroysing vows: 'und wenn ich ihn am Genick mit vorschleifen müsste, ich fang ihn mir wieder. Erst muss ich freilich mit den Herren da drüben abrechnen, die mich aus meiner Höhle geräuchert haben' (229).

Earlier, after a French grenade has killed four of Niggl's soldiers and injured many others, Bertin appeals in vain to Kroysing's sense of responsibility. Kroysing claims that he did need the reinforcement in the Douaumont and that he had only seen to it that he obtained the battalion of Captain Niggl, the composition of which was as little his responsibility as was the war that had claimed the four lives. Moreover, he reminds Bertin that these four belonged to the very people for whose benefit his brother had launched his protest and who in fact had made no gesture to oppose his murder. Finally, Bertin himself had informed Kroysing of the scandal, hoping that the latter would fight for the reconstitution of violated justice. When Kroysing now translates Bertin's desire into action, using the only effective weapons at his disposal, Bertin is shocked. In making use of these arguments Kroysing blames society for the deaths, because it is society that has created the conditions to which he has merely adapted himself.

He points this out even more clearly in his discussion with Father Lochner, who tries to mediate between him and Captain Niggl. Again Kroysing refers to the war. Since Christian morality has been abandoned in its course, the individual, too, can only resort to cynicism and the use of force. He proves his point when he takes the chaplain along on a patrol to the front-line trenches, where he makes him aware of the utter immorality of warfare. The chaplain's Christian confidence is badly shaken during a heavy routine shelling of the trenches. While Kroysing endures it easily in his usual, cynical way, Father Lochner suffers a nervous shock. Later on, when he meets a young man who claims to be a theologian and is moved by the desire to strengthen the young man's confidence, he can only think of the somewhat banal phrase: 'Unser Herrgott wird seine Hand auch weiter über Sie halten' (200). However, the young man has armed himself with a cynicism equal to that of Kroysing. He replies: 'Das glaube ich beinahe auch; vorläufig passiert uns nichts. Aber am Morgen vor dem Waffenstillstand, da fällt unsereiner.' Faced with 'diese Probe der hier gültigen Weltanschauung,' Father Lochner finally understands Kroysing's bitterness. He gives up his attempts to convert him but proposes a simple transaction instead. He promises to help Kläre, who is a Catholic, to obtain a divorce so that she can marry Kroysing if the latter will at least desist from persecuting his enemy Niggl, whom he will not forgive. Kroysing agrees with the naïveté of a beast that is fascinated by the prey within reach and indifferent to everything else. Father Lochner, it is obvious, has likewise developed a pragmatic attitude as a result of his close encounter with war.

In the final analysis it is, time and again, the war that has brutalized man and caused the breakdown of moral principles. Since Zweig and the characters in his novels repeatedly interpret war as a temporary intensification of the incessant struggle among human beings, the question arises as to whether war is to be considered a medium in which man displays his true nature, or whether the brutalization war brings about alienates him from his true being. Kroysing is of the first opinion; he considers war to be the primeval state of man: 'Ich fühle mich wieder als halbwüchsiger Junge, voll von Blutrache und Tatendrang. Richtig hassen, über Vierteljahre hinweg einen Menschen verfolgen, konnte man ja doch nur damals. Es mag sein, der Krieg hat in uns den Urwaldjäger wieder blossgelegt, der aus dem Schädel seines Feindes seinen Abendtee trinkt. Wenn man zwei Jahre dabei ist, braucht man sich darüber nicht zu wundern.' To Bertin's question whether he approves of this development, he answers: 'Ich heisse alles gut, was mein Leben verlängert und den Feind hinhaut' (131). Even Bertin experiences at times the fascination of fighting. In the midst of heavy shelling in the front-line trench he feels that his heart trembles with fear, while at the same time he is 'hingerissen von der Wucht, mit der der menschliche Zerstörungstrieb sich austobte' (199).

Judge Advocate Dr Posnanski, the successor to Mertens and like him a civilian at heart, is of the other opinion. After he has acquainted himself with the case of Christoph Kroysing, he maintains that this scandal is symptomatic of the breakdown of the moral law in times of war. When he imagines the protest such a crime would provoke in times of peace, he comes to the conclusion that only the moral law as it prevails in peacetime can safeguard a truly human existence. It is worthwhile to follow his argumentation in detail.

Setzte man an die Stelle des Armierungsbatallions in seinem Aufgabenkreis einen grossen Industriekonzern, der seine Arbeiter durch eigene Warenhäuser und Kantinen kleidete und ernährte, behauste und verarzten liess, so war die

Gelegenheit für Durchstecherei und Schiebung auf Kosten der Arbeitermassen ebenso gegeben wie bei den Preussen. Steckte man den jungen Kroysing in die Tracht eines Praktikanten und zukünftigen Ingenieurs, der so lange auf gefährliche Arbeitsstellen geschickt wurde, bis seine Mitwisserschaft durch einen Betriebsunfall erlosch, half man diesem Betriebsunfall nur ganz wenig nach, mit Sachverständnis und Tücke, so hatte man den genauen Abdruck des Vorgangs, wie er sich nach Posnanskis Überzeugung abgespielt hatte. Aber wehe den Arbeitgebern, in deren Umkreis dies geschah. Bei einem gut regierten Volk wären sie alle ins Zuchthaus gewandert, in einem unterminierten, vom Anprall der Ausgebeuteten erschütterten Staate hätte ein Massenaufstand bis weit ins Bürgertum hinein gedroht, ein ungeheurer Ruck das Volk aufgerüttelt, in England oder Frankreich wären Neuwahlen des Parlaments notwendig geworden und ein Wechsel des Systems. Selbst im deutschen Vaterland hätte ein solcher Fall weite politische Folgen gezeitigt; keine der herrschenden Gruppen hätte gewagt, den Schuldigen beizuspringen. Ohne grosse Mühe konnte sich ein erfahrener Berliner Zeitungsleser den Ton der konservativen, der liberalen und nun gar der sozialdemokratischen Presse dabei vorstellen. Im Frieden ... Im Krieg aber türmte sich das Unrecht, verübt von Volk zu Volk, die Gewalttat, losgelassen von Gruppe zu Gruppe, so bergehoch, dass ein Eimer voll Unflat einfach verschwand. So sehr standen die Interessen des nackten Lebens auf dem Spiel, die Frage des puren Daseins und Weiterlebens für die herrschenden Schichten und also schliesslich auch für die beherrschten, dass man zugeben musste, das Recht des Einzelwesens auf Leben und Ehre sei bis auf weiteres vertagt, bis zur Wiedereinsetzung der Zivilisation auf ein Nebengeleise gezogen. Natürlich bedeutete das einen Rückfall in die Zeiten der Völkerwanderung, eine entscheidende Niederlage angesichts der sinaitischen Gesetzgebung (382ff.).

Both sides agree that war is a relapse; what they disagree about is its evaluation. Kroysing regards it as the restoration of natural behaviour among human beings, while Posnanski, who believes in progress, regards it as a deplorable setback.

At the end of the novel Kroysing is killed. His development until his death reveals once again his contempt for mankind in its present state. He wants to be a pilot. This is only logical, for he believes that a pilot is 'seinen Feinden überlegen, übergeordnet, besser, ein Wesen höherer Ordnung' (238). When this idea first occurred to him, he was so disgusted with the world that he addressed it in this way: 'Weisst du, wozu allein du taugst? Zum Sprungbrett, zu nichts Besserem. Mit dem Fuss muss man dir ins Gesicht treten und hochsegeln, davonsausen' (239). This is what Judge Advocate Mertens had done, with the important difference that Kroysing's formulation applies to Mertens's suicide in a much more figurative sense than it does to Kroysing's plans. However, at the very moment that Kroysing becomes conscious of this desire, he is stuck in a swampy terrain, unable even to lift his feet. In this symbolic situation he is hit by shrapnel. Later on in hospital he continues to nourish his dream. To Father Lochner, who makes yet another attempt to civilize him, he says, 'der Pater wisse doch, was für ein Heide er sei; voll und ganz bekenne er sich zur Religion des Totschlagens. Statt weiter auf der Erde herumzuhumpeln, wolle er lieber in die Wolken aufsteigen und rächende Blitze auf die Köpfe seiner Feinde pfeffern' (410).

But he does not get that far. For ironically, the French plane that he sees in the sky and that prompts him to make this remark returns at night, misses the nearby loading station, and mistakenly bombs the hospital after Kroysing, having made a conquest of Kläre, has just triumphantly returned to his room. He hears the plane; he also hears the whistling of the bomb. Certain of his approaching death, he grabs a lamp and, with a curse, hurls it against the ceiling, which is at the same moment shattered by the bomb. This defiant gesture documents the fact that his outlook on life never changes. However, he does not die in chivalrous single combat above the clouds, as he had imagined he would, but is destroyed mechanically without being able to defend himself. In the face of the mechanization of warfare, his philosophy proves to be totally anachronistic. In retrospect, Kroysing's courage and his lust for combat remain ineffective, except for his having conquered Kläre. Niggl escapes, and the Douaumont fortress is lost to the French. In the end, Niggl, who always shrewdly looks after his personal advantage, is promoted, while Kroysing dies.

IV

Von Lychow had resigned after his unsuccessful attempt to stem the destruction of justice, while Kroysing, the strong, morally unrestrained individual who is not given to resignation, fails in his attempt to face the new situation and to prevail over the many weaklings, cowards, and liars by whom he is surrounded. His fate could serve as a perfect illustration of Nietzsche's judgment of modern society. The tragic dimension in von Lychow and Kroysing makes them aesthetically the most fascinating figures in Zweig's novels, with one exception: that of Sergeant Grischa Iljitsch Prapotkin. Through him, a perspective is opened up in Zweig's first novel that transcends the defeat of von Lychow and the destruction of Kroysing.

There are, in all four novels of the 'tetralogy,' also representatives of the common people, men and women with practical minds and a natural intelligence. Usually they are firmly rooted in the popular cultural traditions into which they were born, and they unwaveringly take the side of the wronged and the humiliated. Grischa and Babka are the most obvious examples: since they are Russians, Zweig had in their case an excellent opportunity to rely on available clichés in portraying a mixture of vitality, naïveté, mother wit, kind-heartedness, and a deep-rooted sense of being part of a family, a social class, and a popular tradition. He made subtle and effective use of this opportunity. In the case of Babka these characteristics are linked to her emancipation, to her being politically enlightened, and to her sympathy with the revolution. These are elements that were to become more and more dominant in Zweig's portrayal of common people. Even at the end of his first novel, the last word is not that of von Lychow's resignation. The novel concludes with a scene entitled 'Abgesang,' which is hardly integrated into the plot at all. It has manifestly been added in order to provide an optimistic outlook for the future.

A German private, loaded down with luggage, with his gun and helmet, stumbles panting and sweating towards the railway station of Merwinsk. He has managed to obtain a few days of leave and now fears that he may miss the train, for, because of a spiteful trick played on him, he did not get his delousing certificate in time. When he has almost reached the station, the train starts to move; standing at a barrier, he watches the locomotive slowly glide past. Some officers in a first-class compartment poke fun at the miserable creature, who waves his pass in sheer desperation. But the stoker has seen him, and the engine-driver applies the brakes in obvious violation of a very strict order. While the train comes to a stop, he shouts: 'Mach man rin, du Dussel!' (504). The door of a third-class compartment opens and the private is hoisted in, whereupon some of the officers contemplate the possibility of reporting the engine-driver so that he may be sent to the trenches. But, as one of the officers comments, engine-drivers have become irreplaceable; and another officer ponders: 'Die Leute haben den Finger am Ventil des Krieges. Sie wissen es noch nicht ... Und wenn sie es erst wissen' (504).

In *Erziehung vor Verdun*, this trend is continued. Two comrades of Bertin, Pahl the type-setter and Lebehde the innkeeper, are class-conscious socialists. Unlike Bertin and Kroysing, they have recognized the political and economic basis of the war. They think pragmatically; they act like comrades, and they are concerned about Bertin's well-being as well as his political enlightenment. While it is obvious that they like him, they also recognize that his poetic talent might be useful in the propagation of their ideology. Compared to the spontaneity of the social attitudes of Grischa and Babka, the political contributions of these two characters already reflect Zweig's increasingly theoretical preoccupation with Socialism. Their textbook Marxism, which is evident in what they say rather than in the ways they act, appears artificial. Lacking the originality they otherwise display, it is manifestly out of harmony with the overall portraits of these two typical Berliners. They are probably the first characters in Zweig's narrative prose who are symptomatic of the ways in which his developing ideological ties were to infringe upon his narrative talent. The result of this development in Zweig's later novels is hardly controversial.

His unequivocal adoption of socialism as his political creed resulted from the destruction of the moral basis of the social order in Germany by the war, as that destruction was first formulated in *Der Streit um den Sergeanten Grischa* and in *Erziehung vor Verdun*. To Zweig socialism appeared to be the alternative to the resignation of von Lychow and the useless defiance of Kroysing. At the time he wrote his novels it was a well-established pattern that the educated bourgeoisie, who had become aware of the destruction of the principles on which their society was built and of the futility of their attempt to change this situation, still remembered the values of the common people. They tried to overcome their relativism and fatalism by sharing the material and intellectual restrictions imposed upon the people. Büchner's *Lenz* clearly represents such an attempt, and Dostoevsky desperately tried to believe in the God of the Russian people, after having realized the futility of his political activities. In both cases, these intense endeavours probably did not yield the unequivocal result for which the authors were hoping, but they certainly resulted in great works of literature. Zweig, it seems, found his solution to the problem more easily. In doing so he ceased to be a seeker, but turned into a preacher instead. However, this was after he had written the two novels discussed in this paper. They point to his later development only as to a possibility. Aesthetically, Zweig's portrayal of the two other attitudes, resignation and defiance in the face of destruction, is more convincing.

NOTES

1 In 1953, Zweig intended to publish the original version, so that young writers might learn from the comparison. However, his manuscript was returned to him by his publisher, the Aufbau Verlag. He then re-examined his political

attitudes of 1930 in the light of his publisher's criticism and made certain changes to the manuscript. This revised version of the original draft was published in 1954 under the title *Die Feuerpause*. In an afterword, Zweig explained why he rewrote the novel in 1934: he thought it appropriate to change the subjective account of his personal experience into a more objective presentation of the conditions of military life during the war. This leaves the introduction of Eberhard Kroysing unexplained, since this new central character is a highly exceptional individual rather than a typical officer. It may well be concluded that Zweig, from his political vantage point of 1953, no longer accurately recalled his reasons for rewriting the novel in 1934.

2 Hans-Albert Walter, 'Auf dem Wege zum Staatsroman; Arnold Zweigs Grischa-Zyklus,' *Frankfurter Hefte* 23 (1968) 564–74.

3 *Der Streit um den Sergeanten Grischa* (Berlin: Aufbau 1961) 494. Further references in the text will be to this edition. References to *Erziehung vor Verdun* will be to the edition published by the Aufbau Verlag (Berlin 1955).

4 George Salamon, *Arnold Zweig*, Twayne World Authors Series, no. 361 (Boston: Twayne Publishers 1975) 109. Salamon's book, to which I am indebted, is the only comprehensive publication on Arnold Zweig that is perceptive and objective at the same time.

5 T.J. Reed, 'Nietzsche's Animals: Idea, Image and Influence,' in *Nietzsche: Imagery and Thought: A Collection of Essays*, ed. Malcolm Pasley (London: Methuen 1978) 159–219. A.W. Riley kindly drew my attention to this recent article. I would also like to thank him for his other very helpful comments and suggestions.

MANFRED KUXDORF

Mynona versus Remarque, Tucholsky, Mann, and Others: Not So Quiet on the Literary Front

Krieg, sagte der Irrsinnige, Krieg ist unmöglich – ist ewig unmöglich.
Mynona, 1917

Erich Maria Remarque's sensational war novel *All Quiet on the Western Front* has to this day remained an enormous publishing success. Asked about the total number of copies sold, Remarque was able to reply nonchalantly in an interview in 1966 that it had been twenty to thirty million in approximately forty-five to fifty languages.[1] When the book first appeared in 1929 it became an immediate success, any bookseller's dream. The reception that *Im Westen nichts Neues* received in reviews and public announcements was, however, highly controversial. Foremost among the critics ranks the writer of satirical short stories, the romancier and philosopher Salomo Friedlaender, who, under his literary pseudonym Mynona (an anagram of the German word *anonym*) wrote a devastating attack on this work, entitled *Hat Erich Maria Remarque wirklich gelebt? Der Mann, das Werk, der Genius. 1000 Worte Remarque.*[2] Mynona considered Remarque not only a mediocre writer, but accused him of tragically misrepresenting war. Remarque's publishers, the Propyläen Verlag of the Ullstein AG, stood accused of devious manipulations for creating a work of 'Geldliteratur' instead of 'Weltliteratur' (21). Moreover, an entire host of personalities on the contemporary literary scene and its 'Kulturbetrieb' were drawn into this controversy, whose mediocrity was exemplified by that of Remarque. Mynona's book of protest did not remain unchallenged. His scathing wit and his biting satire may have contributed to the fact that the seriousness of his arguments was overlooked. Public denunciations of his book were published by Robert Neumann[3] and by Kurt

Tucholsky, who called Mynona's critique an indecency.[4] Mynona was deeply hurt by what seemed to him vicious attacks and deliberate misrepresentations. He sent his reply to the *Weltbühne* but Tucholsky refused to publish it, while at the same time continuing his attacks on Mynona under the heading 'editorial replies.'[5] This in turn led to yet another book by Mynona, *Der Holzweg zurück oder Knackes Umgang mit Flöhen.*[6] While the book jacket had the inscription 'Gegen Tucholsky,' the title should be taken as a take-off on Remarque's subsequent novel, *Der Weg zurück* (1931). The allusion to fleas in the title will be explained later in our discussion.

The real issues in this literary feud that raged during the declining years of the Weimar Republic have so far received sparse attention. From the present vantage point it seems particularly significant that Mynona had not attacked Remarque primarily from a biographical point of view, as Tucholsky had claimed and as had been widely believed, but that he had critically analysed Remarque's novel from a literary as well as a moral position, that of a Kantian philosopher. With moral indignation Mynona stressed that Remarque had essentially failed in his obligation as a writer to enlighten the public. This view is presented in what seems a self-righteous manner, quite reminiscent of the Lessing-Goeze struggle. Mynona had himself alluded to this similarity and was pleased when one critic linked his polemics to those of Gotthold Ephraim Lessing.[7]

Before going into detail on Friedlaender-Mynona's arguments, his satirical method, and the underlying motives that promoted him to write two books on these issues, a few notes on this relatively little-known figure and his development as a writer and philosopher seem in order.

Salomo Friedlaender was born into a physician's family in Gollantsch (northeast of Posen) on 4 May 1871. This made him some ten to twenty years older than most other expressionists, who, like Otto Flake, saw in him something of a father figure. Tucholsky, on the other hand, in his mock interview 'Hat Mynona wirklich gelebt?' presents him as being plagued by bouts of senility. Friedlaender had studied philosophy and received his doctorate with a dissertation on Schopenhauer in 1902 from the University of Jena. Most of his works on philosophy were published under the name Friedlaender, while his lyric poetry (some one hundred poems) and his satirical writings (mostly short narrative prose and four novels) were published under his pseudonym, Mynona.

As he explained in his autobiography, 'Ich-Autobiographische Skizze. 1871–1936,'[8] Friedlander had experienced a change or conversion in his ideological outlook, from being formerly a wayward *bohemien* who had frequented the artists' circles of Berlin. He developed from

Schopenhauer via Nietzsche to Kant, and finally accepted fully the moral tenets of the Königsberg philosopher, a process that was completed only in his sixty-fifth year.

Today one is struck by the foresight and insight that Friedlaender displayed vis-à-vis the rise of National Socialism, but also by his judgment of contemporaries such as Remarque or, for that matter, Thomas Mann. While he had been a staunch advocate of pacifism throughout his life, Friedlaender did not adhere to a blind concept of pacifism that would maintain disarmament at all costs, in the face of the rearmament of opponents. He felt that a change in attitude, a change of heart, was needed, something similar to the regeneration of man as it was advocated by the expressionists, before a lasting peace could be achieved. This stance places him close to writers such as Georg Kaiser, who believed that a change of society had to begin on an individual level.

In the light of Friedlaender's tenets as stated in his primer *Kant für Kinder. Fragelehrbuch zum sittlichen Unterricht*,[9] his feeling of outrage at the novel *All Quiet on the Western Front* can be better understood. Here, for example, he does away with the notion that there are 'chosen people.' In an appeal to reason, he stresses the human bond that unites all people when he says: 'Sittlichkeit aber bewirkt notwendig den Frieden zwischen allen Menschen. Auch Ausländer, wenn man in ihnen *zuerst den Menschen* sieht und nicht den Fremden, den in Bausch und Bogen verachteten Juden oder Deutschen oder Franzosen oder Neger, sind liebenswürdig. Der Mensch ist vor allen Dingen *Mensch* und erst in *zweiter* Linie vaterländisch, deutsch, französisch usw' (33). The achievement of peace is considered difficult but possible, and above all an ethical postulate. The most significant point, however, is that to see war as a necessity is simply unethical (32).

Mynona had become familiar with Remarque's *Im Westen nichts Neues* by way of its instalment publication in the Berlin *Vossische Zeitung* from 10 November to 9 December 1928. Yet his satirical apotheosis, *Hat Erich Maria Remarque wirklich gelebt?*, probably was brought on by an incident that he later related in *Knacke*:

Ich las zufällig wieder einmal zu meiner Erholung von der lieben Moderne Jean Paul: Feldprediger Schmelzle. Das ist ein Wesen, das seine Minderwertigkeiten immerfort überkompensiert. Zugleich flog auf meinen Tisch – 'Nichts Neues im Westen', das Tages- und Nachtgespräch ... Plötzlich pochte es an meine sympathische und besch-eidene [sic] Tür (vor der meine Mäzene und Verleger einander immerfort die Hacken abtreten), und herein spazierte Paul Steegemann, um mir den Vorschlag zu machen, gegen den Ullsteinschen Remarquerummel etwas zu tun. A tempo lehnte ich, trotzdem man mir Millionen bot, ab. Nicht etwa aus Solidarität mit den guten (wo sind sie heut?) Geistern, achnein [sic], Herr Neumann, sondern weil mir Remarque gegen Jean Paul unendlich banal abstach ... Paul Steegemann weinte heisse Tränen und bat mich, die Sache zu überschlafen. Tatsächlich schenkte mir Jean Paul über Nacht einen Einfall, der mich humoristisch elektrisierte: Remarque als Floh im Sonnenmikroskope Kants (29–30).

It should be added here that Paul Steegemann had two foremost satirists, namely, Hans Reimann and Mynona. For Steegemann it was not unusual to look for an author after he had already publicized a book title. This happened, for instance, in the case of a novel entitled *Raffke*, which had alternately been advertised with Reimann and with Mynona as authors. The novel finally appeared as *Raffke & Cie*, written by yet another author, Artur Landsberger.[10] At the end of a sarcastic review of one of Reimann's parodies on Edgar Wallace, *Männer, die im Keller husten* (1929), Robert Neumann had slyly suggested that Reimann should write a parody on Remarque: 'Und ich flüstere ihm, dass eine Parodie auf Remarque seiner geschätzten Feder entstammend, zweifellos ein Geschäft sein wird.'[11] As we know now, the book was not written by Reimann, but rather by Mynona. It did not turn out to be a parody but a satire, which was later appropriately advertised by Steegemann as 'eine Denkmalsenthüllung.' Mynona supplied further epithets and descriptions of what he had attempted with this work. In *Knacke* he spoke of 'humoristisch literarisches Attentat auf Remarque' (25), 'stilistisches Bravourstück' (48), and with a good measure of frustration, he countered the argument of Neumann that he had been bought: 'Der Mann, für den Sie mich bisher gehalten haben, wäre nicht fähig, sich dingen zu lassen. Sondern es ist mir gelungen, gegen allen modernen Strom schwimmend, ein durchaus inopportunes Buch zu veröffentlichen, das mir von den grossen Lieblingen schweigende, von den Kleineren, wie man sieht, laute Verachtung (und meinem Verleger nicht einmal Geld) einbringt' (28).

In his correspondence with his sister Anna Samuel, Mynona expresses his gratitude towards his publisher for giving him the opportunity to reply: 'Mein Verleger befreit mich von dem Maulkorb, den mir meine Gegner angelegt haben.'[12] Referring to Tucholsky's refusal to publish his reply in *Die Weltbühne*, Mynona uses one of his favourite satirical devices, namely that of twisted expressions, when in this case he speaks of 'der Ring der Knebelungen' (*Knacke* 30). Mynona's wit comes to the fore when he describes in a letter his idealistic intention and the subsequent dismal result: 'Der Donnerkeil, aus dem meine Blitze gegen diese Geist-Canaille

fahren könnten, wird mir in eine Art Klosettbürste verschandelt.'[13]
Equally witty is the image alluded to in a quote preceding *Knacke*, when
the need for a giant clean-up of the literary scene is pointed out: 'Selten
erscheint ein genialer kritischer Staubsauger, der auf ganz kurze Zeit
Reinlichkeit schafft wie Lessing – (gottbehüte, nicht etwa Theodor!!!)'
(*Knacke* 9). Once more Mynona picks up the idea that his work was
intended to have a lightning effect through the bolt of reason, which in
turn was inspired by his philosopher friend Ernst Marcus: 'Auf dieser
modernen Weltbühne schnarchen nicht nur die Tucholskys. Mein Buch
ist eine Art "Vernunftgewitter" à la Marcus: erwacht endlich zur Selbst-
erkenntnis, wie sie Kant lehrt! Ihr bleibt sonst unrettbar mittelmässig und
kriegt höchstens Nobelpreise. Aber die Weltbühne schützte sich durch
den wrobeligen Blitzableiter und begrub den himmelhohen Blitz in nied-
rigen Kot' (16). The same metaphor is picked up a little later: 'In meinem
verlästerten humoristischen Vernunftgewitter habe ich die Blitze dorthin
niederzucken lassen, wo die Geistigsten der Moderne mit der dummen
Masse Mensch dicht zusammengedrängt stehen' (67).

The severe criticism that Mynona levelled against what he called the
darlings of modern times included, apart from Remarque, a number of
prominent writers: 'unsere Manns, Döblins, Unruhs, Molos, Haupt-
manns ... bleiben, da sie vorkantisch orientiert sind, nur brave Zeit-, nicht
Ewigkeitsgenossen. Remarque war mir nur das allerbequemste Mono-
gramm ihrer Triumphe' (*Knacke* 23). He had taken swipes at Gerhart
Hauptmann as the 'Literaturhauptmann von Köpenick,'[14] and had
reviewed Thomas Mann's *Zauberberg* as 'Zauber-Bergpredigt eines
ungläubigen Thomas an Mannbare: Rezept zum Kitsch allererstens
Ranges.'[15] During the time of the Remarque controversy and even earlier,
Thomas Mann had been the target of Mynona's attacks. One should
remember that it was Mann who had received the Nobel Prize for literature in 1929, an award of which Mynona speaks derogatorily in the
quotation above.[16] At the end of a manuscript entitled, 'In welchem
Jahrhundert und in welcher Form möchten Sie gelebt haben?'[17] Mynona
raises the question: 'Ist der Nobelpreis Ruhm oder Ehre?' and maintains
that he would have preferred to have lived in the eighteenth century. He
continues by alluding to Remarque's one-time position as advertising
manager for the rubber company 'Continental': 'als Reklamechef und
Ullstein der Kantischen Philosophie: das xix. und xx. wären dann
weniger sensationell als vernünftig und der Weltkrieg wäre ausgefallen.'
At the heart of this discussion is a quotation that Mynona attributes to
'Heinrich, der Bruder des letzten Nobelpreismannes,' who had ad-
monished him that the world was not ready to listen to truths all the time:

'Die Welt duldet beim Schriftsteller weder Überhebung noch harte Zurechtweisung. Man muss den rechten Augenblick erfassen, um sie auf den Weg des Besseren zu geleiten. Sogar ihre Fehler muss man zeitweilig mitmachen und verklären.' Mynona, however, prefers the dogmatic approach and does not want to hear these voices of moderation. His answer follows the quotation: 'Ach, Heinerich, mir graut's vor dir! Köstlich naiv hast du den Witz ausgeplauscht, wodurch dein Bruder den geistigen Kopernikus übertroffen hat: – Bravo! Ihr modernen, klug gemässigten Koperniküsse!' Why have I been so untimely, Mynona wonders, with my *Kant für Kinder* and my *Anti-Remarque*? Remarque provides the prime example of one who had taken the middle-of-the-road approach, 'der stets rechtzeitig, weder zu früh noch zu spät kommt,' always maintaining a measured balance between dying fighters and happy pigs.

The aversion that Mynona harboured for Thomas Mann went deeper than could be explained in terms of envy or jealousy. There were clearly distinguishable character and ideological differences that stood between the two personalities. One might be reminded that Mynona had frequented those Berlin literary and artistic circles where such disrespectful couplets attributed to John Höxter were recited:

> Wenn mancher Mann wüsste,
> Wer Thomas Mann wär',
> Gäb mancher Mann Heinrich Mann
> Manchmal mehr Ehr'.[18]

Personal animosities notwithstanding, Mynona chastizes Thomas Mann above all for calling war a necessary evil: 'Thomann sagt, der Krieg sei ein Übel, aber ein notwendiges. Heimann findet ihn auch übel, aber nicht notwendig ... Heimann proponiert Abrüstung. Thomann weigert sich; solange die Abrüstung nicht allgemein sei, müsste er bewaffnet bleiben' (*Hat Remarque?* 36–7). As a result of these duelling brothers, Mynona sees Remarque as the winner: 'Was wären die Kriegsroman-kitscher erst ohne ihren Gegenstand! Eben drum bleiben sie auch pisper-leisestill, wenn es sich weder um Kriegsvorteile noch -schäden, sondern um Kant, um Vernunft und Sittlichkeit, d.i. praktische Vernunft handelt, um diejenige Gesetzlichkeit, die der echte Grund aller Tapferkeit ist, und die auch allein allem Militär den Garaus machen soll' (37–8).

Towards the end of his book Mynona refers to a number of war apologists, among whom he includes Thomas Mann. He quotes the lat-ter's 'wunderschöne Kriegssehnsuchtsworte' ('Gedanken im Kriege'

[1914]): 'Krieg! Es war Reinigung, Befreiung, was wir empfanden, und eine ungeheure Hoffnung ... was die Dichter begeisterte, war Krieg an sich selbst, als Heimsuchung, als sittliche Not' (223). Mynona is understandably outraged at such pronouncements: 'Solche Leute gibt es ... Sie würden auch versuchen, *den* Roman zu schreiben, um den Nobelpreis zu kriegen. Sie würden sich zu diesem Zwecke auf ein gewisses Stühlchen in der Dichterakademie setzen, abwarten, auch Tee trinken. So aber wähnen sie sich Propheten, weil faule Zauberberge zu ihnen gekommen sind' (224).

From his hopeless situation in his Paris exile (1933–46), Friedlaender's rage had not died down, as is indicated in a letter to his sister Anna Samuel, dated 28 September 1934.[19] Here he refers to a statement by Thomas Mann, published in the *American Hebrew and Jewish Tribune*, to the effect that occidental culture is based on Greek and Christian, and in turn on Jewish culture. Since Nietzsche and Goethe were such 'treffliche Protestanten,' and since Faulhaber as a Catholic was so fond of Jews, there could be no doubt that reason would prevail. In hopeless despair, Mynona writes: 'Ist es nicht entsetzlich, dass die allgemein anerkannte höchste "Spitze" der modernen Literatur, mit Nobelpreismarke imprägniert, zum schauerlichen Chaos diese furchtbare und banale Konfusion hinzufügt!'[20]

Mynona realized that Thomas Mann would never forgive him for his public attacks, although he would have wished him to react as Wieland did when he embraced Goethe after he had written *Götter, Helden und Wieland*: 'Hätte er 'Götter, Helden und – Thomas Mann' geschrieben, so hätte Thomas ihn nicht umarmt, als vielmehr ihm Gelegenheit gegeben, 'Über allen Gipfeln ist Ruh" zu konzipieren' (*Knacke* 73). Thomas Mann did not accept Mynona's motto 'Es ist Arznei, nicht Gift, was ich dir reiche' (*Knacke* 11); instead he remained firm in his resentment even when René Schickele appealed to him, on behalf of the political refugee Friedlaender, to assert his influence in helping him emigrate to the United States in 1938. Thomas Mann replied: 'Mynona mag ich nicht und wünsche ihn bei uns nicht zu sehen. Er hatte immer ein freches Thersites-Maul, und seine Art von "angeblichen" Hitler-Gegnern zu sprechen, die seinen Kantianismus nicht teilen, ist auch schon wieder höchst unangenehm. Lassen wir ihn seine "entscheidenden Dinge" schreiben.'[21]

It must be doubted that Mynona was aware of Schickele's intervention on his behalf, but his isolation in exile became even more pronounced than it had been before. In a postcard to his wife Lise he conceded already in 1931 that financial help from official organizations such as the

Dichterakademie was not forthcoming: 'Jetzt, nach *Knacke*, wird alles vollends unmöglich,'[22] and in the letter to Doktor Rukser he intimated: 'Summarisch hat man mich [*sic*] bedeutet, dass ich isoliert wäre, weil ich in zwei Broschüren die prominente Moderne verspottet habe; und weil ich gewisse bezahlte Farben (wie die komm. oder zionistische) nicht bekenne.'[23]

Even though Mynona had reached his most prolific years as a writer during the time of the First World War and well into the early twenties, he had no illusions about this time, which was considered by many to be pregnant with the hope for a better society. This sentiment is echoed by A. Natan in his article, 'The "twenties" and Berlin,' where he summarizes: 'Who thinks today of Berlin only as an exciting and sparkling dream, as a perpetual "happening" of mental and physical high-powered "trips" misses the under-current of the revolution that never was. Anyone who was born in Berlin and sang in 1918 "Mit uns zieht die neue Zeit" perceived the pulse-beat of the disillusions and frustrations of the restored "good old days" underneath the glittering, alluring but so deceptive façade in the "twenties"'.[24] Responding critically to Fritz von Unruh's contention that the soldier and the cameraderie as presented by Remarque were 'die Keimzelle einer neuen Gemeinschaft, aus der einmal die Nation, das Volk, die Völker erst ihren wahren Völkerbund schliessen werden,' Mynona writes with understandable indignation: 'Und dieser Zweck, Herr von Unruh, heiligt alle noch so blutigen Mittel? Bitte, Herr von Unruh, studieren Sie, bevor Sie solche jesuitischen Naivetäten [*sic*] vornehm pathetisch herausbringen, das allergenialste, allerdings beträchtlich weltunberühmte, radikalst unmoderne Kulturwerk: Ernst Marcus' "Kategorischen Imperativ"!' (*Hat Remarque?* 213).

For Mynona, Remarque's war novel was a 'Synthese aus Krieg, Tod, Kommissbrot und Liebe': he had not, as Unruh would have it, 'an den Nerv der Dinge gerührt' (*Hat Remarque?* 215). Following this discussion, Mynona suggests that with this accolade on Remarque, Unruh had placed a Persian rug on a dung pile (218) and, appealing to Unruh's sense of smell, Mynona elaborates on his own motivation for writing grotesque stories: 'Als das Leben, Herr von Unruh, mir zu sehr stank, genoss ich's nur noch im *Reflex der Groteske*. War es meine Marotte oder mein Schicksal, immer nur stinkendes Original spielen zu müssen? ... Schliesslich macht es mir Spass, lauter stänkerisches Zeug in meinem Groteskenspiegel zu desodorieren' (218).

We should turn for a moment to some of the prose writings of Salomo

Friedlaender-Mynona in which he expressed his views on war in general and the causes of war in particular. Unlike the contemporary expressionists, Mynona was not a writer given to publishing manifestos and programmatic outcries as was so very popular during the first two decades of our century. In several cases he turned to writing in his familiar medium, the *Groteske*, or he resorted to writing satirical pamphlets.[25] We intend to show that in these writings his anti-war feelings conformed in essence to those expressed in his polemics against Remarque.

Such is the case in an essay published early during the war, entitled 'Geist und Krieg.'[26] Here Friedlaender develops his thoughts on war and its prevention in terms of Walt Whitman's idea of the all-powerful forces of the soul, which Friedlaender calls 'die Allmacht des Herzens.' Friedlaender believes that the reactivation of the forces of the soul can prevent and overcome belligerence among nations. Similar sentiments are expressed in an unpublished manuscript, 'Weltfriedenswettbewerb,' in which he visualizes a 'detoxification' of man's heart as the necessary prerequisite to disarmament. Here again, this regeneration of mankind must be initiated by the individual: 'Der gemeine Mann muss, wenn er den Frieden der Welt herbeiführen will, eine Revolutionierung mit sich selbst vornehmen: er muss um äusserlich abrüsten zu können, innerlich aufrüsten!'[27] Mynona is not so naïve as to believe that this would be an easy struggle. That can be seen by the warlike terminology that he employs in these anti-war essays. In a letter written in Paris on 23 June 1934 to his sister Anna Samuel, Mynona stresses that, in the fight for peace, real heroism is needed. He emphasizes 'dass nicht nur der Krieg, sondern auch der Frieden soldatische Tugenden verlangt.' It is, indeed, touching that Friedlaender, who often signed his letters to his sister as 'Paix des pays,' would have emphasized in this time of turmoil the need for the realization that 'friedliche Kultur ist der Sinn des Menschenlebens.' For the emigré publication *Deutsche Freiheit* he composed an anti-Nazi version of Schiller's heroic 'Reiterlied,' which in his own words was 'pazifiziert von Schiller-Mynona':

> Wohl ab, Kameraden, vom Pferd vom Pferd,
> Aus dem Feld in die Freiheit gezogen,
> Im Frieden, da ist die Uniform nichts mehr wert,
> Da wird das Herz nur gewogen,
> Da tritt keine Waffe mehr für dich ein,
> Auf dir selber stehst du, – doch nicht allein!

The eight verses are concluded with a rousing appeal to dismount and rid the breast of thoughts of Hitler:

> Frisch auf, eh der *Geist* noch verdüftet!
> Und setzet ihr nicht den *Frieden* ein,
> Nie wird euch das *Leben* gewonnen sein.[28]

No less serious but much more satirical are the two subsequently discussed prose writings, 'Neues Kinderspielzeug' and 'Der nachträgliche Heldentod.' The latter work reminds one of Heine's 'Die beiden Grenadiere,' when even the dead in their graves feel 'dass unser Deutschland in Gefahr ist.'[29] The former consists of a straight-faced proposal to produce more realistic toys for children, particularly more realistic war toys. Mynona ironically begrudges the fact that children are not prepared for everything in the world. Faint-hearted minds must have designed toys in the past, for they left out the gory aspects of battles. Mynona proposes:

Man führe Blut ein (natürlich künstliches!), und sofort macht es den Kindern mehr Spass. Das ist kolossal leicht: man verfertige hohle Soldaten mit siebartigen Öffnungen. Purzeln sie um, so verspritzen sie rotgefärbtes Wasser. Um granatenartige Wirkungen zu erzielen, nehme man magneteiserne Soldatchen, deren Glieder sich, auf einen Anprall hin, loslösen; man repariert sie rasch ... Das Massengrab darf in keinem Soldatenkästchen fehlen, so wenig wie ein gutes Musterungslokal, ein Lazarett mit gut imitierten Verwundeten, an denen die kleinen Ärzte Operationen, Amputationen u. dgl. vornehmen können. Ich liess für meine Kleinen von ehrsamer Handwerkerhand einen Lazarettzug mit Leichnamen, Verwundeten, Ärzten, Schwestern, mitreisenden Witwen, Waisen und anderen schwarzgekleideten Trauerpüppchen anfertigen und erregte damit Jubel über Jubel.[30]

Children who grow up with these types of toys will be better prepared for the genuine grief of times to come, and furthermore, Mynona adds, no mother will have to wonder at Christmas time, 'Was schenke ich meinem Helmut zu Weihnachten?' (45).

Such Swiftian satire was also employed in a story entitled 'Friedensberichterstattung,' published by the *Pariser Tageblatt* in 1936 during a time of impending war.[31] Reporting from a fictitious world peace conference, Mynona heaps ridicule on such major proponents of peace as the 'Geschwaderchef Giauring' and 'Hidolf.' The conference participants unfold their programs: 'Aber unser jetzt herannahender Weltfriedenskrieg wird sämtlichen Unhelden, sprich Zivilisten, die der vorige in falscher Humanität noch verschonte, radikal ausrotten. Der bare Unsinn neutraler Schweizerei darf nicht weiter bestehen ... Kein militärisches Aas (pardon!) denkt an Krieg anders als im humanen Sinn dieses heldenwürdigen, alles Zivilistenungeziefer vertilgenden Friedens' (3).

Not quite as direct as this attack on the Nazi hierarchy had been Mynona's satirical treatment of the German preoccupation with flag-waving during the First World War. Judging from the title of his book *Schwarz-Weiss-Rot*, there seemed to be little doubt that this would be a nationalistic work on the German colours and not a collection of *Grotesken*, of which only the first one was called 'Schwarz-Weiss-Rot oder Deutschlands Sieg über England unter Goethes Farben.'[32] In a number of previous essays, Mynona had presented Goethe's 'Farbenlehre' as superior to Newton's teachings. He maintained that the mere lack of bright light does not explain darkness (as Newton had ascertained), but that the very existence of intermediate shades of light, such as light grey, violet, blue, and green, would indicate the possibility of varying degrees of brightness, as had been maintained by Goethe.[33] This controversy over natural phenomena between two opponents is ironically carried into the realm of the international conflict that was raging at the time:

Ein grosser Rechenmeister war dieser englische Fürst der Geister, Newton. Aber er hat ausgespielt, wenn Deutschland auf preussische Manier und mit Goethes Augen Schwarz-Weiss sehen lernt: es wird sich dann das Rot noch göttlicher herausrechnen, wenn es erst sieht, dass dieses freudig errötende Grau zwischen Schwarz und Weiss so wenig aus dem Lichte allein stammt wie das preussisch nüchterne, das ja ganz unverkennbar eine Mischung aus Schwarz und Weiss ist. Lasst Euch doch nicht von englisch perfekter Rechenkunst betören, die auf Lug und Trug, auf Augentäuschung beruht, und führt Eure Farben auch zum Sieg deutscher Gründlichkeit unter dem Farben-Generalfeldmarschall Goethe, diesem Über-Hindenburg aller Farbenlehre! (6)

Mynona carries this satirical analogy even further when he maintains that the colour black represents truthfulness and the genuine. He continues his argument:

Und ist es nicht kerndeutsch und Goethisch, dass Meister Schwarz das Pulver erfunden hat: und dass, genau so wenig wie Grau, sich Farbe bloss aus Weiss, sondern bloss aus der Vermischung von Schwarz mit Weiss gewinnen lässt, deren innigstes Kind Rot ist? – Wenn Deutschland alle Welt versöhnen, vermählen will,

will England, um selber zu herrschen, überall entzweien; so wie Newton lieber das Licht in sich selbst entzweit (7).

Perhaps only minds of the calibre of Kurt Tucholsky were fully able to appreciate the subtleties of this type of humour. Under his pseudonym, Peter Panter, he reviewed this collection of grotesque stories, referring to Mynona as the 'Heilige Grotescus.' Elaborating on Mynona's sense of humour, he contends: 'Seine Komik ist schwer zu fassen, sie ist ganz unterirdisch. Zunächst fallen einmal alle Hemmungen weg, der Himmel öffnet sich, der liebe Gott selbst streicht sich seinen weissen Bart, aber er und der Bart sind aus Glas, man sieht durch sie hindurch in den zweiten Himmel ... Dass unsere Erde bei einer solchen Betrachtungsweise nicht immer gut wegkommt, lässt sich wohl denken. Die wird es verwinden. Aber der Schreck, wenn auch schon dieses Verwinden wieder bespöttelt ist![34] Tucholsky concludes his review by recommending to his readers yet another of Mynona's stories: 'Vielleicht reizt es manchen, sich Rosan, der schönen Schutzmannsfrau (auch bei Kurt Wolff) zu verbinden. Sie wird ihm helfen, die grosse Zeit zu vertreiben' (13).

When Mynona refers to Germany's role as peacemaker and 'Weltversöhner' during a time of bitter warfare, one is reminded of the Jove episode in Grimmelshausen's *Simplicius Simplicissimus* (bk. 3, chaps. 3–6), where a deranged person with Messianic delusions intends to bring lasting peace to a Utopian world in which everyone will have to learn German. Mynona, too, in a time of war, created a madman who, however, conceives of war as the result of man's imperfect perception: 'Krieg, sagte der Irrsinnige, Krieg ist unmöglich – ist ewig unmöglich.'[35] In this grotesque story we find a reversal of Grimmelshausen's reformer, in that this madman turns out to be the only truly sane person. It is interesting that this character, named humorously 'Hastenpiep,' a one-time author of a war novel (!), has now been committed to an asylum after having been hit by what Mynona terms a 'feindliche Christenkugel' (53). The impact of the bullet brings about a change of perception in him: from a former sense orientation he turns now to a 'Geist' orientation. No longer does he see war as holy or as a judgment of God, as he had formerly done, but explains to his visitor, Mynona: 'Aber der Geist ist nicht der "Genius des Krieges", wie ihn der Mund des Volkes nennt, sondern des Friedens, und Sinne und Leib sind gelehrige, aber widerspenstige Schüler dieses Geistes. Ihr habt so gut wie geistlose Sinne. Daher nehmt ihr eine Menge Unsinn wahr. Eure Wahrnehmung ist Falschnehmung' (55).

Views uttered by this newly enlightened, but assumedly insane person are similar to thoughts that Mynona compiled in his *Schöpferische Indifferenz*.[36] They were the result of his association with von Pannwitz and zur Linde during the years ranging from 1905 to 1908, which might be identified as his *Charon* years.[37] Friedlaender had stressed the power of the creative ego in contrast to the empirical ego, an idea echoed in Hastenpiep's explanations. Hastenpiep wants to convert Mynona (in this case Friedlaender's alter ego) to his enlightened stage of perception: 'Denken Sie über den berühmten Kerl nach, der durch einen Schlag verrückt, aber durch einen etwa entgegengesetzten wieder normal wurde. Herrschaften, mein Kopf, meine Sinne, mein ganzer Leib wurde gesund geschossen wie die Soldaten in Goethes "Neuem Paris"' ('Krieg,' 59). Against the advice of the director of the asylum, Hastenpiep proceeds to apply a vigorous massage on Mynona's head, thereby giving him a temporarily enlightened perspective according to which he sees gory battle scenes presented in a film as 'paradisische Idyllen' (65). What had begun as bloody slaughter turns into a harmonious constructive happening: 'Aus explodierenden Granaten wurden zusehends ... Baumeister: sie bewirkten nämlich, wo sie auch einschlugen, die wundervollsten Architekturen, und getroffene oder gar zerplatzende Leiber waren sekundenlang übel genug anzusehen, reorganisierten sich aber rasch desto harmonischer' (65). Peace triumphs over war; the military vanish into the background, and what might be called in Leibnizian terms a pre-established harmony is reinstated. Hastenpiep reiterates that being peaceful is superhuman, is divine: 'Es ist allzumenschlich, sich in dieser Göttlichkeit kriegerisch gehen zu lassen. Der Krieg ist nur die Gedächtnisschwäche des Friedens selber' (62). While being led away by the orderly, Hastenpiep remains convinced, 'Krieg ist unmöglich – ist ewig unmöglich' (67).

The moral obligation of the writer to his audience was always of paramount concern to Mynona. This dearly held view is amplified in a statement on the purpose of the grotesque stories:

Der groteske Humorist hat den Willen, die Erinnerung an das göttlich geheimnisvolle Urbild echten Lebens dadurch aufzufrischen, dass er das Zerrbild dieses verschlossenen Paradieses bis ins Unmögliche absichtlich übertreibt. Er kuriert das verweichlichte Gemüt mit Härte, das sentimentale mit Zynismus, das in Gewohnheiten abgestandene durch Paradoxe; er ärgert und schockiert den fast unausrottbaren Philister in uns ... Der Groteskenmacher ist davon durchdrungen, dass man diese Welt hier, die uns umgibt, gleichsam ausschwefeln muss, um sie von allem Ungeziefer zu reinigen; er wird zum Kammerjäger der Seelen.[38]

When taking Mynona's overall pacifist orientation into consideration, only a publisher's added prompting was needed, as it appeared in the commission of Paul Steegemann to initiate the writing of the anti-Remarque polemics. Since the publishers of *Im Westen nichts Neues* had, in Mynona's view, manipulated the image of Remarque in glowing colours, he decided to provide a well-researched documentary appendix for skeptical readers to his *Hat Erich Maria Remarque wirklich gelebt?* (251–8). Subscribing in a diary entry dated 9 August 1929 to the motto of Paul Kornfeld that the biography of the writer is public, Mynona came to the astounding conclusion that, according to the registry of Osnabrück, there had in Remarque's year of birth in fact been no Erich Maria Remarque, but rather only an entry for Erich Paul Remark, a boy born to the bookbinder Peter Franz Remark and his wife Anna Maria Remark, both Catholics.[39]

Mynona was, moreover, eager to show that Erich Paul Remark had at one time aspired to nobility by registering as 'Erich Freiherr v. Buchwald gen. Remark,' while his wife (the former dancer Zambona) was named as 'Frau Freiherr von Buchwald, Ilse geb. Zambona.'[40] He therefore used the subtitle for his documentation: 'Von Adam Remark bis zu Erich Freiherr von Buchwald' (251). As to Remarque's military career, Mynona was able to show that he had not returned from the war as a lieutenant, that he had not been in the 'Infanterieregiment 91,' and that neither the EK I nor the *Friedrich-August-Kreuz*, first class, had been bestowed on him, all part of the myth that had been happily circulated as authentic information by the Propyläen Verlag.[41] As a result of public insistence, however, the publishers later corrected their earlier release. It must be said to the credit of Remarque that he revealed in a statement the fact that he had merely been a common soldier on the western front: 'wurde dort mehrfach verwundet, einmal so, dass ich heute noch an den Folgen leide.'[42]

Even before those major attacks on Remarque had appeared, the one by Mynona and one by Gottfried Nickl, *Im Westen nichts Neues und sein wahrer Sinn*,[43] the various camps were taking aim at Remarque, particularly the rightists, who considered him a defeatist. Tucholsky as Kaspar Hauser ridiculed these attempts at defamation of character by publishing a mock attack on Remarque, 'Endlich die Wahrheit über Remarque,' in *Die Weltbühne* on 11 June 1929. Tucholsky introduces this 'traitor' as 'Erich Salomon Markus' and identifies him falsely as 'Judenknäblein.' Basing his information on the research of a fictitious professor of the *Süddeutsche Monatshefte*, Tucholsky gives the following account of Remarque's development: 'Salomon Markus trieb sich zunächst stellungslos in Berlin umher; er versuchte beim Theater unterzukommen und soll auch bei seinem Rassengenossen Reinhardt mehrere Male alle Titelrollen in den Brechtschen "Verbrechern" gespielt haben. Ferner war der junge Markus in Berlin als Bonbonhändler, Zuhälter, Hundehaarschneider und Redakteur tätig. Markus ist Freimaurer und Jesuit' (902). As a soldier he was supposedly never in contact with the enemy, but was only employed as a bureaucrat. Tucholsky plays up all possible prejudices; he even leaves it open to the reader to speculate on an association with the mass murderer of the time, Haarmann: 'Nach dem Kriege hat er sich in Osnabrück als Damenschneider niedergelassen, dann war er Hilfsbremser am jüdischen Leichenwagen in Breslau und ist später nach Hannover gegangen; Professor Kossmann lässt die Frage offen, ob Markus etwa Haarmann gekannt und vielleicht auch unterstützt hat ... (903). In his parody Tucholsky makes clear in which camp he places Remarque's antagonists: 'Salomon Markus ist gerichtet. Sein Werk ist durch die unvergängliche Veröffentlichung der Süddeutschen Monatshefte als das gekennzeichnet, was es ist: als eine vom Feindbund und den Marxisten bezahlte Pechfackel, die dem blanken Panzer der deutschen Wehrhaftigkeit nicht das Wasser lassen kann – !' (904).

This satire directed against Remarque's antagonists was published before Mynona took up his pen against the author of *Im Westen nichts Neues*. It does, however, explain Tucholsky's indignation when he found Mynona on the side of Remarque's critics, even though he was there for different reasons. Robert Neumann, too, felt that Mynona had violated the unwritten law of the 'guten Geister' of the time: 'Bei allem Respekt lehne ich Mynonas Buch ab, weil er die Zeit meint und Remarque sagt, und weil er so Wasser leitet auf die Mühle von Leuten, auf deren Mühle Wasser zu leiten an sich schon ein Verstoss gegen die Solidarität aller guten Geister ist.'[44] The German ethnic press had indeed registered these attacks against other pacifists with gleeful satisfaction. A reviewer of *Deutsches Volkstum* took the occasion of Mynona's *Knacke* to grind his own axe with Tucholsky when he wrote: 'Wenn Tucholsky böse wird, kommt der Schlamm der Pfütze zu Tage ... Das ist das jüdischfranzösische Schema für alles spezifisch Deutsche ... Ich begreife die Wichtigkeit des Flöheknackens nicht. Das ist schliesslich eine orientalische Beschäftigung. Aber da Mynona mit tiefer Überzeugung und mit kalauerndem Witze knackt, sieht man ihm interessiert zu. Tucholsky wird hundertmal geknackt.'[45]

From Mynona's point of view it had been a grave mistake to identify

Remarque as a pacifist. The ambiguous position that Remarque took in the political sphere has to this day not been fully explored. This is indicated by a recent biography that presents Remarque almost as an anti-fascist.[46] Remarque left Germany for Switzerland in 1930 and not in 1933 as Baumer claimed. It was the Swiss tax haven that prompted Remarque's exit, not his political stance. 'Euer Liebling ist kein Bekenner,' writes Mynona in *Knacke*, where he quotes Remarque in an interview in Paris with *Nouvelles Littéraires*: 'je n'ai aucune opinion sur Hitler' (62). In 1931, even Tucholsky finally became disappointed in Remarque after the latter had left Germany: 'Auf Remarque als Kämpfer können wir nicht zählen, seit er sich von dem Kammerjäger Goebbels so leicht hat besiegen lassen. Da hat nun schon mal einer von uns so einen grossen Erfolg.'[47]

We would be amiss if we failed to mention at this juncture that the brown shirts had caused a disturbance at the première of the film *Im Westen nichts Neues*, that Remarque's books were burned publicly in 1933, and that he (just as Thomas Mann) had been stripped of his German citizenship in 1938.[48] It was his sister who bore the brunt of the Nazi rage, however. She was condemned for 'defätistische Reden' by the infamous *Volksgerichtshof* and executed in 1943.[49] In spite of Remarque's later pronounced opposition to fascism, as expressed in his writings during the time of his exile,[50] and in spite of Tucholsky's assertion to the contrary, Remarque's early writings had consistently expounded the views of the political right, just as Mynona had correctly pointed out. Mynona must have seen him clearly in the camp of the Hugenberg press, for which he wrote frequent articles in *Sport im Bild*, *Die Schönheit*, *Scherls Magazin*, *Berliner Lokalanzeiger*, and *Der Montag*. The heroism of the soldier was stressed by Remarque in a review of Ernst Jünger's *In Stahlgewittern* in *Sport im Bild* (Heft 12 [1928]). Looking for a publisher of his war novel *Im Westen nichts Neues*, Remarque had significantly turned first to the Scherl Verlag before going to S. Fischer and finally to Ullstein, which accepted the work. Mynona registers this fact as: 'Auf der Stammburg derer von Ullstein saust ... eine Fahne hoch' (*Hat Remarque?* 237). A cartoon by E. Schilling in the satiric journal *Simplicissimus* depicted under the caption 'Die Sieghaften' both Adolf Hitler and his press tsar Hugenberg (after the election defeat of the NSDAP) riding on horseback: 'Man sieht es ihnen gar nicht an, dass sie eine Niederlage erlitten haben – Sie wissen es ja auch noch nicht, sie lesen doch bloss ihre eigenen Blätter.'[51]

Hardly concealable anti-Semitic and anti-Slavic sentiments on the part of Remarque had surfaced in an early artist's novel entitled *Traumbude*,[52] a work extensively quoted by Mynona. This book must have been an embarrassment to Remarque's new publishers for, as Mynona writes, the remaining copies of this edition were bought up by Ullstein: 'am 9.3.28 von Ullstein in aller Stille aufgekauft' (*Hat Remarque?* 255).

The concern of Mynona's anti-Remarque writings is, therefore, not so much with the person as such, but with the ideology that this writer represents. War for Remarque had become a 'Konjunkturthema' (*Hat Remarque?* 20) which had been 'romantisiert' (36); war had even been made to look elegant. Mynona alludes to an article by Remarque on the mixing of cocktails[53] when he refers to the ingredients of the novel: 'verquirlt Ullstein mit Scherl, Pädagogik mit Gummi, Krieg mit Eleganz' (182). Although Remarque had claimed to be a member of the generation, 'die vom Kriege zerstört wurde, auch wenn sie den Granaten entkam' (the motto of *Im Westen nichts Neues*), he stands accused of being the *arbiter elegantiarum* of war:

Und so hat hier Marquis Remarque, der vom Krieg bis auf die seelischen Grundfesten zer- und verstörte Genius, noch den Adel, bei einem nur ordinären Menschen eine Talmieleganz zu konstatieren. In solchen kleinen Zügen verrät sich die übermenschliche Beglaubigung unverkennbarer als durch noch so dicke, viel Lärm um nichts neues im Westen, Osten, Süden, Norden verbreitende Kriegsscharteken ... Und eben dadurch, dass er zwar innerlich längst zerstört ist, äusserlich aber immer tipptopp à quatre épingles weiterbeharrt, erweist sich der Halb-Mensch oder vielmehr Halb-Gott Maria Remarque als Berufensten ... Ein Zerstörer, der elegant nonchalant über seine eigene Vernichtung hinwegtaumelt (179–80).

Apart from the comradeship extolled by Remarque mentioned earlier, Mynona finds fault in the fact that war serves as a foil 'zur Erhöhung des Lebensgenusses' (40), that the dangers inherent in peace are depicted as being greater than those of war (44), and that war turns out to be a more efficient instrument of education than the school (43). Commenting on Remarque's description of artillery fire and the growling of cannons, Mynona comments: 'Denn bitte unterscheiden Sie mal, geliebter Leser: – ist das hier Krieg oder Frieden oder Konzert oder einfach alles zusammen, also Sport? ... Das Wort Krieg sollte verschwinden, und die Wörter Sport, ja wenn es knallt, Konzert (z.B. europäisches oder Kriegskonzert) an seine Stelle treten, und die brünstigste Umschlingung von Krieg und Frieden würde pazibellizistisch resultieren' (147). In *Knacke* Mynona emphasizes, 'Remarques Buch enthält, statt des rationalen Ideals des ewigen Friedens (das radikale Esel für eine Kirchhofsdevise ansehen), nur geschickt mit pazifistischen Seufzern montierten Militarismus' (17), or his work shows, as formulated in a Nietzschean parody: 'die Geburt der Uniform aus dem Geiste der Erotik' (*Hat Remarque?* 127).

For Mynona it is disturbing that this work should receive such a mass interest.[54] Despairingly, he seeks refuge by applying his sarcasm to man and work when expressing his fear that the infatuation with Remarque may create a host of consumer products, such as 'Remarque-würstchen' (*Hat Remarque?* 93) or *Remarqueierkognak, Cacao Remarque*, or even 'Remarquepistolen, Remarque-combinations, Remarquebinden, Remarque-elastiks, per- oder unperforiertes Remarquepaper in Rollenform (mit 1000 Worten Ullstein)' (92).

Remarque never publicly responded to these attacks, but Mynona was convinced that he had read his book for, as he was able to point out, Remarque had made changes in his follow-up novel, *Der Weg zurück*, between the instalment edition in the *Vossische Zeitung* and the book edition: 'Im zweiten Kapitel des ersten Teils der Zeitungsausgabe benehmen sich die lieben Belgier förchterlich [*sic*] tückisch, sie schiessen meuchlerisch ... In der Buchausgabe kommen aber diese belgischen Meuchelmörder unendlich zu kurz, nämlich garnicht vor. Cui bono? Das ist eben der Holzweg zurück ... Remarque [bewährt sich] hier als Meister der Doppelwegigkeit' (*Knacke* 11). One might add here a famous quotation, restructured à la Mynona: 'Quod licet Remarquo Jovi, non licet Mynonae bovi' (73). Mynona indeed raised a prophetic voice when he discussed the concept of sense of duty: 'Die Pflicht hat ein schönes Organ und pflegt mit lautester Stimme zu rufen, wenn die verehrten Damen und Herren da droben neue Weltkriege für spruchreif halten – : 1933 Kriegspflicht??? ... Na, einstweilen ist noch Zwischenzeit der Launen und unberechenbaren Einfälle. Sie brachte uns "Nichts Neues"' (156–7). 'Does a critic need experience at the front in order to criticize Remarque?' wonders Mynona rhetorically in response to Tucholsky's question: 'Was weiss Mynona vom Krieg?' (*Knacke* 50). Mynona responds: 'Jetzt, Herr Wrobel, jetzt eben bin ich an der Front ...'

Yet no one wanted to listen to Mynona, for unlike Remarque he obviously wrote not for, but against his time.

NOTES

1 Marcel Reich-Ranicki, 'Sein Geschmack war der von Millionen. Zum Tod Erich Maria Remarques,' *Die Zeit*, no. 40 (6 October 1970).

2 Berlin: Paul Steegemann 1929. Further references to *Hat Remarque?* appear in the text.

3 'Die Meute hinter Remarque,' *Die Literatur* 32 (1929-30) 199–200.

4 Ignaz Wrobel (Tucholsky), 'Hat Mynona wirklich gelebt?' *Die Weltbühne* 1, no. 15 (1930) 1218. Reprinted in Kurt Tucholsky, *Werke III 1929–32*, ed. Mary Gerold Tucholsky and Fritz J. Raddatz (Hamburg: Rowohlt 1961) 282–6.

5 *Die Weltbühne* 1, no. 26 (1930) 373.

6 Berlin and Leipzig: Steegemann 1931. Further references to *Knacke* appear in the text.

7 Franz Blei had sent a manuscript to Friedlaender in which he made the above comparison. *Die Literarische Welt* had allegedly refused to publish it. Cf. *Knacke* 47.

8 Manuscript, typescript, Deutsches Literaturarchiv, Marbach, especially 35–53. This autobiographical sketch is partially contained in Ellen Otten (ed.), *Rosa die schöne Schutzmannsfrau und andere Grotesken* (Zürich: Arche 1965).

9 Hanover: Steegemann 1924. Further references appear in the text.

10 Jochen Meyer, *Der Paul Steegemann Verlag* (Stuttgart: Eggert 1975) 36–9, has revealed these amusing details concerning the publisher Steegemann.

11 *Die Literatur* 32 (1929–30) 15–19.

12 A postcard dated 4.2.1930, Deutsches Literaturarchiv, Marbach.

13 A letter to Salomon and Anna Samuel dated 25.11.1930, Deutsches Literaturarchiv, Marbach. The frequently used aliases of Tucholsky (Panter, Tiger, Ignaz Wrobel, and Kaspar Hauser) were derided by Mynona with such disfigurations as 'Weltbühnentigerchen-Theaterpantherchen, pöbel-wröbelhafte Aufnahme,' 'Ignaz Illoyola,' and 'Kasperlehauserle' (*Knacke* 15, 51, and 54 respectively).

14 Undated and unpublished MS, 'Der Literaturhauptmann von Köpenick,' Archiv der Akademie der Künste, Berlin.

15 *Die neue Bücherschau* 6, 4. Folge (1926) 186.

16 While in Paris exile Salomo Friedlaender attempted in earnest to find a nominating sponsor to suggest him to the Stockholm committee. In a letter to Dr Rukser, an archivist, dated 31 May 1935 (Archiv der Akademie der Künste, Berlin), he gives the following reasons: 'Sie wissen, dass hinter meinem Wunsch, dem Nobelpreiskomité empfohlen zu werden, keine ordinäre Eitelkeit steht. Ich sehe aber nicht mehr ein wie man noch heutzutage die allein richtige geistige Orientierung durch Immanuel Kant wirksamer, mindestens der geistigen Moderne gegenüber, plakatieren könne.'

17 Undated typescript copy, one page, Deutsches Literaturarchiv, Marbach.

18 Quoted by Paul Raabe (ed.), *Expressionismus. Aufzeichnungen und Erinnerungen der Zeitgenossen* (Olten and Freiburg: Walter 1965) 200.

19 Archiv der Akademie der Künste, Berlin.

20 Instances in which Thomas Mann clearly distinguishes between Germans and Jews are brought out in a quote from Mann's recently published diary notes. See Gerd Bucerius, 'Die Leiden des Helden, Herrscherliches Urteil eines intelligenten Schriftstellers über alles,' *Die Zeit*, no. 15 (14 April 1978).

21 *Thomas Mann. Briefe 1937–1947*, ed. Erika Mann (Frankfurt: S. Fischer 1963) 109.

22 26 May, Archiv der Akademie der Künste, Berlin.

23 Cf. n. 16.

24 In R.W. Last (ed.), *Affinities: Essays in German and English Literature, dedicated to the memory of Oswald Wolff 1897–1968* (London: Oswald Wolff 1971) 288.

25 In *Knacke* (24), Mynona recalls that Thomas Mann had allowed the writer of the pamphlet great literary freedom in his criticism, provided that it be 'geistreich und ein Produkt der Leidenschaft.'

26 'Geist und Krieg,' *Der Sturm* 6 (1915–16) 54.

27 Unpublished and undated manuscript, Deutsches Literaturarchiv, Marbach. A similar idea is expressed in an essay entitled 'Der Allgemeingeist,' *Die weissen Blätter* 2, No. 2 (1915) 252–3.

28 *Deutsche Freiheit* 2, no. 18 (23 January 1934).

29 This theme is treated satirically in 'Der nachträgliche Heldentod,' *Die Sichel* 1, Heft 2 (1919) 26–8.

30 'Neues Kinderspielzeug,' *Die weissen Blätter* 5, Heft 1 (1918) 45. It may be of some interest that Thomas Mann had written autobiographical notes on 'Kinderspiele,' which were published in *Das Spielzeug im Leben des Kindes*, ed. Paul Hildebrandt (Berlin: G. Söhlke 1904).

31 *Pariser Tageblatt* 4, no. 873 (1936) 3.

32 'Der jüngste Tag 31' (Leipzig: Wolff 1917), 5–8.

33 Cf. Salomo Friedlaender, 'Goethes Farbenlehre,' *Der Almanach der Neuen Jugend auf das Jahr 1917* (Berlin: Neue Jugend 1917) 112–21.

34 'Die Sekt Eule,' *Die Schaubühne* 13, no. 1 (1917) 12.

35 The *Groteske* was entitled 'Krieg, sagte der Irrsinnige, Krieg ist unmöglich – ist ewig unmöglich,' *Der Almanach der Neuen Jugend auf das Jahr 1917* (Berlin: Neue Jugend 1917) 53–67. Further references to 'Krieg' appear in the text.

36 Munich: Müller 1918.

37 Mynona considered himself a collaborator of Otto zur Linde, the editor of the journal *Charon*. Cf. Mynona's autobiographical notes and Helmut Röttger, Die Freunde Otto zur Lindes' (Magisterarbeit, Bonn University, n.d.).

38 Mynona, 'Grotesk,' *Der Querschnitt durch 1921*, ed. Alfred Flechtheim (Dusseldorf, Berlin: Propyläen 1922) 54.

39 The denominational designation is significant in view of Remarque's claim to Huguenot derivation. Cf. Franz Baumer, *E.M. Remarque* (Berlin: Colloqium 1976) 21. Further to the name Remarque, see Robert M.W. Kempner, 'E.M. Remarque: Der Ursprung des Namens,' *Aufbau* (New York) 41, no. 49 (1970) 6.

40 Cf. *Hat Remarque?* 254.

41 'Buchhändler-Börsenblatt,' 21 May 1929. Quoted by Mynona in *Hat Remarque?* (253).

42 'Erich Maria Remarque über sich selbst,' *Die Literarische Welt*, 14 June 1929, quoted by Mynona in *Hat Remarque?* (253). On page 141 Mynona comments on these statements: 'Das ist nicht wohlgetan, mein lieber Remarque, sich künstlich zu verkleinern ... Sie sind der grosse Unbekannte Soldat, somit der allerbekannteste. Zerstören Sie diese Legendenbildung, diese Investierung sämtlicher Kriegsgewinne in Ihrer einzigen Person, so gefährden Sie den Erfolg, den ich Ihnen hier präpariere.' In *Knacke* (25) Mynona remarks apologetically: 'Seine Biographie enthielt gewisse für den modernen Snobismus typische Charakteristika.' Baumer, *Remarque* (37), maintains that, according to a photo, Remarque must have been decorated with both EK II and I.

43 Published in Leipzig and Graz (1929).

44 Robert Neumann, 'Die Meute hinter Remarque.' *Die Literatur* 32 (1929–30) 200.

45 Anonymous, 'Mynona: Der Holzweg zurück oder Knackes Umgang mit Flöhen,' *Deutsches Volkstum* (Hamburg: Hanseatische Verlagsanstalt 1931) 565.

46 Baumer, *Remarque* 62–76. Pointing out the inconsistencies and inaccuracies of this Remarque study, a recent reviewer calls for increased research on Remarque's biography and particularly about the 'zwiespältige Aufnahme von *Im Westen nichts Neues*.' Cf. Armin Kerker, 'Im Westen nichts Neues und so weiter. Eine verfehlte Remarque-Biographie,' *Die Zeit*, no. 47, (18 November 1977).

47 Kurt Tucholsky, *Werke III 1929–32* 862.

48 Cf. Hans Habe, 'Nachbar Remarque. Schöne Frauen und schöner Zorn: Ein einsamer Weltmann feiert.' *Der Abend* (21 June 1963). See also Baumer, *Remarque* 64.

49 Baumer, *Remarque* 93.

50 The most recent account of Remarque's time in exile is by Hans Wagener, 'Erich Maria Remarque,' in *Deutsche Exilliteratur seit 1933*, ed. J.M. Spalek and Joseph Strelka (Bern and Munich: Franke 1976), vol. 1, 591–605.

51 *Simplicissimus* 37, no. 2, (1932).

52 Bücherei der Schönheit: Munich 1920.

53 'Über das Mixen kostbarer Schnäpse. Essay,' *Störtebecker*, Heft 2 (1924) 37.

54 Reich-Ranicki, *Die Zeit*, comments in this regard: 'Remarque hat auf seine Art Hemingway mit Karl May und Ganghofer verbunden und das Endergebnis mit einem handwerklichen Können serviert, das seinesgleichen sucht. Er war kein zynischer, wohl aber ein routinierter Erzähler. Er wusste, wie man eine Szene aufbaut, wie man Requisiten, die auch der Klassenletzte als Symbole erkennt, verwendet, wie man einen Dialog führt, auf Pointen zusteuert und Höhepunkte vorbereitet.' Baumer, *Remarque* (10), quotes the author: 'Man glaubt nicht wie schwer ich es mir mache, so verständlich zu schreiben. Was sich am Ende so leicht und – hoffentlich – mühelos liest, ist das Ergebnis langen Feilens, Vereinfachens und Korrigierens. Gerade wenn "Lieschen Müller" mich versteht, habe ich mein Ziel erreicht.'

ANTHONY W. RILEY

The Aftermath of the First World War: Christianity and Revolution in Alfred Döblin's *November 1918*[1]

Faith is a miracle, and yet no man is excluded from it; for that in which all human life is unified is passion, and faith is a passion. Søren Kierkegaard, *Fear and Trembling*

I

At the time of writing, in the summer of 1978, the one hundredth anniversary of Alfred Döblin's birth (10 August 1878) was soon to be celebrated. On 10 June, Günter Grass gave a brilliant lecture at the opening of the Alfred Döblin Exhibition at the Schiller-Nationalmuseum, Marbach am Neckar (where Döblin's *Nachlass* is deposited), having also established a well-funded Alfred Döblin Prize for Literature to commemorate the writer whom Grass considered his teacher. But it is worth recalling that 1978 also marks various other anniversaries, all of which are connected with the novel that is the subject of the present article. Sixty years ago the terrible carnage of the First World War came to an end; 9 November 1918 was not only the date of the announcement of the German Emperor's abdication, but also the day on which the first German Republic (under somewhat tragicomic circumstances) was twice proclaimed: first, and almost by accident, by Philipp Scheidemann from the balcony of the Reichstag, and for a second time only two hours later, from the former Imperial Palace by the leader of the Spartacist Union Karl Liebknecht.[2] This was the signal for the beginning of the short-lived but bloody revolution that Döblin, some twenty years later, was already using as the subject-matter of the first volume of his cycle of novels, later to be entitled *November 1918. Eine deutsche Revolution.*

Exactly thirty years ago, in 1948, the first volume of the three-volume edition of this trilogy appeared.[3] Thus 1978 seems an appropriate year to take critical stock and attempt to throw some light on what is not only Döblin's longest narrative work (over two thousand printed pages), but the one that took him longest to complete (from 1937 to 1943). In addition, it is probably the least known of all the novels of his vast *œuvre*, and has remained (with a few notable exceptions) neglected by scholars and mainly ignored by the reading public. A glance at the assessments of those critics and journalists who reviewed the novel when it first appeared in 1948–50 will demonstrate the great divergence of opinion it provoked; the critiques range from praise to thinly veiled contempt, and from appreciative understanding to almost total incomprehension of the work's aesthetic qualities and underlying message.[4] True, most of these contemporary reviews (after which years of critical silence followed) cannot easily be divorced from the special atmosphere prevalent in Germany immediately after the Second World War, when émigrés, who like Döblin were now able to publish works that had been written in exile, became the cause of extraordinarily vehement expressions of rejection or equally passionate feelings of approval, depending on the political or philosophical attitudes of the individual critics concerned. One thinks in this connection of the furore raised by the publication of Thomas Mann's *Doktor Faustus* in 1947.

Nevertheless, even in the 1970s, *November 1918* remains a stumbling-block to some Döblin scholars and critics, the majority of whom are not only far too young to have witnessed the aftermath of the First World War, but who also experienced the immediate post–Second World War period as children or adolescents. Some of the reasons why the novel is still a 'scandal' and has remained 'exasperating' will soon become evident. Obviously, a brief essay of this kind cannot possibly do justice to the truly vast canvas of *November 1918*, a novel of such complexity in structure and content that only a full-length scholarly monograph (which has still to be written) could adequately elucidate it. Our aim is therefore a very limited one: to concentrate primarily on the final volume of the trilogy, entitled *Karl und Rosa*, which was written in Hollywood after Döblin's conversion to Christianity in 1941, and to attempt to illuminate Döblin's portrayal of Rosa Luxemburg, who, in the words of Ossip Flechtheim, 'was one of the last great humanists of the 19th Century (which did not end until 1914!),'[5] and who – it is easy to forget this – was only seven years older than Döblin himself.[6] In order to provoke discussion, the content of the present article will be presented in the form of three interlocking theses. The first is that the novel can only be considered 'historical' in a very restricted sense; the depiction of Rosa Luxemburg, in which the fictional element is far more important than the factual or historical element, may be regarded as paradigmatic for Döblin's special concept of the role of historical and poetic truth. The second thesis is that religion and politics, in an unusual Döblinesque synthesis, are the determining factors not only of the message of the novel but also of its composition, which is of a musical nature. The third thesis is that, in the case of the two main characters of the novel who are redeemed in a Christian sense, the influence of Søren Kierkegaard can hardly be overestimated; the timeless topicality of Döblin's message will not be lost even on those of his readers for whom the events of November 1918 are merely the stuff of history textbooks.

II

The historical framework of *November 1918* is at once simple and complicated. The time-frame is fairly straightforward: a depiction of the events in Berlin (and to a lesser extent in Alsace) approximately from the day after the abdication of the Emperor (10 November 1918) until 15 January 1919, the day that Karl Liebknecht and Rosa Luxemburg were murdered, signalling the end of the Spartacist Revolution. But this is merely the external frame, for within it Döblin creates a plot (or rather plots) of immense complexity and scope. In view of this, it may perhaps be useful to give a brief listing of some of the various groups of people by means of whom Döblin attempted to analyse and reflect, almost in the manner of a kaleidoscope, the totality of the events of the revolution.[7]

First, on the historical level, there are members of the provisional Social Democratic government in Berlin (for example, Reichskanzler Ebert, Scheidemann, and Noske); the reactionary counter-revolutionary officers in Kassel (Hindenburg, Groener, Schleicher); members of the *Spartakus-Bund*, later to become the Communist Party of Germany (Liebknecht, Luxemburg, and the Soviet emissary, Radek); politicians and officers from the victorious camp of the Allies (for example, Woodrow Wilson and Marshal Foch); and the victor of the Russian October Revolution, Lenin. Second, on the fictional level, are representatives of the proletariat (the Imker family); the bourgeoisie (for example, the *Schuldirektor* and his colleagues); typical war profiteers (Motz and Fingerl); the German poet and aesthete Stauffer, whose story provides some comic relief within the generally sombre tenor of the novel; and last but not least, the actual protagonist or hero of the novel, the former Lieutenant and *Studienrat* Dr

Friedrich Becker, who together with millions of German soldiers returns home from the war, seriously wounded, and must adjust to civilian life as a teacher of classics amidst the turmoil of the revolution in Berlin. Third, on what may be termed the supernatural level, devils and angels appear, spirits and ghosts (of, for example, the medieval Strasbourg mystic Johannes Tauler, or of Rosa Luxemburg's dead lover) – all manifestations of good and evil that in part bridge the gap between the historical and fictional figures listed above. We shall return to this web of religious themes and motifs later.

It is important to note that Becker (like Rosa Luxemburg, who was released from long years of imprisonment during the war for her political activities almost at the same time that he was demobilized) is a *Heimkehrer* (there is no single English word for the expression), a person who returns home after facing death, usually, but not always, in battle. This ancient motif of world literature, reaching back to the *Odyssey* or indeed to the Gospel according to St. Luke, occurred with great frequency in German novels and plays of the period after the two world wars. One recalls such examples of *Heimkehrerliteratur* as novels by Wassermann, Remarque, Ina Seidel, and Böll, or dramas such as Toller's *Hinkemann*, Borchert's *Draussen vor der Tür*, or Brecht's *Trommeln in der Nacht* (1919), which was originally entitled *Spartakus*. Indeed, it might not be too far-fetched to consider Döblin's Spartacus trilogy as his belated answer to the message of Brecht's drama, whose *Heimkehrer*, the soldier Kragler, clearly prefers the 'large, white, broad bed' he shares with his mistress to the dangers of the proletarian revolution. For Döblin's hero Becker does get involved in the street fighting in Berlin, gives aid and comfort to his fellow-men on the side of the revolutionaries, but dies a wretched death after the revolution has been crushed. Brecht's famous lines, put into the jeering mouth of his 'hero,' Kragler – 'Mein Fleisch soll im Rinnstein verwesen, damit eure Idee in den Himmel kommt? Seid ihr besoffen?'[8] – express exactly those sentiments that Döblin, in his retrospective artistic recreation of the Spartacist Revolution, totally and utterly rejects, though under very different auspices from those of the later Brecht.

Whereas Brecht, from 1938 to 1943, in Scandinavian and Californian exile, was working as a convinced propagator of Marxist ideology on such plays as *Leben des Galilei, Mutter Courage*, or *Der gute Mensch von Sezuan*, Döblin – during almost exactly the same period, as an émigré in France and California (Brecht and he were almost neighbours there) – was creating his trilogy on the November Revolution, a work that, like all of his writings after 1941, was unmistakably imbued with the spirit of Christianity. For Friedrich Becker is single minded in his passionate pursuit of truth, struggling with doubts and self-questioning like so many of the heroes of Döblin's works. In a hitherto unpublished letter of 23 July 1951, Döblin places Becker at the centre of his novel:

... und als Gegenspieler nur die ganze andere tobende Welt. Das ... Thema wird: Wie dieser Friedrich Becker willentlich und unwillentlich sich dem Christentum nähert und schliesslich Christ wird und nun nicht für sich selbst Christ bleibt, sondern hinausgeht in das wilde Leben seiner Zeit und sein Christentum zu vertreten und durchzusetzen sucht. Es wird, wie vorauszusehen, nicht eine Tragödie, sondern ein Martyrium. Er erliegt dem Teufel, der ihn schon in den Klauen hält, nicht.[9]

Echoes of Franz Biberkopf's 'new life' in *Berlin Alexanderplatz* (1929) after his release from prison and the promise, albeit an ironical one, of the beginning of yet another life in the closing sentences of the novel ('Es geht in die Freiheit, die Freiheit hinein, die alte Welt muss stürzen')[10] are to be heard in *November 1918*. For Becker and Rosa Luxemburg begin new lives, too, though as the motto of *Karl and Rosa* ('Mitten wir im Leben sind / mit dem Tod umfangen ...') suggests, Döblin has now arrived at very different conclusions. His question is (to paraphrase words from his essay 'Christentum und Revolution'): How does a Christian behave in times of revolution; how does he react to a revolution?[11] Döblin might well have expanded this question by asking: How does a Christian *writer* react to a revolution, that is, to political and social problems in times of revolutionary upheaval? His answer is to be found in *November 1918*, for part of Becker's (and Rosa Luxemburg's) dilemma in some ways bears striking similarities to Döblin's own, the dilemma of a formerly agnostically inclined and politically active writer who has now undergone a religious conversion.

The problem of the *écrivain engagé* in times of violent social upheaval and revolution has been examined in detail by Gerd Müller in his study *Literatur und Revolution*;[12] Müller, however, covers only what may be termed the secular dimension of the problem. In his stimulating discussion of individual writers from the end of the Enlightenment to the 1960s (for example, Schubart, Forster, Büchner, Heine, Heinrich Mann, Peter Weiss, and Tankred Dorst), Müller raises questions, for example, about the effect that a revolution has on a writer's or intellectual's view of himself, or on his aesthetic principles and literary practice. What is lacking in Müller's study is the religious, or more specifically the Christian dimension of the problem. And it is precisely this dimension that is of paramount importance in Döblin's case.

As a medical officer in Alsace during the First World War, Döblin had experienced the senseless slaughter of the battlefields at first hand, just as he was later to witness the November Revolution in Berlin after his demobilization. His deep and active involvement in the left-wing political and literary life of the Weimar Republic is well documented by the numerous articles and glosses he wrote in the 1920s and early 1930s.[13] His enforced exile in 1933, as a Jew whose books were later publicly burned by the Nazis, his escape from Paris in 1940 just before the victorious German armies entered the city, and his long and perilous journey through France, Spain, and Portugal before finally arriving in America in 1940, are the subjects of his autobiographical *Schicksalsreise*, a book that also throws light on the troubled process of his conversion, which took place a year later.[14] To attempt to explain religious conversions, whether the method used be psychological, socio-political, philosophical, or literary, is basically futile. For religious conversion (unless it occurs for purely practical or material purposes – the case of Heine's baptism comes to mind) must remain by its very nature a mystery, an act of faith that is inexplicable by means of rational analysis.[15] Certainly Döblin derived no material advantages from his conversion; quite the opposite. In the last years of his life, from his return to Germany in 1945 until his death in 1957, Döblin's religious convictions (like those of Becker) gave rise to enmity and opprobrium, both from his erstwhile friends of the Left and from many of his right-wing orthodox co-religionists during the era of the Adenauer Restoration, the period that came to be identfied with the Cold War after two new German republics had been established in East and West.[16] But these latter events took place long before Döblin had completed his *November 1918*, a work that in his own almost prophetic words was written 'zur Warnung und Erinnerung'[17] – as a warning to present and future generations to remember the past and not to repeat the mistakes Döblin's own generation had made.

Thanks to Manfred Auer's painstaking study of Döblin's later works, particularly *November 1918* and *Hamlet*, it is unnecessary to go into any detail about the historical sources Döblin used when writing his trilogy; the study also provides us with a reliable and illuminating scholarly examination of the artistry of *November 1918*.[18] Auer – and I gladly acknowledge my debt to him – also successfully demolishes the myth

(accepted and propagated by several Döblin scholars) that Döblin's religi-
ously inspired *Spätwerk* should be regarded as an example of the 'artistic
decline' of a once-great novelist.[19] More than this, Auer was the first
scholar to analyse Döblin's portrayal of Rosa Luxemburg in detail, and to
come to the conclusion that (as with the majority of the historical characters in the novel) Döblin depicts 'einen Zug ihres Charakters, der absolut
gesetzt wird.'[20] In other words, Döblin depicts Rosa Luxemburg, 'einheit-
lich ... wie sie sich in ihren Briefen aus dem Gefängnis präsentiert.'[21] This
point of Auer's will be taken up later on.

In the present article, historical facts about Rosa Luxemburg have
primarily been taken from what is probably the best and certainly the most
comprehensive biography available, J.P. Nettl's two-volume study of
1966.[22] A quotation from Nettl's introductory chapter neatly sums up
problems many readers of *November 1918* will have – that is, that they are
not really in a strong position to judge how 'true to life' Döblin's portrayal
of the famous revolutionary is. Nettl writes:

Many people actually know Rosa Luxemburg's name, but its associations are
vague – German, Jewish, and revolutionary; that is as far as it goes. To those
interested in the history of Socialism she emerges in clearer focus, as the spokes-
woman and theoretician of the German Left, and one of the founders of the
German Communist Party. Two aspects of her life seem to stand out: her death –
which retrospectively creates a special, if slightly sentimental, interest in a woman
revolutionary brutally murdered by the soldiery; and her disputes with Lenin in
which she appears to represent democracy against Russian Communism.[23]

Certainly, the two aspects of her life that Nettl stresses are present in
Döblin's trilogy – the 'sentimental' and the political. But there is a third
aspect, which, as we have already indicated in general terms, is much more
significant for Döblin: a mystical, emotionally charged, religious facet of
her character. And it is precisely this element that many critics have
attacked and condemned, despite the fact that it is part and parcel of the
overall religious tenor of the trilogy as regards both its message (that is,
the author's intention) and its narrative structure. In this connection, it is
worth quoting again from Nettl's book, for in a brief résumé of the plot of
the final volume of the trilogy, *Karl und Rosa* (a résumé that has not to my
knowledge been noticed by Döblin scholars), Nettl demonstrates (uncon-
sciously and almost paradigmatically) the way in which a professional
historian can misjudge and misinterpret a literary work of art: 'A not
insensitive but gaudy dramatization of Rosa Luxemburg's prison years in

fictional form. Though it establishes her as a powerful, dramatic figure in German history, the story departs substantially from the truth and grossly over-emphasizes her love-life.'[24]

One must assume that Nettl did not read all of the novel and perhaps relied on a potted summary of it obtained from some other source. First, Döblin's novel does not only dramatize Rosa Luxemburg's years in prison, but is equally concerned with the months she spent in Berlin after her release. Second, Döblin's concept of the 'truth' is substantially different from that of any professional historian. It seems hardly necessary to mention that Shakespeare or Schiller, for example, both 'departed from the truth' in their major historical dramas; and yet this age-old difference between poetic and historical truth could hardly be unfamiliar to an historian of Nettl's rank and reputation. The third point Nettl raises – that Döblin grossly over-emphasizes Rosa's love-life – is important since it is exactly the 'weakness' seized upon by the most vociferous critical opponents of *Karl und Rosa*. Müller-Salget, for example, speaks of frightful stylistic lapses ('ärgsten stilistischen Entgleisungen')[25] in Döblin's portrayal of love scenes, and does not mince his words when attempting to ridicule them in his condemnation of the novel:

Wenn Döblin schliesslich im letzten Band auf den geschmacklosen Gedanken verfällt, Rosa Luxemburg im Gefängnis vom Geist ihres gefallenen Freundes Hans Diefenbach (im Roman: Hans Düsterwald) heimsuchen und sexuell bedrängen zu lassen, wenn er den also Malträtierten während des Gespenster-Koitus schwärmen lässt: 'Du nimmst mich armen Hannes auf' ... dann ist wohl doch die Grenze dessen überschritten, was noch erträglich genannt werden kann.[26]

Quite apart from the fact that Müller-Salget's own style, with its vindictive turns of phrase ('sexuell bedrängen') and sarcastic neologisms ('Gespenster-Koitus') – worthy, one might add, only of *Der Spiegel* – hardly qualifies him to pontificate on Döblin's 'lack of taste,' it must be pointed out that he is also guilty of tearing passages from their context to suit his purpose. Blinded by his aesthetic sensibilities about Döblin's lack of taste (although it could be cogently argued that the ghostly love scene is both moving and tender), Müller-Salget fails to see the crux of all such scenes in which Rosa meets, in various guises, the spirit of her dead lover. For in the final volume of the trilogy it is Döblin's aim to emphasize the *human* side of Rosa's personality – her weaknesses, her over-wrought emotions, her dreams and nightmares, the deterioration of her health during her long years in prison, and her deep love for Hans Diefenbach, the news of whose death in action had reached her in November 1917.[27]

As has already been indicated, the most important source Döblin used in his portrayal of the 'inner' Rosa Luxemburg was her *Briefe aus dem Gefängnis*, first published in 1920.[28] The appearance of these letters in print so shortly after her death was certainly not without political implications: the letters were intended to change her public image. Until 1920, the Rosa Luxemburg who impinged upon the non-Marxian consciousness was that of *die blutige Rosa*, the woman who preached and practised violence, a tribune of the people whose brilliant intellect was used solely to promote world revolution. Now, with the publication of the letters, all of this changed. As the editors of the letters are at pains to point out in the fulsomely sentimental language of their introduction:

The adherents and fellow-combatants of Rosa Luxemburg have a right to know the richness of her untiringly flowing heart. They shall see how this woman, raising herself above her own sufferings, encompasses all beings of the creation with understanding love and poetic power, how her heart trembles at the call of birds, how verses of winged language echo in her, and how the fate and daily lives of her friends are safe and secure within her.[29]

There is no doubt that the *Briefe aus dem Gefängnis*, like other collections of her letters published subsequently,[30] were attempts to counter the effects of official, party-line biographies, which always played down the 'human' side of her character in favour of her political theories and revolutionary activities. Indeed, the political legacy of Rosa Luxemburg, or Luxemburgism as it is called, became the centre of bitter controversy within the Communist Party in the Soviet Union, in Germany, and elsewhere, a controversy that has continued into the 1970s.[31] It may be added that Döblin was well aware of this controversy, since in *Karl und Rosa* he shows Rosa in her prison cell, writing her famous treatise, *Die russische Revolution*, which was published posthumously in 1922 but incurred Lenin's ire and forced him to write a reply pointing out her errors.[32] The details need not concern us here, but it is worth noting that Döblin quotes several passages (almost, but not quite verbatim) from *Die russische Revolution*, in which Rosa vehemently attacks the suppression of democratic freedoms in Soviet Russia: '"Die wirkliche Diktatur,"' Rosa concludes, '"unsere Diktatur, besteht in der Anwendung der Demokratie, nicht in ihrer Abschaffung." Und das war ein Satz, an dem sie sich labte' (Vol. 3, 91).[33]

Examples of this sort of *montage* of quotations by Döblin – there are others, for example from her *Spartakus-Briefe* (Vol. 3, 38–9) – do tend to counter Auer's previously cited argument that Rosa Luxemburg is 'uniformly' portrayed as she is revealed in her *Letters from Prison*. Nevertheless, Auer's claim is, with certain qualifications, generally a valid one. The *Letters from Prison* are used by Döblin (and were used by those who originally published them) to confront readers with a choice: between a political, public Rosa and an all-too-human private Rosa. There is, Nettl comments, an error in this way of thinking; this is 'to see her political writings as artefacts, the letters as natural, bursting through in a torrent of temperament.'[34] Nothing could be further from the truth, Nettl continues, since in fact 'there was nothing spontaneous about these letters at all. They were written quickly, but writing them was as disciplined and deliberate as any of her political work ... Every syllable serves a purpose. The real, the only spontaneity of which Rosa was ever capable was – silence.'[35]

To some extent, Nettl's arguments are convincing. If one reads *all* of Rosa's letters, it becomes obvious that, despite emotional and sentimental outpourings about frozen wasps or mistreated animals or the beauty of flowers or poems or music, the tone and contents of each letter are finely tuned to the probable reaction of its recipient. On the other hand, it is important to take into consideration the psychology of letter-writers throughout the ages (which Nettl does not do) and remember that the majority of them (whether poets, businessmen, intellectuals, or university professors) always try to do the very thing that Nettl implies is reprehensible in Rosa's case – that is, to establish empathy with their correspondents, to feel their way into the particular situation of each individual recipient. Surely it is unfair of Nettl to expect more (or less) of Rosa. Again, it must be borne in mind that Rosa wrote her letters in the loneliness and isolation and often harsh conditions of incarceration. Her letters were not simply her only means of contact with the outside world, but also the sole method available to her of expressing her thoughts and emotions in a concrete manner. From a psychological standpoint, her letters written in prison may be viewed, at least in part, as vital to her mental health, or as an essential means to sublimate her emotions.

Even the casual reader of Rosa's letters will, however, be struck by her silences, to which Nettl draws our attention. For whenever an event occurs that moves her deeply (especially the death of Hans Diefenbach), her inability to write about it – she is usually so fluent and loquacious on almost any subject – is almost uncanny. In a letter to Sonja Liebknecht, written on hearing the news of her lover's death, all she is capable of saying is: 'das Beste und Feinste in solchen Fällen ist, mir schleunigst aber kurz und einfach die zwei Worte zu sagen: er ist tot – das kränkt mich, doch Schluss damit.'[36] There are many other examples in her letters of this kind of reluctance.[37] As an historian, Nettl rightly states that 'silence cannot be quoted or recorded';[38] but this is precisely what a creative writer like Döblin can and does do.

The inner life of Rosa in her prison cell, her fears, her dreams, and hallucinations – in short, that which is 'unspeakable' for her – comprise a major part of Döblin's portrayal, and, it must be added, not without basis in fact. Manfred Auer has gone into this question in some detail, so that one quotation will suffice to illustrate the point. On 24 November 1917, Rosa wrote to Luise Kautsky: 'Ich lebe ... weiter im Traum, dass er [Hans Diefenbach] da ist, ich sehe ihn lebendig vor mir, plaudere mit ihm in Gedanken über alles, *in mir* lebt er weiter.'[39] In fact, Döblin himself stressed that it was sentences similar to the one just quoted that struck him while he was writing *Karl und Rosa* in California. Döblin continues: 'Ich folgte ihren [Rosas] Gedanken, und über seinen [Diefenbachs] Tod hinaus habe ich sie ihn suchen lassen, und sie fand und hatte ihn bald (im Traum), aber das wurde keine Liebesgeschichte, sondern eine schreckliche, grausige Begegnung, im Geisterreich.'[40]

These encounters with the supernatural, which, as has been indicated, play an extraordinarily important role in Döblin's trilogy, are the very thing that some critics can neither accept nor understand. Just as Klaus Müller-Salget rejected such scenes mainly on aesthetic grounds, Klaus Schröter, whose monograph on Döblin was published as recently as the spring of 1978, objects to them for political reasons as well: 'In [*November 1918*] wird die politische Geschichte zum Kampf des satanisch *Bösen* mit den Engeln um die Seele des Menschen verdünnt.'[41] Schröter even goes further and (in what must surely be one of the most careless and cavalier critical judgments of 1978) dismisses *November 1918* as being 'von rohester Kunstlosigkeit und diffusem Gehalt.'[42] Regrettably, Schröter does not see fit to back up his laconic generalization with any arguments whatsoever, and it can only be assumed that he does not have more than a nodding acquaintance with the novel.

For it is with consummate artistry that Döblin draws together the hundreds of threads of plot and sub-plot, weaving a huge tapestry depicting a host of major and minor characters whose individual destinies combine to mirror the events of the Spartacist Revolution. In a more fundamental sense, Schröter has misunderstood Döblin's basic position: the battle between the forces of good and evil, between Satan and the angels, is the crux of the novel; in other words, the German Revolution of 1918 must be understood as the historical framework, the foundation, as it were, upon which Döblin constructs the edifice of his special concept of poetic truth – the timeless truth of faith. Döblin did not by any means 'dilute' the political aspect of his novel but added to it, 'thickened' it with a deeper level of human existence, that religious dimension of life that may be rejected by agnostics, atheists, materialists, or liberal humanists, but the existence of which cannot be denied. *November 1918* is in many ways the artistic *summa* of Alfred Döblin's philosophical, political, and religious views in his later years. In the final section of this article, we shall turn to the synthesis of politics and Christianity Döblin achieves, and to an aspect of the novel that illustrates the ways in which its thematic structure and religious message are intertwined.

III

The paths of Friedrich Becker and Rosa Luxemburg never cross within the plot of the novel; thematically, however, their separate fates, their ultimate martyrdom, intertwine. Rosa Luxemburg's political struggles, and above all her passionate search for truth during her spiritual development, parallel those of Becker. It is important to grasp, as Auer points out,[43] that Döblin skilfully employs, particularly in the final volume of the trilogy, the fugal technique of the *stretto* (in Döblin's own words, an 'Engführung der Themen')[44] by means of which Becker (the subject or *dux*) is imitated in close succession, with the answer, Rosa (the *comes*), entering before the subject is completed. Another earlier and most perceptive critic, Dieter Baacke, was probably the first to suggest that the 'geometric point' at which the destinies of Rosa and Becker meet is in their relationship to Sophocles' Antigone, whose solicitude for the dead serves as a model for both of them. Rosa continually thinks of her unburied lover and tries to give his restless spirit human warmth; Becker is almost the only one of his colleagues who attends the funeral of his high-school principal, the cause of whose untimely death will be discussed later.[45] Baacke's arguments, however, can be taken a step further, so that Antigone is not merely considered the geometrical point of intersection but, in a musical sense, precisely the point at which the dovetailing of fugal *dux* and *comes* produces an extraordinary intensification of the thematic structure of the work. More than this: Döblin's contrapuntal technique (which can easily hold its own with Thomas Mann's more famous use of counterpoint in his great novels – *Doktor Faustus* again comes to mind) includes a further major voice that, though never expressly named, dominates the composition of the novel. This voice is that of Søren Kierkegaard.

At first glance, the subject matter of *November 1918* seems to be as far removed from Kierkegaard's unpolitical and highly personal philosophy as Heaven is from Hell. Rosa Luxemburg and Kierkegaard: can this be more, one may well ask, than a contrived *coincidentia oppositorum*? Yet we know from Döblin's own testimony that he had begun to read *Either/Or* in Paris in 1935,[46] and that he continued his study of Kierkegaard in American exile. In September 1941, less than two months before his conversion to Catholicism and while he was writing *November 1918*, Döblin specifically mentions the fact that his increasing interest in Christian mysticism and philosophy occurred 'im Anschluss an Kierkegaard.'[47] Indeed, it is now almost a convention among Döblin scholars to draw attention to Kierkegaard's influence on his later works; but few have gone into the question in any detail (for example, M. Weyembergh-Boussart, who demonstrates Döblin's *montage* of Kierkegaard quotations in *Hamlet*),[48] and nobody to my knowledge has actually gone to Kierkegaard's texts in order to examine their reflection in *November 1918*.[49] True, Mark Goldberg, in his unpublished doctoral thesis of 1969, was probably the first scholar to indicate that Kierkegaard's three 'stages,' of the aesthetic, ethical, and religious man, can be fruitfully applied to the three sets of moral principles that characters in Döblin's trilogy 'impute as guides in their renovation and as justification for their actions.'[50] Thus the aesthetic stage is represented by the poet Stauffer; the ethical by the revolutionaries (and, one may add, by their opponents, both reactionary and moderate); and the transition from the ethical to the religious stage by Becker and Rosa Luxemburg. What Goldberg overlooks is that Kierkegaard's idiosyncratic and modern interpretation of Sophocles' *Antigone* (contained in the section of *Either/Or* entitled 'The Ancient Tragical Motif as Reflected in the Modern') is mirrored in *November 1918*.

When Rosa Luxemburg, at the beginning of the final volume of the trilogy, exclaims in the darkness and despair of her prison cell in Breslau: 'Wie Antigone bin ich in die Brautkammer gesperrt und lebend eingemauert. Wer rettet mich?' (vol. 3, 12), the reader is aware that these words echo two preceding Antigone motifs, both concerning Becker. In one of the first chapters of the first volume of the trilogy, Becker, now convalescing in a military hospital from his war wounds, recalls happier days before 1914 when he taught Sophocles to his admiring pupils. He then quotes from the first *stasimon* of *Antigone*, beginning where the chorus of Theban Elders proclaims: 'Vieles Gewaltige lebt, und nichts ist gewaltiger als der Mensch' (26).[51] At this point Becker is still (in Kierkegaardian terms) at the ethical stage in his development; much later, having returned to Berlin, he attempts in total despair to commit suicide by hanging himself from a nail in his room that had formerly supported a bust of his mentor Sophocles. As he hammers in the nail to make it firmer, egged on by one of the many supernatural manifestations of evil that visit him (Satan in the shape of a rat), he again quotes from Sophocles' chorus but this time utterly rejects the *hubris* contained in its opening lines: 'Vieles Gewaltige (Schlag) lebt (Schlag), doch Nichts (Schlag) ist gewaltiger (Schlag) als der Mensch (Schlag), als der Mensch (Schlag)' (vol. 2, 261). Becker rejects the temptations of Satan and does not take his own life; he is now prepared for the transition to the religious stage of his development, the point at which he ceases in the Kierkegaardian sense *to be* a Christian and begins *to become* a Christian. With subtle artistry, Döblin takes up the theme again towards the end of the third volume of the trilogy: the terrible blows with which the soldier Runge's rifle butt shatters Rosa Luxemburg's skull in the last moments of her life on earth are to be understood in the same Kierkegaardian context. Like Becker, Rosa rejects the temptations of the devil (who had previously appeared to her frequently in the guise of her dead lover) and, dying, passes from the ethical to the religious stage – her martyrdom. Objective truth (in Rosa's case, Marxism) is rejected in favour of Kierkegaard's subjective truth – that is, a belief in and love of God, the Absolute Thou. Through their actions, both Rosa and Becker, in analogy to Abraham's teleological suspension of the ethical in *Fear and Trembling*, have 'overstepped the ethical entirely and possessed a higher *telos* outside of it.'[52]

This, however, is only to scratch the surface of the virtuosity of Döblin's technique of literary counterpoint. Reference has already been made to Rosa's *Briefe aus dem Gefängnis*. At the beginning of the third volume of the trilogy, there is a skilful use of *montage* of phrases from one of these letters to Sonja Liebknecht, in which Rosa describes a scene she has witnessed in December 1917, when a brutal soldier beats Roumanian buffaloes in the prison courtyard unmercifully until their hides are broken and bloody.[53] As Manfred Auer remarks, Döblin – in an extraordinarily successful and masterly use of his historical source – deliberately omits at this point in the narrative one key sentence of the original letter, in which Rosa identifies herself with the poor mistreated animal: 'O, mein armer Büffel, mein armer, geliebter Bruder, wir stehen hier beide so ohnmächtig und stumpf und sind nur eins in Schmerz, in Ohnmacht, in Sehnsucht.'[54] Hundreds of pages later, Döblin introduces the scene of Rosa's murder by repeating the paraphrase of the quotations he had used ('Sonja, es waren schöne rumänische Büffel, sie waren an Freiheit gewohnt' [3, 609]), but allows his readers to make the analogy of self-identification that the historical Rosa had made in her letter. For just before she dies, Rosa recognizes that the soldier who had pitilessly mistreated the buffaloes and her own murderer, Runge, are one and the same person, or rather that they are both manifestations of Satan himself: 'Sie speit ihm in sein tyrannisches Gesicht ... und schreit ihm ihren Abscheu entgegen: Du hast keine Macht über mich' (610).

Auer, however, neglects two further points in the novel where this leitmotif is used; once, in the middle of volume three, when Rosa, tirelessly working for the revolution, thinks of the scene in the prison courtyard ('der junge Soldat schlug [den Büffeln] mit dem Peitschenstiel über den Rücken, unbarmherzig' [290]), she realizes that her work is in vain. As the title of the chapter suggests: 'Die Revolution [war] schon vor der Schlacht geschlagen' (289). A further, and even more subtle use of the motif occurs before this, involving the thematic linking of Becker, Rosa, Antigone, and Kierkegaard. To cite our musical analogy again, the theme is repeated as in a mirror fugue, with introversion and retrogression, and with inversion and augmentation of the melody.[55] In book three of the third volume, Becker is giving his first lesson at school – on Sophocles' *Antigone*. Led by Schröter, the reactionary *Klassenprimus*, most of the pupils are for Creon and against Antigone, since Creon represents the state – we recall that the time is January 1919 and the Spartacist Revolution is nearing its bloody climax – whereas Antigone symbolizes the right of the individual against the state. 'Antigone ist ein Weib,' one of Becker's pupils sneers, 'das nicht die mindeste Ahnung davon hat, was ein Staat ist. Dass man sich seine Gefühle zu verkneifen hat, wenn es um die Allgemeinheit geht und dass sich manche für den Staat opfern, das geht in ihren kleinen Gehirnkasten nicht hinein' (201). In vain, Becker attempts to convince his class that Antigone can be interpreted in a way that transcends the obvious political arguments his pupils put forward. (One of the few socialist students in the class calls Antigone a 'modern type,' since she fights against political tyranny just as Wilhelm Tell does in Schiller's play [201–2].) But Becker counters both left and right by arguing: 'Antigone kämpft überhaupt nicht. Sie fühlt sich als ein Instrument. Sie dient dem göttlichen Gesetz ... Und damit leitet sie, ohne es zu wissen, auch die Auflösung des schrecklichen Erbfluches ein. Sie unterwirft sich dem göttlichen Gebot' (202). Creon, on the other hand, Becker continues, acts against the supernatural, invisible powers that have placed their laws in the safest place possible, in the human heart: 'Auf solch ungeschriebenes Gesetz beruft sich Antigone. Alle Menschen wissen von diesem Gesetz, auch Kreon. Er glaubt, sie brechen zu können, und Antigone muss in den Tod gehen. Aber er selbst erhält eine furchtbare Lehre' (204).[56]

The dovetailing of different motifs in book three of the third volume, significantly entitled 'Antigone und die Schuld der Ahnen,' is much more complex than a brief summary of Becker's lesson can suggest. It is important to know that, shortly before he begins his exegesis of Sophocles' drama, Becker is sitting in his study looking at his small crucifix, and realizes in a flash of insight that Christ is the truth that goes beyond the confines of the visible: 'Du thronst über den Zeiten. Dich berühren keine Kriege und Revolutionen' (185). Becker has made his Kierkegaardian 'leap of faith,' his miraculous venture over the abyss, just as Döblin himself had done in the French city of Mende in 1940 when, like Saul on the road to Damascus, he saw the crucifix in the cathedral.[57]

We now come to the second time Döblin uses the buffalo motif. After the *Antigone* lesson at school, the *Klassenprimus* not only objects to Becker's views on the delicate topic 'Antigone gegen den Staat' (230), but even more to the guilty conduct of the school principal, whose homo-erotic relationship with a pupil (rather on the lines of Stefan George's aestheticism) is becoming a public scandal. The principal is finally hounded to suicide by intolerant colleagues, pupils, and parents; before this happens, Becker thinks of the fate of Antigone in the course of a conversation he has with the principal shortly before his death. 'Becker sah: mein armer Bruder ... mein eigenes Bild von früher' (231). As if to underscore the connection between the self-identification of Becker (who had ultimately rejected suicide by the power of faith) and the principal on the one hand, and between Rosa Luxemburg and the ill-treated buffaloes on the other, the chapter is entitled 'Mein armer Bruder' (230) – a cryptic quotation, as we know, from Rosa's letter to Sonja Liebknecht. The web of point and counterpoint created by Döblin grows in its complexity and intensity.

To return again to Becker's interpretation of Antigone, Döblin's projection of mythological motifs into a modern, Christian context is not merely a favourite device employed throughout his later works, but it is also precisely the device used by Kierkegaard in his interpretation of Sophocles' tragedy. For the Danish philosopher, too, Antigone is 'modern' – that is, he creates his own Antigone whose name, he writes, 'I will retain from the ancient tragedy, which for the most part I will follow, although from another point of view, everything will be modern.'[58] Kierkegaard, like Becker, focuses his attention on the question of Antigone's guilt, and although his arguments are far more subtle, closely knit, and complicated than Becker's, both arrive at some similar conclusions. Kierkegaard, for instance, stresses that 'tragic guilt is something more than merely subjective guilt, it is inherited guilt; but inherited guilt, like inherited sin, is a substantial category, and it is exactly this substantiality which makes the sorrow deeper.'[59] Becker also draws the analogy between the inherited guilt of the kin of Oedipus and the Christian concept of original sin. (In German translations of Kierkegaard, the concept of 'inherited sin' is rendered as 'Erbsünde' – the exact equivalent of 'original sin.') 'Einer, ein einzelner, hatte in der Vergangenheit also eine Schuld begangen,' Becker instructs his pupils, 'wie in der Biblischen Geschichte Adam. Aber diese eine Schuld ... war gross, weil sie sich gegen die göttliche Macht richtete' (vol. 3, 196).

Time and again, Kierkegaardian ideas are worked into the fabric of *November 1918*. In Becker's interpretation Antigone does not follow a blind impulse when burying her brother but is led by universal and moral laws; yet even if the Antigone of the Greek tragedy does not know of her inherited guilt ('Erbschuld'), the reader of Döblin's trilogy realizes that Becker himself is acutely aware of 'Erbsünde' in the Christian sense. Kierkegaard's own, modern Antigone (in contradistinction to Sophocles') knows about her inherited guilt and silently carries this knowledge as a 'secret under her heart, hidden and concealed.'[60] This secret, Kierkegaard says, is borne in her heart 'like an arrow which life unrelentingly has driven in deeper and deeper without depriving her of life, for as long as it remains in her heart she can live, but the moment it is drawn out, she must die.'[61] The 'silence' of Döblin's Rosa Luxemburg, as we have noted, is portrayed in her dreams and visions; so, too, with Kierkegaard's Antigone: 'Her life does not unfold like that of the Greek Antigone; it is not turned outward but inward, the scene is not external but internal; it is an invisible scene.'[62] In the German translation of this latter passage, 'invisible scene' is rendered by 'Geisterszene.' Rosa Luxemburg's and Friedrich Becker's (to reiterate Döblin's own words) 'grausige Begegnung[en] im Geisterreich,' their encounters with the supernatural in nightmarish visions, in a word, the internal, invisible world of the mind, can easily be understood in a Kierkegaardian sense. Rosa's inner struggles, like those of Becker, are basically those of a person passionately searching for the truth, emerging from the cocoon of the merely ethical, and, ironically in Rosa's case, reaching the final religious stage at the very moment of her death. Becker lives a little longer than Rosa, but his life until his death is that of a Kierkegaardian 'Knight of Faith.' (It is interesting to note that Döblin, a convert to Catholicism, makes his hero a Protestant – perhaps to suggest Becker's proximity to Kierkegaard's special and unorthodox brand of Protestantism?)

The two main protagonists of *November 1918* accurately reflect the Kierkegaardian ideal of being a 'scandal,' that is, of being witnesses and martyrs to the 'paradox of faith' that 'begins precisely there where thinking leaves off.'[63] This, too, is a paradox, since neither Kierkegaard nor Döblin could be accused of ceasing to think: their huge literary and philosophical *œuvres* bear witness to their keen intellects and to a fruitful use of human *ratio*. And yet *November 1918* – a novel in which the multitudes of those who died in two world wars and in their aftermaths are never far from the author or his readers – contains the essence of Döblin's own profession of faith. As a Catholic, he remained a thorn in the flesh of his contemporaries, an 'exasperation' to those who did not wish to be prodded out of the rut of conventional thinking. Politically, Döblin's view of the German Revolution of 1918 is 'scandalous,' but it is also timeless, as a mere glance at the strife-torn, violent world of the late 1970s will tell us. In the pages of the trilogy, the professing Protestant Becker and the writer who created him, the professing Catholic Alfred Döblin, and before them both, Kierkegaard, are united in the passion of the way they view the world. Liselotte Richter's description of the path Kierkegaard took can be aptly applied to that of Döblin: 'ohne bürgerlichen Beruf, wie Sokrates, durch die Strassen schlendernd, seiner Zeit auf die Finger sehend, seine Zeitgenossen ärgernd, indem er sie aus gewohnten gedankenlosen Ideenassoziationen herausriss durch den spekulativ nicht auflösbaren Widerspruch der menschlichen Existenz.'[64] And could Döblin's Rosa Luxemburg (and the millions of human beings, Jews and gentiles alike, who have since followed her in imprisonment and martyrdom) have a more fitting and highly topical epitaph than the following words from the first of Kierkegaard's *Two Minor Ethico-Religious Treatises*, written on the eve of an earlier revolution, that of 1848?

Among the many ludicrous things in these foolish times, perhaps the most ludicrous is the utterance ... that in our age it is not even possible to become a martyr, that our age lacks sufficient energy to put a man to death, *sie irren sich*! It is not the age which needs the energy to put a man to death or to make him a martyr; it is the martyr, the martyr in process of becoming, who must have the energy to impart to the age sufficient passion, the passion of exasperation in this case, to put him to death.[65]

The sentence with which Christoph Eykman concludes his evaluation of Döblin's *November 1918* – 'Das geschichtliche Ereignis des Aufstandes bleibt ohne Sinn'[66] – is only true if one excludes or downgrades the religious message of the trilogy. Historically, the revolution may have been 'senseless' (and Döblin was, of course, well aware of this when he wrote his novel). But one can only penetrate to the heart of the meaning of *November 1918* if one is prepared to follow Döblin's acceptance of the paradox of eternal truth, which transcends the merely historical and, rejecting secular pessimism, leads to the hope born of despair, to the miracle of faith's passion, in which all of human life is unified.

NOTES

1 Other versions of this article in English and German were given as lectures or papers (under slightly different titles) as follows: at the University of Winnipeg (28 March 1978); at Marbach am Neckar, Deutsches Literaturarchiv (9 August 1978); and at the Fourteenth Congress of the International Federation for Modern Languages and Literatures (Aix-en-Provence, 28 August to 2 September 1978); an abstract of the latter version will be printed in the federation's *Proceedings*. I gratefully acknowledge the award of a travel grant made to me by the Advisory Research Committee of Queen's University, Kingston, which enabled me to give the lectures in Germany and France.

2 For a very readable account in English of the events of 9 November 1918, see Richard M. Watt, *The Kings Depart. The Tragedy of Germany: Versailles and the German Revolution* (New York: Simon and Schuster 1968), esp. 170–200. The literature on the revolution is vast, but a comprehensive collection of the relevant original historical documents can be found in: Herbert Michaelis et al., *Ursachen und Folgen. Vom deutschen Zusammenbruch 1918 und 1945 ... Eine Urkunden- und Dokumentensammlung zur Zeitgeschichte* (Berlin: Dokumenten-Verlag n.d. [1959ff.]), esp. vols. 1–3. Döblin's own use of historical sources is discussed in full by Manfred Auer (see n. 18 below).

3 Alfred Döblin, *November 1918. Eine deutsche Revolution. Erzählwerk*, 3 vols. (Munich: Karl Alber 1948–50), vol. 1, *Verratenes Volk* (1948); vol. 2, *Heimkehr der Fronttruppen* (1949); vol. 3, *Karl und Rosa* (1950). Further references in the text and notes of this article will be to this edition. To avoid complicated explanations of the novel's history of publication, we shall follow Manfred Auer's arguments (see n. 18 below) and refer to *November 1918* as a trilogy, rather than as a tetralogy, although it must be borne in mind that in fact the first volume of the projected cycle was published on the eve of the Second World War and entitled *Bürger und Soldaten 1918* (Stockholm and Amster-

dam: Bermann-Fischer/Querido 1939); the 'Vorspiel' of vol. 1 of the trilogy is a revised version of the introductory chapter of *Bürger und Soldaten 1918*. Until the summer of 1978, when dtv (Munich) published a new, four-volume paperback edition of *November 1918* (which was unavailable to me at the time of writing), the work had neither been reprinted nor reissued since 1950. It is to be hoped that the dtv edition will serve to revive interest in the novel.

4 For a useful collection of typical reviews of that period, see Ingrid Schuster and Ingrid Bode, (eds.), *Alfred Döblin im Spiegel der zeitgenössischen Kritik* (Bern and Munich: Francke 1973) 399–416.

5 Rosa Luxemburg, *Politische Schriften*, ed. Ossip K. Flechtheim, 3 vols. (Frankfurt, Vienna: Europäische Verlagsanstalt/Europa Verlag 1966–8), vol. 3, 'Einleitung,' 20 (my translation).

6 Rosa Luxemburg was born on 5 March 1871, in the same year as Karl Liebknecht and Friedrich Ebert – all three of whom were to play decisive roles in the November Revolution.

7 In the following list, I have adapted that of Dieter Baacke, whose brief but seminal article helped to pioneer appreciative scholarly criticism of *November 1918* ('Erzähltes Engagement. Antike Mythologie in Döblins Romanen,' *Text + Kritik* 13–14 [1966] 22–31; here 24–6).

8 Bertolt Brecht, *Trommeln in der Nacht* (Frankfurt: Suhrkamp 1953) 187.

9 Unpublished letter (four typed pages), dated Mainz, 23 July 1951, to Fr Matthew A. Hoehn, OSB (1898–1959), then editor of a reference work, *Catholic Authors*. Döblin's letter contains a brief *curriculum vitae* supplied to Hoehn for translation into English, editing, and inclusion in a forthcoming volume of *Catholic Authors*. Although the *vita* was published (*Catholic Authors: Contemporary Biographical Sketches* [Newark, NJ: St Mary's Abbey 1952], vol. 2, 133–5), it contains a number of errors in translation and is not a complete version of Döblin's original text (for example, it does not contain the passage on *November 1918* quoted in the present article). I am grateful to Rev. Theodore J. Howarth, OSB (Newark Abbey, NJ, where the files of the late Fr. Hoehn are deposited) for supplying me with photocopies of Döblin's letter of 23 July 1951 and also of a second letter of 3 October 1951 (in which he approves the text of the English version of his *vita*).

10 Alfred Döblin, *Berlin Alexanderplatz. Die Geschichte vom Franz Biberkopf*, ed. Walter Muschg (Olten and Freiburg: Walter 1964) 501. Similar echoes can be found in Döblin's last great novel, *Hamlet oder Die lange Nacht nimmt ein Ende* (1957), whose hero, the war-amputee Edward Allison, returns home to England after 1945 to begin a new life. Here again, the closing sentences of the novel suggest the beginning of yet another 'new life' for the novel's hero. (For detailed discussion of this problem, see A.W. Riley, 'Zum umstrittenen Schluss

von Alfred Döblins *Hamlet oder Die lange Nacht nimmt ein Ende,'* *Literaturwissenschaftliches Jahrbuch*, N.F. 13 [1972] 331–58.)

11 Cf. Alfred Döblin, 'Christentum und Revolution' (1950), in *Aufsätze zur Literatur*, ed. Walter Muschg (Olten and Freiburg: Walter 1963) 379–83, esp. 380. Further references to Döblin's essays will, unless otherwise specified, be to this edition and indicated by *Aufsätze*.

12 Gerd Müller, *Literatur und Revolution. Untersuchungen zur Frage des literarischen Engagements in Zeiten des politischen Umbruchs*, Acta Universitatis Upsaliensis 14 (Uppsala, 1974).

13 A useful collection of these can be found in Alfred Döblin, *Schriften zur Politik und Gesellschaft 1896–1951*, ed. Heinz Graber (Olten and Freiburg: Walter 1972); see also Döblin's full-length essays *Der deutsche Maskenball* (von Linke Poot) [1921] and *Wissen und Verändern!* [1931], ed. Heinz Graber (Olten and Freiburg: Walter 1972). For further details on Döblin's political activities before 1933, see Leo Kreutzer, *Alfred Döblin. Sein Werk bis 1933* (Stuttgart: W. Kohlhammer 1970) 134–62 et passim.

14 Alfred Döblin, *Schicksalsreise. Bericht und Bekenntnis* (Frankfurt, 1949); the book has recently been reprinted in Alfred Döblin, *Autobiographische Schriften und letzte Aufzeichnungen*, ed. Edgar Pässler, Jubiläums-Sonderausgabe (Olten and Freiburg: Walter 1977) 103–426.

15 Hans Jürgen Baden, in his study *Literatur und Bekehrung* (Stuttgart: Ernst Klett 1968), devotes a chapter to Alfred Döblin (162–97), which is probably one of the most sensitive discussions of the complicated issues involved in religious conversions ever written. Citing Döblin, Baden points out that there is 'a (divine) reality, which can never be comprehended by human reason' (163), but that one can distinguish between the actual, historical, biographical fact of conversion and its 'invisible preludes' – 'ihre (unsichtbare) Vorgeschichte, die der Bekehrte meistens erst post festum zu dechiffrieren vermag' (164).

16 For a brief discussion of the antagonisms aroused by Döblin's conversion and subsequent religious convictions, see A.W. Riley, 'The Professing Christian and the Ironic Humanist: A Comment on the Relationship of Alfred Döblin and Thomas Mann after 1933,' in *Essays on German Literature in Honour of G. Joyce Hallamore*, ed. M.S. Batts and M.G. Stankiewicz (Toronto: University of Toronto Press 1968) 177–94.

17 See letters to Arthur Rosin, dated Hollywood, 2 February and 2 March 1942, in Alfred Döblin, *Briefe*, ed. Heinz Graber (Olten and Freiburg: Walter 1970) 269, 272; in the second of these letters, Döblin uses the variant 'Zur Mahnung und Erinnerung.' Further references to this edition will be indicated by *Briefe*.

18 Manfred Auer, *Das Exil vor der Vertreibung. Motivkontinuität und Quellenproblematik im späten Werk Alfred Döblins*, Abhandlungen zur Kunst-, Musik- und

Literaturwissenschaft 254 (Bonn: Bouvier Verlag Herbert Grundmann 1977).

19 In particular by Klaus Müller-Salget; the title of one of the sections of his Döblin monograph is 'Der künstlerische Abstieg,' referring to those works written after 1933 (*Alfred Döblin. Werk und Entwicklung*. Bonner Arbeiten zur deutschen Literatur 22 [Bonn: Bouvier Verlag Herbert Grundmann 1972] 357).

20 Auer, *Das Exil* 78.

21 Ibid. 77.

22 J.P. Nettl, *Rosa Luxemburg*, 2 vols. (London, New York, Toronto: Oxford University Press 1966).

23 Ibid., vol. 1, 1.

24 Ibid., vol. 2, 918.

25 Müller-Salget, 'Der künstlerische Abstieg,' 378.

26 Ibid. 378.

27 See Nettl, *Rosa Luxemburg* 674 et passim.

28 Rosa Luxemburg, *Briefe aus dem Gefängnis* (1920), ed. Exekutiv-Komitee der Kommunistischen Jugendinternationale (Berlin: Verlag der Jugendinternationale 1929).

29 'Zur Einführung,' *Briefe aus dem Gefängnis* 8 (my translation).

30 For example, *Briefe an Karl und Luise Kautsky (1896–1918)* (Berlin: E. Laubsche Verlagshandlung 1923); *Briefe an Freunde* (Hamburg: Europäische Verlagsanstalt 1950). It is worth noting that Döblin reviewed this latter edition of Rosa's letters in the journal he founded and edited, *Das Goldene Tor*; the review has been reprinted in *Schriften zur Politik und Gesellschaft* (see n. 13 above) 463–7.

31 Cf. Charlotte Beradt (ed.), 'Einleitung,' *Rosa Luxemburg im Gefängnis. Briefe und Dokumente aus den Jahren 1915–1918* (Frankfurt: S. Fischer 1973) 7–13. Beradt cites (8) an amusing example of the worst sort of popular journalism, portraying Rosa as the 'world's greatest lover'; the banner headline of an article in *Der Stern* (15 November 1970) reads: 'Die blaue Blume der Roten.'

32 Nettl discusses *Die russische Revolution* and the resulting feud with Lenin, quoting part of Lenin's reply (*Pravda* [16 April 1924]) as well as tracing the later controversies with Stalin and others (cf. Nettl, *Rosa Luxemburg*, vol. 2, 696–705, 792–3 et passim).

33 It is worth noting that Döblin made a significant change when quoting Rosa's words; the original text reads: 'Jawohl: Diktatur! Aber diese Diktatur besteht in der *Art der Verwendung der Demokratie*, nicht in ihrer *Abschaffung* ...' Luxemburg, *Politische Schriften*, vol. 3, 139 [italics in the original]). Döblin's omission of the word 'Art' makes Rosa's statement more 'democratic' than it really is. In fact, if one compares all of the quotations (or paraphrases of quotations)

Döblin culls from *Die russische Revolution* with the original text *in toto*, it becomes obvious that his process of selection tends to bolster up his own view of Rosa as an opponent of all that Leninism stood for in practice. This is, of course, not entirely in accordance with the historical facts, and is a further example of Döblin's poetic truth versus historical truth.

34 Nettl, *Rosa Luxemburg*, vol. 2, 675.

35 Ibid. 675.

36 Letter dated 'Mitte November 1917,' *Briefe aus dem Gefängnis* (n. 28 above) 52.

37 Cf. Nettl, *Rosa Luxemburg*, vol. 2, 675: letter to Karl and Luise Kautsky of 15 November 1917. Nettl also points out that Rosa's silence was not confined to her letters on Diefenbach: the same is true of a letter, written on the occasion of her father's death, to Minna Kautsky (30 December 1900). Rosa admits that the blow shook her so much that she 'could not communicate for many months either by letter or word of mouth.'

38 Nettl, *Rosa Luxemburg*, vol. 2, 675.

39 Cited by Auer, *Das Exil* (77).

40 Alfred Döblin, 'Rosa Luxemburg, Briefe an Freunde' (1951), *Schriften zur Politik und Gesellschaft* (n. 13 above) 465.

41 Klaus Schröter, *Alfred Döblin in Selbstzeugnissen und Bilddokumenten*, rowohlts monographien 266 (Reinbek: Rowohlt Taschenbuch 1978) 125.

42 Ibid. 130.

43 Cf. Auer, *Das Exil* 62, 85–8.

44 'In diesem Schlussband sollen nicht ... die deutschen Zustände weiter breit dargestellt werden, sondern der Abschluss soll, wie in der Musik bei der Fuge, in einer "Engführung" der Themen erreicht werden' (Alfred Döblin, 'Inhaltsskizze im Marbacher Nachlass'; cited by Auer, *Das Exil* [62]).

45 Baacke, 'Erzähltes Engagement' (n. 7 above) 30.

46 Alfred Döblin, 'Epilog' (1948), *Aufsätze* 392. Döblin also writes that he 'verschlang einen Band [Kierkegaard] nach dem anderen ... zog lange Partien aus, schrieb Hefte voll. Er erschütterte mich. Er war redlich, wach und wahr' (394).

47 Letter dated 17 September 1941 to Elvira and Arthur Rosin, *Briefe* 258.

48 See Monique Weyembergh-Boussart, *Alfred Döblin. Seine Religiosität in Persönlichkeit und Werk*, Abhandlungen zur Kunst-, Musik- und Literaturwissenschaft 76 (Bonn: Bouvier 1970), esp. 336–7, 348–50. This monograph, the best available on Döblin's religious beliefs, also mentions the possibility of Kierkegaard's influence on *November 1918* and *Die Pilgerin Aetheria* (written c. 1947–9), but without going into great detail. The latter *Erzählung* was recently published (for the first time in its complete form) in a volume of the 'Ausgewählte Werke in Einzelbänden,' ed. A.W. Riley, *Der Oberst und der Dichter oder das menschliche Herz/Die Pilgerin Aetheria* (Olten and Freiburg: Walter 1978).

49 Various scholars have suggested that Kierkegaard's influence is present – for example, Robert Minder, who writes: 'L'influence de Kierkegaard y est très sensible,' but does not expand on the question ('Hommage à Alfred Doeblin,' *Allemagne d'aujourd'hui*, no. 3 (1957) 10.

50 Mark Goldberg, 'The Individual and Society in the Novels of Alfred Doeblin,' (Dissertation, New York University, 1969) 137; Goldberg's discussion of *November 1918* is well worth reading.

51 I have not been able to determine which of the many German translations of Sophocles' *Antigone* Döblin used. Regrettably, many of the books in Döblin's private library were given away or sold after his death; lists of his books still in the possession of his sons Claude and Peter Döblin were compiled in 1977 and are deposited in the Döblin-*Nachlass* at Marbach (Deutsches Literaturarchiv), but neither Sophocles nor Kierkegaard appears in the lists. Within the context of *November 1918* it is fortunate that Döblin used a German translation of *Antigone* that rendered the difficult words 'πολλὰ τὰ δεινὰ'/'δεινότερον' of the original as 'Vieles Gewaltige'/'gewaltiger' (Hölderlin, for example, uses 'Ungeheuer'); all of the English versions I have consulted render the Greek expression with terms like 'many marvels' or 'many wonders' – all of which would be inappropriate for Döblin's particular purposes.

52 Søren Kierkegaard, *Fear and Trembling and The Sickness unto Death*, trans. Walter Lowrie (Princeton, NJ: Princeton University Press 1974 [1941]) 69.

53 Letter dated Breslau, 'Mitte Dezember 1917,' *Briefe aus dem Gefängnis* (n. 28 above) 63–5. Döblin's quotations, it must be stressed, are not always direct. Some sentences are paraphrases; some are taken almost verbatim from two different parts of the letter – for example, from its postscript, where the historical Rosa writes: 'So ist das Leben und so muss man es nehmen, tapfer, unverzagt und lächelnd – trotz alledem' (65); Döblin's version (vol. 3, 10) reads: 'Aber so ist das Leben, Sonja. Trotz alledem, man muss es tapfer und unverzagt nehmen.'

54 *Briefe aus dem Gefängnis* 65. This particular letter, it is worth noting, became a *cause célèbre* when it was reproduced in Karl Kraus's *Die Fackel* in 1922, provoking extremely hostile reactions from correspondents and also an impassioned defence by Kraus himself. (For details, see Nettl, *Rosa Luxemburg*, vol. 1, 14–15.) It is quite possible that Döblin may have first become aware of *Briefe aus dem Gefängnis* at this time, when they were having such a strong public impact.

55 Matthias Prangel rightly points out that Döblin's *Gespräche mit Kalypso. Über die Musik* (first published in *Der Sturm* in 1910, but regrettably never reprinted since) are of inestimable value in understanding Döblin's theories of the relationship between literature and music, especially in his discussion of the

117 Christianity and Revolution in Döblin

musical problem of integration, the solution to which he saw in the transformation of the 'Hintereinander des Zeitlichen in ein Nebeneinander' and by
means of the unifying 'Gesetz des Gegensatzes und der Mannigfaltigkeit' (cf.
M. Prangel, *Alfred Döblin*, Sammlung Metzler M105 [Stuttgart: Metzler 1973]
21–2). *November 1918* would be an ideal subject for research on this topic.

56 In a nutshell, this is also the theme of Döblin's *Der Oberst und der Dichter* (cf. n.
48 above), which was written in 1944 just after *November 1918* had been
completed.
57 Cf. *Schicksalsreise* [1949] (n. 14 above) 212–14.
58 Søren Kierkegaard, *Either/Or*, trans. David F. Swenson and Lillian Marvin
Swenson, (Garden City, NY: Doubleday, Anchor Books 1959) 151.
59 Ibid. 148.
60 Ibid. 155.
61 Ibid. 162.
62 Ibid. 154–5.
63 Kierkegaard, *Fear and Trembling* 64.
64 Liselotte Richter, 'Einleitung,' in Sören Kierkegaard, *Die Leidenschaft des
Religiösen. Eine Auswahl aus Schriften und Tagebüchern*, ed. Heinz Köpper
(Stuttgart: Reclam 1958) 10–11.
65 Søren Kierkegaard, 'Has a Man the Right to let himself be put to Death for the
Truth?' [1847], in *The Present Age and Two Minor Ethico-Religious Treatises*,
trans. Alexander Dru and Walter Lowrie (London, New York, Toronto:
Oxford University Press 1940) 120.
66 Christoph Eykman, 'Zwischen Pessimismus und Christentum. Alfred
Döblins historische Romane,' *Geschichtspessimismus in der deutschen Literatur des
zwanzigsten Jahrhunderts* (Bern and Munich: Francke 1970) 57.

COLIN BUTLER

Mr Britling Sees It Through: A View from the Other Side

Mr Britling Sees It Through[1] was an instant best seller. Begun towards the end of 1915 and first published in September 1916, it had gone through thirteen editions by Christmas of that year, and American royalties alone grossed over £20,000.[2] 'For the first time,' wrote an anonymous reviewer in *The Times Literary Supplement* of 21 September 1916, 'we have a novel which touches the life of the last two years without impertinence. This is a really remarkable event, and Mr Wells's book, with all its many obvious imperfections, is a proud achievement.'[3] Galsworthy declared it a 'fine, generous, big-hearted book'; and in a letter from Petrograd dated end of December 1916/beginning of January 1917, Maxim Gorky judged it 'the finest, most courageous, truthful and humane book written in Europe in the course of this accursed war.'[4] It is a book that is unusual in a number of respects. The work of a non-combatant man of letters in his late forties, it was written and published before Wells had ever seen a battlefield; it is set not at the front but in England; its temper is wholly civilian; and, in the midst of war, it attempts to present the Germans in as sympathetic a light as possible (in the majority of English war novels, the Germans are the principal enemy and the western front the principal theatre of war, with the eastern Mediterranean the most prominent 'side-show' – cultures, like politics, have their blind spots). There are passages in it that are as poignant today as they were on the day it was published. Yet they are only part of its raison d'être, though an important one for all that, as we shall see; for, typically, the book aspires to instruct as well as to move. Its immediate preoccupation with the Britlings of Matching's Easy and their circle is, as its title implies, inseparable from the larger issue of the state of the nation at a given moment in its history. In short, *Mr Britling* is very much a Wellsian war novel, and one way to arrive at an understanding of it is to approach it via its antecedents.

Wells was born on 21 September 1886 in what is now very much the South London suburb of Bromley. His mother had been a lady's maid at Up Park in West Sussex, and his father had worked there as a gardener. A cousin had sold them a china shop, Atlas House, in Bromley High Street, and they had moved in on 23 October 1853, having sunk their entire savings in the business. It was in Atlas House that Wells learned from personal experience what it meant to be poor in the country that had led the world in industrialization and that was to remain extremely rich even after that lead had been largely surrendered to newer nations. He also learned there that in an age of insistent individualism, many people could have at best only very limited control over their economic circumstances, and consequently over the nature and quality of their lives; for no amount of Smilesean self-help on the part of his parents in the cramped, laborious, and insanitary rear quarters of their china shop could do more than protract the years' long but inevitable decline into bankruptcy of the essentially insolvent business. There is no doubt that the sight of so much unmerited hardship and pain engendered in Wells not only the desire to escape such a fate himself but to discover, and replace, the 'vast unsuspected forces'[5] that had made his family life what it was. After his father had accidentally broken a leg, his mother saved the Wellses from the ever-present nightmare of the English lower-middle class – becoming part of the obscure proletariat, which all his life Wells saw through nineteenth-century middle-class eyes as 'inherently barbarous and hateful'[6] – by returning to Up Park for a further twelve years as a (rather incompetent) housekeeper. If it was life in Bromley that had turned Wells against laissez-faire capitalism and the doctrine of self-reliance, and thereby made him typical of a generation of discontent with the whole socio-economic structure of contemporary England, it was 'from the eighteenth-century civilisation revealed at Uppark [sic]' during his visits to his mother that Wells derived the 'ideals of spaciousness and intellectual freedom' that consistently inform his conception of how society must be if universal human happiness is to be attained.

For most of his life, albeit with a sense of urgency increasingly bordering on desperation,[7] Wells remained convinced that reality can be changed by changing men's minds – a conviction that ultimately justified his life as a writer and profoundly affected his attitude to the nature of the arts. As was by no means unusual for the times, his own formal education was 'a queer discontinuous series,'[8] even though belated attempts at modernization had been made in England, chiefly as a means to counter the upsurge of foreign technological competition that marked the latter part of the nineteenth century. In a retrospective appraisal, in *Experiment in Autobiography*, of education in England at this time, Wells found that it had paid far too little attention to science and technology, and that it had failed to develop a guiding rationale. He, in contrast, was persuaded that it was precisely on science and technology, as areas essential to social progress, that it *should* concentrate, and that it should be planned throughout, *as should society at large*. The latter idea doubtless owed a lot to his private reading, not least in the 'free thinker's'[9] library at Up Park, in the enlightened atmosphere of which he read, among others, Plato, whose *Republic* afforded him a life-long model of a society run efficiently from the top on behalf of the majority, and Henry George, whose *Progress and Poverty* (1879) was then replacing Smiles as a lodestar of social thinking in England.[10]

George maintained that evil was not natural but the result of inequality, and that inequality was an inevitable concomitant of laissez-faire capitalism; he concluded that if an end were to be put to a situation in which the poor wasted their energies acquiring sustenance and the rich wasted theirs on ostentatious luxury, laissez-faire capitalism would have to be replaced by much more deliberately ordered arrangement. George was influenced in his thinking by the assumption that 'man is social in his nature', that 'mind is the instrument by which man advances, and by which each advance is secured and made the vantage ground for new advances,'[11] and (understandably for his time) that material improvement was the key to man's general well-being. All of these points recur in Wells.

A greater influence on Wells than George, however, was T.H. Huxley, whose course of lectures on biology Wells attended during 1884–5 as a science teacher in training at the Normal School of Science in South Kensington. The *locus classicus* of Huxley's thought is his Romanes Lecture, 'Evolution and Ethics,' of 18 May 1893 and its 'Prolegomena' of 1894, the theme of which, expressed in the new fundamentalism of Darwinism, was the mastering of natural evolution by means of nature's own gift – reason. Huxley's 'ideal polity' would improve upon the blind processes of nature 'not by gradually adjusting the men to the conditions around them, but by creating artificial conditions for them; not by allowing the free play of the struggle for existence, but by excluding that struggle.' 'In place of ruthless self-assertion,' Huxley argued, 'it [the "ethically best"] demands self-restraint; in place of thrusting aside, or treading down, all competitors, it requires that the individual shall not merely respect, but shall help his fellows; its influence is directed, not so much to the survival of the fittest, as to the fitting of as many as possible to survive.' And in order to realize this ideal polity, Huxley postulates 'some administrative authority, as far superior in power and intelligence to men, as men are to their cattle.'[12]

To Wells, scientific novice, economic casualty, and would-be social improver, nothing was more obvious than that, if the contemporary free-for-all could be replaced by the best brains acting in the interest of the remainder, then the best of all possible worlds would automatically come into being. 'In civilised man,' he wrote in an early essay, 'we have (1) an inherited factor, the natural man, who is the product of natural selection ... and (2) an acquired factor, the artificial man, the highly plastic creature of tradition, suggestion, and reasoned thought. In the artificial man we have all that makes the comforts and securities of civilisation a possibility.'[13] This 'acquired factor,' for Wells as for Huxley a novelty in the evolutionary process, confers on man the ability to make evolution irreversible and to direct all future change in accordance with his own perceived interests (something that neither evolution alone, nor its implicit analogue, capitalism, could guarantee). Such thinking originates in a divided view of man – natural man, living on in contemporary man as predatory egotism, is to be overcome by artificial man, the collectivist improver – and Wells's work is never wholly free from its tension. But if his dream of a better future *is* ever to be realized, a function of education, construed in the largest possible sense, will be not only the dissemination of functional skills but the imparting of the vision they are to help make a reality: 'Education ... obviously should be the careful and systematic manufacture of the artificial factor in man.'[14]

It was the belief that 'man-making [is] a human enterprise rather than a natural process'[15] that led Wells for a time into the Fabian camp. He deplored the Liberals as 'a diversified crowd ... a vague and *planless* association' (italics added);[16] he felt that the Marxists' reliance on the working out of forces inherent in society was far too providentialist to be worth supporting; and the many forms of well-intentioned egalitarianism being devised as 'cures' for the ills of late-Victorian society amounted in his opinion to no more than sinking to the level of the incompetent masses, '[whose] range of incapacity tempts and demoralises the strong.'[17] Fabian gradualism, on the other hand, offered 'a vision of extreme seductiveness – of a world run by the intelligent'[18] that was consistent both with his neo-Huxleyan ethical Darwinism and his own benign but peremptory psychology. Before too long, Wells lost patience with Fabianism for being altogether *too* gradualist, while his sexual life made it in any case difficult for him to remain one of what was, after all, not a political party but a congeries of more or less like-minded reformers in constant personal contact with each other.[19] But it is clear that there was, and remained, no little affinity between Wells and the undemocratic, managerial, and intellectual Fabians, an affinity that was not lessened by Wells's own awareness of the discrepancy between the class from which he had risen and the class by which he was by now being taken up.

Wells had achieved this rise with his pen. Had he followed an orthodox career he would either have remained all his life in something like the genteel helotry of drapery, in which trade he was sporadically apprenticed, or become a teacher: the higher professions would have been closed to him, and manual labour, even had his health been better, would have been beneath him. However, a general increase in literacy – a consequence of the growing artificiality of society that Wells looked to with such great expectations – and the corresponding growth of a popular press to cater to it, afforded Wells the opportunity rapidly to acquire wealth and reputation as an entertaining and informative journalist and writer of scientific romances. By the turn of the century he was a rich man, and a national voice by 1912. As such, he was able to exercise considerable influence in two ways. Bruno Schultze has remarked in *H.G. Wells und der Erste Weltkrieg* that, whereas in Germany events have to become history before they may be treated fictionally, in England the man of letters is traditionally far less isolated. In that country, success brings an author not only wealth but social standing and ready access, as table companion and fellow clubman, to holders of public office.[20] For a time, along with Grey, Haldane, Bertrand Russell, Sidney Webb, and the like, Wells was a member of the 'Coefficients' dining club, and he felt all his life that, by virtue of his status as a writer, he was entitled to the ear of the mighty. In addition, of course, there was his large, popular readership, which he could address directly through an unending flow of publications.

For his fiction, Wells developed a technique of writing that allowed him to reach, if not the proletariat, then at least the lower strata of the middle class. Since the novel had established itself during the nineteenth century as *the* pre-eminent genre, it was, for a time, as a novelist that Wells, too, wished to make his mark. It is well known that he took (for him) a great deal of trouble over *Love and Mr Lewisham* (1900),[21] and although that level of assiduity was not maintained, he still managed to produce during this period a series of works that, like *Mr Lewisham* itself, have become minor classics in the language: *Kipps, The Story of a Simple Soul* (1905), *Tono-Bungay* (1909), and *The History of Mr Polly* (1910), for example. Much of the appeal of these novels results from what Edward Ponderevo might call their 'woosh': the way their best characters speak, dress, feel, and blunder catches something that is so much a part of life that it compels an instinctive, immediate response from the reader. It was this unattenuated vitality that Henry James recognized and praised in letter after letter to the younger writer, even though, being James, he never, for all his fulsomeness, entirely surrendered the right to analyse and to insinuate qualifications (of *Marriage* [1912] he wrote that it was 'more convulsed with life and more brimming with blood than any [work] it is given me nowadays to meet ... I consume you crude and whole and to the last morsel').[22] It was the same vitality that gave Wells the confidence to set his face against the 'genre of nervous exhaustion'[23] characteristic of fin de siècle decadence and, in a climate of religious uncertainty, to maintain that life could nevertheless be lived purposefully.

That Wells had something real to offer with his 'far-flaring even though turbid and smoky lamp'[24] is indisputable; yet it was an offering of a limited sort, as a glance at Lawrence will show. What Lawrence was supremely successful in communicating was dynamic: the primary *processes* of living, unfolding in accordance with their own inherent logic; whereas what Wells was attracted to was by comparison static and complete in itself, and therefore less amenable to growth than to repetition. Hence his designs for the future, with their emphasis on external reorganization, seem less than satisfactory, not because society did not (and does not) need reorganization but because they conceal a lack of insight into the fundamental movements of human nature. Wells's Utopia is very much the product of the late nineteenth century in its marked aversion to the natural world as well as to the natural man, both of which are to be overcome by conscious effort if the best kind of future for mankind is to be achieved. In this, of course, it is completely the reverse of the Romantic Utopia (including Lawrence's Rananim), which sought to be close to both by setting up small 'organic' communities in rural settings, and which was inspired by the belief that man's best interests lay in saving the natural man from the corrupting artificialities of modern civilization.

However, Wells's capacity for a certain kind of positive, unmediated experience should not be underestimated. It imparts to his novels as to his tracts their enthusiastic and practical character, and their assurance that the future can and should be shaped in such a way as to secure indefinitely that inner glow that was so important to their author. It also accounts for the fact that, under his pen, novel and social propaganda rapidly converged in the hybrid discussion novel. In Wells's view – this was the crux of his quarrel with James – the 'pure' artist was socially irresponsible. The artist's function was to pass beyond the moral education of discrete figures to a form of writing suitable to the new spirit of reform en masse. The discussion novel – the treatment of experience simultaneously as an intensely personal matter *and* as a matter of impersonal public projects – was Wells's response to his sense of their necessary connection. His determination to assert the continuity of the individual and the social – in formal terms, of the novel and the tract – as comprehensively as possible led him logically to the 'condition of England' novel, in which the state of the nation is itself made the subject of the story;[25] this in turn led to the 'condition of the world' novel, as the scale of planning was increased sufficiently to subsume all possible dimensions of conflict. That *Mr Britling* partakes of the former kind has already been noted. But since for Wells the war was the international extension of man's seemingly endless failure to see the advantages of acting in concert, *Mr Britling* inevitably gravitates towards the latter as well.

The England of the years before the First World War was, in Henry Pelling's words, 'prosperous, by all previous standards, and yet ... not advancing.'[26] Its agriculture had long since declined, thanks not least to improved technical means of bringing in cheaper foodstuffs from abroad; its industrial productivity was relatively poor; capital investment at home, though not abroad, was low; industrial re-equipping was inadequate; and the lead was being lost in the development of new industries. Moreover, public life was becoming decidedly fractious. Politically active 'new' unions of largely unskilled workers were readily looking to strike action to further their interests; the militancy of the suffragettes was growing; the Tories had set an example of grossly unconstitutional action to block Liberal social reforms; the Irish question was being exacerbated for party political purposes; and there was, as far as Wells could see, no more of a force existing in twentieth-century public life capable of countering the destructive effects of an 'immer krasser werdenden Klassen- und Gruppenegoismus'[27] than there had been in the nineteenth. And then there were threats of various kinds from the Continent. The days had gone when, 'safe behind the shield of the navy,' Britain could think of 'all the problems of life in terms of peace and security.'[28] Instead, by the turn of the century, Britain could no longer be confident of being able to withstand 'jede denkbare Konstellation möglicher Gegner,' a consideration that gave rise to an amalgam of theories about decadence in foreign affairs, in a spate of books portraying once-mighty Britain as too enfeebled and too ill prepared to defend itself any longer.[29]

H.J. Müllenbrock's examination of the role of Germany in Wells's writings shows that he was presaging armed conflict as early as *The War of the Worlds* (1898), in which British complacency is shown up by the technical superiority of the invading 'Martians.' In the novels that followed, certain points recur: Britain's smug sense of natural superiority is ill founded in view of its class-ridden, old-fashioned, inadequately trained forces, of its general technical inferiority, and of its incapacity to learn from experience. Germany, on the other hand, has implemented a series of praiseworthy domestic reforms, notably in the fields of education and industry; but its well-drilled populace has been induced by its militaristic leaders to support an aggressive, expansionist 'Welt-Politik' (*sic*). Nevertheless, when war actually did break out, Wells was as caught on the hop as anyone. 'I will confess,' he was later to write, 'I was taken by surprise by the Great War. Yet I saw long ahead how it would happen, and wove fantastic stories about it. I let my imagination play about it, but at the bottom of my heart I could not feel and believe it would really be let happen.'[30]

The outbreak of hostilities in August 1914 was for Wells both a defeat and an opportunity. His old fear that natural man – 'invincibly bestial, envious, malicious and greedy' as he was to have one of his fictional characters of the thirties call him, 'the same fearing, snarling, fighting beast he was a hundred thousand years ago'[31] – would not after all be bested by artificial man but would succumb to the lure of local advantage, seemed justified, as did the aspersions he had long cast on inadequate national and international political institutions. At the same time there was the hope that the ensuing destruction would be so great and so horrific that it would annihilate the many self-seeking entities that had stood in the way of total reform, and act as a kind of enforced schooling in the need for rational planning if things were ever to improve. This reliance on a single, sweeping event to clear the way for the World State had already been anticipated in Wells's fiction, notably in *In the Days of the Comet* (1906) and *The World Set Free* (1914), and his 'little real interest in how the necessary changes in society would come about'[32] has been commented on often enough. In part, it is explicable quite simply as a failure of temperament. But it is also in part attributable to the fact that, with the exception of those professional soldiers and sailors who had seen action abroad, very few people of Wells's generation knew from personal experience what armed conflict was. 'Throughout the nineteenth century after Waterloo,' wrote Basil Willey in a contribution to George A. Panichas's *Promise of Greatness*, 'it was possible for Englishmen, despite the

Crimea and other people's wars, to feel that the *Pax Britannica* had come to stay.'[33] Wells's problem was the nation's: to understand, after a century of peace, the reality of strife. Like the nation's, his period of adjustment took some time, during which, in his own words, he produced a good many 'shrill jets of journalism.'[34] The substance of a number of these is included in *Mr Britling*. Many are ironized by their context, and a few are disclaimed altogether; for by late 1915, Wells had found in the war a new order of seriousness by which to measure them.

The opening sections of *Mr Britling* portray 'a soft country. A country with a passion for imperfection. A padded country' (71). It is insular, civilian, and more interested in sweet peas than in hard truths about the outside world. 'Unenterprising and sluggish' (17), it enjoys the benefits of being an advanced industrial nation without thinking too hard about their provenance. The Essex of the book is an updated version of the South of Mrs Gaskell's *North and South*: wholly agreeable, yet not wholly defensible. If it has managed to evade the physical and intellectual consequences of the industrial revolution, it has also succeeded in keeping clear of its aftermath – a well-heeled, non-manufacturing élite, instantiated for Wells by the stockbrokers, company promoters, bookmakers, and newspaper proprietors of Surrey, who derive their income from an economy that is still essentially unregulated and opportunist. But as Mr Direck, the visiting American, points out, the Dower House is not even a working farm any longer: it is merely the very pleasant rural home of an internationally respected high-brow journalist, whose wealth and potential for influence are the fruits of the very social changes that his own countrified existence implicitly denies. As such, it is of a piece with Mr Britling's habit of romanticizing his country's inefficiency, rather than attending to the connection between efficiency and the good life in a competitive world.

The affluence of the symbolical Dower House and the poverty of Atlas House nearly half a century before have a common denominator: the absence of control over the forces that create one's circumstances. Mr Britling has grown too comfortable to promote the radical reorganization of society with the energy and urgency of his younger years; the motor car he can never quite master is the product of better foreign technology; and the sons of the makers of the industrial revolution have become a generation of machine haters, receiving their education not in technical colleges but at Oxford. The sense these early sections of *Mr Britling* convey is that England has only survived so handily because it has managed to avoid any really serious challenge. The significance of even the most prominent evidence that all is not well – labour unrest, the suffragettes, and the self-destructive vehemence of the Irish question – is reduced to nothing by a characteristic, ubiquitous complacency ('And it's just because we are all convinced that we are so safe against a general breakdown that we are able to be so recklessly violent in our special cases' [46–7]); and as for a European war:

It was quite characteristic of the state of mind of England in the summer of 1914 that Mr Britling should be mightily concerned about the conflict in Ireland, and almost deliberately negligent of the possibility of a war with Germany.

The armament of Germany, the hostility of Germany, the consistent assertion of Germany, the world-wide clash of British and German interests, had been facts in the consciousness of Englishmen for more than a quarter of a century. A whole generation had been born and brought up in the threat of this German war. A threat that goes on for too long ceases to have the effect of a threat, and this overhanging possibility had become a fixed and scarcely disturbing feature of the British situation ... He [Mr Britling] had been in France in 1911, he had seen how close things had come then to a conflict, and the fact that they had not come to a conflict had enormously strengthened his natural disposition to believe that at bottom Germany was sane and her militarism a bluff (123–4).

When war does break out, it creates, initially, as much a conflict of conceptions as of arms: the Matching's Easy flower show and the guns, England and continental Europe, a tradition of peace and deliberate national aggression, a family outing in bank-holiday sunshine and carnage, civilization and barbarism. 'These were inconceivable ideas in August, 1914. Such things must happen before they can be comprehended as possible' (205).

They must also last long enough for their meaning to sink in. When war did at last break out, Wells, like many of his compatriots, thought it would all be over by Christmas; his initial reaction was to see it as a form of pedagogy by other means. 'We fight,' he wrote at the time, 'not to destroy a nation, but a nest of evil ideas.'[35] Europe's quarrel was 'with the German state, not with the German people ... The older tradition [that is, before 1871] of Germany is a pacific and civilising tradition. The temperament of the mass of German people is kindly, sane and amiable';[36] but it has been perverted by a combination of national vanity and capitalist arms-dealing ('Kaiserism and Kruppism').[37] Britain's involvement was the unsought consequence of a treaty obligation. But now that Britain *was* involved, the war would be not just another European passage of arms but a war that would be waged 'until the Germans as a people ... are convinced that they have had enough of war.'[38] It was to be an altruistic war, fought on behalf of 'the common sense and the common feeling of humanity.'[39] Its objective was disarmament, not glory. It presented liberalism with an unparalleled opportunity to stamp out 'imperialism and militarism' and to inaugurate the 'Peace League that will control the globe.'[40] China, Italy, and Scandinavia would guarantee 'the final readjustment';[41] and America, which Wells (in a phrase showing how much his political thinking was still coloured by notions of decadence) had earlier referred to as 'the freshest and most valiant beginning that has ever been made in human life,'[42] would take the lead and bring about 'that pacification of the world for which our whole nation is working.'[43]

While these ideas remained largely unaltered, they were soon deprived of their drawing-board facility by the consolidation of trench warfare and the advent of a protracted strategy of attrition. Germany's unexpected military strength and stamina, the lack of international initiative, and the failure of the belligerents to abandon old-style diplomacy when the New Age was waiting to be created, conspired to bring about 'eine nachweisbare Ratlosigkeit und Verzweiflung des Autors am Kriege.'[44] Outraged by reports of German atrocities, irked by not being listened to, and appalled by the cost in casualties, Wells was beset by the dilemma 'dass einerseits eine dauerhafte Weltfriedensordnung ohne eine Versöhnung mit Deutschland und dessen aktive Mitarbeit keine Chance hätte, sich andererseits aber unter dem Eindruck der Kriegsereignisse daran zweifeln liess, ob Deutschland jemals zu einer solchen Mitarbeit bereit wäre.'[45] In his anguish Wells, like Boon, 'could only express his faith that the empire of sanity was spreading ... He had to fall back on prophecy.'[46] So dire did the situation seem, in fact, that he was moved in *Mr Britling* to identify his ideals with God's own purpose, since a closer effective champion was difficult to discern.[47] This, as Wells was later to concede, was something of an aberration. But it gives an idea of the state of mind of a man who had worked and planned with a good old-fashioned nineteenth-century belief in progress for what for him were entirely self-evident ends, and who had lived to see them rendered more and more unlikely as report after report of what was actually taking place came into his hands.

'Report after report ...'; for it should not be forgotten that Wells had no first-hand experience to draw upon. Living in a country that lay outside the main theatres of war, Wells's principal source of information was the press. It might be thought that this would constitute a disqualification for him, and his exasperation at not being able to participate in the directest possible way is nicely recorded in *Mr Britling*, as is the realization that, after all, the war is 'over there' and can therefore, without being taken any the less seriously, of course, be treated at arm's length – as long as one's own are not threatened. But though many of the ambiguities of non-involvement are very exactly explored in the novel, there was no doubt in Wells's mind that to write a book about the war was a useful and legitimate enterprise. The battle for men's minds, as might be expected, was for him as important as the battle for territory; the perspective afforded by a certain remoteness from the action was certainly no disadvantage; and it was just possible that the pen might yet triumph over the sword, provided that it publicized the right ideas. Consequently, a fair proportion of *Mr Britling* – the 'non-novelistic' parts – amounts to no more than an adaptation to new circumstances of the novelist's pleading on behalf of the artificial factor in public life, in, *mutatis mutandis*, the familiar manner of the discussion novels.

But the hortatory elements of the book are 'placed' by their context ('One talks,' Mr Britling said, 'and then weeks and months later one learns the meaning of the things one has been saying' [222]); and perhaps only a work of art, with its peculiar affective properties, could provide the kind of placing Wells required. *Mr Britling* endeavours to explore the war under a number of different headings. But what holds it together, for all its apparent heterogeneity, is the deeply personal element that underlies its attitudinizing and scheming. The war's grim finality compels absolute definitions of what it threatens, and the chief of these is the feeling of human love, not in the abstract but as something vivid in each individual – for the feeling of love, for Wells, by its nature invests living itself with meaning. This is why – very much as a novel – *Mr Britling* turns on two private relationships: between Mr Britling and his son, Hugh,[48] and between Mr Britling and the family's German tutor, Herr Heinrich. Statistically insignificant, these relationships are in terms of human values incomparably bigger than the war that will sever them. And an understanding of this aspect of fighting is not exclusive to front-line combat.

Like Heinrich, Hugh finds himself in a situation that is not of his own making and that has been brought about by forces with which he is profoundly out of sympathy. For him, the war is not an opportunity for heroism, an existential experiment *in extremis*, a source of religious experience, a means to revitalize degenerate Europe, a course in practical Nietzscheanism, or even a simple act of patriotism.[49] Rather, it is boring and dirty, 'necessary sanitation' (245), as he calls it, to be gone through in the interests of a better peace-time civilization. Inherent in Wells's conception of Hugh is his belief, extending right back to his early espousal of ethical Darwinism, that the best of life is to be found not in strife but in its absence. It manifests itself in Hugh's avoiding any appearance of exalting the war, which he represents in a letter to his father as madness made methodical; in his consistently unflattering comparisons of military with civilian life; in the way that attention is drawn to what for Wells are, literally, its brutalizing effects ('There's a kind of hardening not only of the body but of the *mind* through all this life out here' [323], italics added); in a major distinction between the primitive and the fundamental ('Life is very primitive here – which doesn't mean that one is getting down to anything fundamental, but only going back to something immediate and simple' [338]); and in the way that the war is made in the novel visibly to violate what is *truly* fundamental: Britling's love for his son.

Part of Hugh's function is to prepare the mind of the English reader for the possibility of post-war co-operation with the Germans in the World Republic to come, and to this end to offer a conciliatory explanation of the widely reported atrocities that had so inflamed Mr Britling (and Wells) that his attitude to the German people had changed from benevolence to 'a self-righteous indignation that was indeed entirely Teutonic in its quality, that for a time drowned out his former friendship and every kindly disposition towards Germany, that inspired him with destructive impulses, and obsessed him with a desire to hear of death and more death and yet more death in every German town and home' (277). To subdue this kind of partisan ferocity in the interests of his vision of a common humanity with a common political destiny, Wells has Hugh report that 'the great part of the German army in the early stage of the war was really an army of demented civilians ... They were nice orderly clean law-abiding men suddenly torn up by the roots and flung into quite shocking conditions. They felt that they were rushing at death, and that decency was at an end ... They did horrible things just as one does them sometimes in dreams' (321). That these words are obviously special pleading and that the possibility of innate bestiality they imply makes Wells's plans for the future seem naïve should not be allowed entirely to nullify either their local perceptiveness or their general purpose. For if Wells did not have a comprehensive understanding of human nature, he had a sure understanding of some of its best parts; and he was determined that nothing, not even righteous indignation, should lessen their chances of institutionalization.

Between Germany's spurious aggrandizement of war ('They have to see the war as something romantic and melodramatic, or as something moral, or as tragic fate' [322]) and the English idea of the game, more harmless because of its lack of belligerence but in its way just as perverse ('One does not think of the dead body as a man recently deceased ... as something that laughed and cried and didn't like getting hurt. That would spoil everything' [323]), there are moments in the novel where the imperatives of the kind of feeling that Wells set such store by simply take over and make their rightness seem irrefragable. One such is when Mr Britling tries to tell his wife of Hugh's death. Another, slightly less intense, and protracted into a night of effort, is the death of Herr Heinrich. The point of the symmetry – it is in any case unmistakable – is insisted upon: 'His mind took no note of the fact that Heinrich was an enemy, that by the reckoning of a "war of attrition" his death was balance and compensation for the death of Hugh. He went straight to the root fact that they had been gallant and kindly beings, and that the same thing had killed them both' (411).

Herr Heinrich is deliberately 'an unmistakable young German' (21), though to use the word *caricature* would suggest a far less *sympathique* creation than Wells has in fact managed (though *gallant* also seems not quite right). Part of his function is to reinforce Wells's constant criticism of the English, that they are vulnerable as much because of their wilful ignorance as of their lack of practical application. What Heinrich sees is 'a pleasant life but ... not a serious life' (49), and his puzzlement is a counterpart of Wells's personal mixed feelings about a country that is simultaneously so pleasant to live in and so full of faults. As is often the case, Wells brings together considerable acuteness of perception with a (partly perceived) disregard for finding out precisely *why* things are as they are – in this case the very different kinds of historical development undergone by Prussia and England – but, even so, he succeeds with the help of Herr Heinrich in making some pregnant contrasts between the two nations: the one a 'triumph of directive will' (64) – orderly, deliberate, militaristic, and exactly defined in all areas of living, from categories of thought to categories of authority; and the other the product of less obvious political and economic power structures.

Heinrich, of course, is rather more than the typical modern Prussian. His cosmopolitanism, characteristic for Wells of Germany before 1871, reveals itself *inter alia* in his interest in universal citizenship and in a rational, international, man-made language like Esperanto[50] – an interest that causes him to fall foul of the Prussian authorities. That it does so signals a basic difference between the authoritarian Prussian state and what one might have supposed to be Wells's equally authoritarian Utopia, a difference that has been lucidly defined by Bruno Schultze:

Aber das traditionelle Misstrauen des Engländers gegen einen starken und wirkungsvollen Staatsapparat war auch bei ihm [Wells] sehr ausgeprägt. Dies liess ihn ein Bild des neuen Staates entwerfen, dessen Effektivität nicht auf einem starken und zweckmässig aufgebauten Staatsapparat beruhte, sondern auf dem ausgeprägten Staatssinn jedes einzelnen Bürgers. Wo jeder bereit wäre, sein eigenes Interesse hinter das des Ganzen zu stellen, würden sich auch kollektive Aufgaben mit einem Minimum an Staatsapparat bewerkstelligen lassen.[51]

And regarding Wells's conception of a ruling élite without any kind of democratic mandate, Schultze adds:

[Es] zeigt das für ihn typische Misstrauen gegenüber der Masse und seine Bindung an sehr englische Traditionen. Die politischen Geschicke Englands sind bis in die neuere Zeit hinein von einer elitären Schicht gelenkt worden, deren selbstverständlicher Führungsanspruch nicht nach demokratischer Legitimation trachtete. Die herrschenden Klassen in England wussten ihre Herrschaft immer durch die Bereitschaft zu sichern, sich geistig regsame Kräfte aus der Masse des Volkes, die ihnen hätten gefährlich werden können, zu assimilieren.[52]

In a word, Wells's World State is a composite of nineteenth-century English liberalism unified by wholesale voluntary acquiescence in the obviousness of eighteenth-century reason, and of traditional English deference to ruling minorities, the difference being that, in the World State, the right to rule would derive not from wealth or property but from ethical immaculateness. As Wells conceives it, the World State would exist for the benefit of the individual, whereas, as Herr Heinrich's predicament makes clear, in Prussia the individual is seen most definitely to exist for the state.[53] Though Wells's dream of a supranational, suprapolitical, centrally directed World State was derisory in its innocence, its informing intention was not;[54] and it is an important part of Herr Heinrich's function to underline just what this intention was. He achieves this, like Hugh, by being a source of bereavement ('one small life uprooted' [166]). The attempt in Mr Britling to devise a practical response to such anguish as the death of Herr Heinrich occasions, may be as defective, for all the qualifications that attend its working out, as any of Wells's other political master plans; but its origin in his acute sense of pain as an irreducible, terrible reality is sufficiently well communicated to make it wholly comprehensible. From Atlas House to the western front, human suffering was, quite simply, more than Wells could bear.

The Great War is justly named. How is its immense complexity to be encompassed in a fictional narrative, and how, when all is said and done, is such an undertaking to be validated? What needs to be emphasized, muted, deliberately omitted, or simply not known or thought of before continuities can be established and attitudes struck? W. Warren Wagar has rightly remarked that 'the war found Wells on the brink of forty-eight, too old and too well prepared for it intellectually to be made over again.' The product of what felt itself to be an age of opportunity, Wells had by 1914 long since become accustomed to analysing events in accordance with a basically unchanging system, and was unable to adjust to any other set of options than those that had looked so promising during his younger years. 'But,' continues Wagar, Wells was still 'young enough to be deeply affected';[55] and this is the heart of the matter.

Mr Britling is, deliberately, not a 'timeless' work of art as the disputatious Wells would have understood the term. Rather it is, like the journalism he pointedly liked to identify with, a specific response to a specific historical situation, and therefore theoretically expendable once it has served its purpose. Yet the feelings that are responsible for the book's key discriminations, and that allow a certain way – though by no means the only way – of rendering at least parts of the war intelligible by means of fiction, are, if not timeless, then as perdurable as human existence itself. Understandably, they made *Mr Britling* à propos at a time when personal loss had replaced dreams of glory as an outstanding characteristic of the war. But they also ensured that, in addition to whatever documentary or political merit it might have, the book would exceed the tacit limitations of its immediate intentions, and retain its worth long after the First World War itself had become a part of the historical process that *Mr Britling* was so anxiously written to keep in the control of reasonable men.

NOTES

1 H.G. Wells, *Mr Britling Sees It Through* (London, New York, Toronto, Melbourne: Cassell 1916). Further references to this edition appear in the text.
2 Jeanne and Norman MacKenzie, *The Time Traveller: The Life of H.G. Wells* (London: Weidenfeld and Nicolson 1973) 311. I have been greatly assisted by this book, as I have by Lovat Dickson, *H.G. Wells: His Turbulent Life and Times* (London: Macmillan 1969); Samuel Hynes, *The Edwardian Turn of Mind*

(Princeton, NJ: Princeton University Press, and London: Oxford University Press 1968); H.J. Müllenbrock, *Literatur und Zeitgeschichte in England zwischen dem Ende des 19. Jahrhunderts und dem Ausbruch des Ersten Weltkrieges*, Britannica et Americana, (Hamburg: Cram, de Gruyter 1967), vol. 16; Norman Nicholson, *H.G. Wells* (London: Barker 1950); Bruno Schultze, *H.G. Wells und der Erste Weltkrieg*, Britannica et Americana, (Berlin: Cram, de Gruyter 1971), vol. 18; and Wells's own *Experiment in Autobiography*, 2 vols. (London: Gollancz and Cresset Press 1934).

3 Reprinted in Patrick Parrinder (ed.), *H.G. Wells: The Critical Heritage* (London and Boston: Routledge and Kegan Paul 1972) 236–8.

4 MacKenzie, *The Time Traveller* 311; and *Maxim Gorky: Letters*, ed. P. Cockerell, trans. V. Dutt (Moscow: Progress 1966) 96.

5 *Experiment in Autobiography* 65.

6 Patrick Parrinder, *H.G. Wells* (Edinburgh: Oliver and Boyd 1970) 7.

7 Dieter Wessels, for one, has rightly insisted that pessimism is never far from optimism in Wells's reflections on the future (*Welt im Chaos: Struktur und Funktion des Weltkatastrophenmotivs in der neueren Science Fiction*, Studienreihe Humanitas [Frankfurt: Akademische Verlagsgesellschaft 1974] 50–3).

8 *Experiment in Autobiography* 83.

9 Parrinder, *H.G. Wells*. See also *Experiment in Autobiography* 177–81.

10 See Henry Pelling, *Modern Britain 1885–1955* (Edinburgh: Thomas Nelson and Sons 1960) 22.

11 Henry George, *Progress and Poverty: An Enquiry into the Cause of Industrial Depressions, and of Increase of Want with Increase of Wealth. – The Remedy* (London: Kegan Paul, Trench, Trübner 1905) 360, 358.

12 T.H. Huxley, 'Evolution and Ethics,' in *Evolution and Ethics and Other Essays*, vol. 9 of *Collected Essays* (London and New York: Macmillan 1901) 20, 82, 17. Wells's Huxleyan adaptation of Darwinism is extensively discussed in Otto Barber, *H.G. Wells Verhältnis zum Darwinismus* (Leipzig: Tauchnitz 1934), and Georg Roppen, *Evolution and Poetic Belief: A Study in Some Victorian and Modern Writers*, Oslo Studies in English, no. 5 (Oslo: Oslo University Press 1956).

13 H.G. Wells, 'Human Evolution, an Artificial Process,' *Fortnightly Review* n.s. 60 (October 1896) 590–5, reprinted in *Early Writings in Science and Science Fiction by H.G. Wells*, ed. Robert Philmus and David Y. Hughes (Berkeley, Los Angeles, London: University of California Press 1975) 211–19.

14 Ibid.

15 Philmus and Hughes, *Early Writings* 186.

16 *The New Machiavelli* (1911). Quoted in Hynes, *The Edwardian Turn of Mind* 12.

17 *Anticipations* (1901). Quoted in Hynes, *The Edwardian Turn of Mind* 95.

18 Hynes, *The Edwardian Turn of Mind* 92. Dr J. Bronowski has tartly called this 'the Houyhnhmns administering the Yahoos' (quoted via Anthony West by

Bernard Begonzi in *The Early H.G. Wells* [Manchester: Manchester University Press 1961] 172).

19 See Hynes, *The Edwardian Turn of Mind* 87–92.

20 Schultze, *H.G. Wells* 9–10. For a comprehensive analysis of the opportunities of the man of letters in English society, see Malcolm Bradbury, *The Social Context of Modern English Literature* (Oxford: Blackwell 1971). Wells himself noted: 'Success with a book ... means in the English-speaking world not merely a moderate financial independence but the utmost freedom of movement and intercourse' (H.G. Wells, 'Mr. Wells explains himself,' *T.P.'s Magazine* [December 1911], quoted in Parrinder, *H.G. Wells* 6).

21 See Gordon N. Ray, 'H.G. Wells Tries to Be a Novelist,' in *Edwardians and Late Victorians*, English Institute Essays 1959, ed. Richard Ellmann (New York and London: Columbia University Press 1960) 106–59.

22 Letter of 18 October 1912. Reprinted in *Henry James and H.G. Wells*, ed. Leon Edel and Gordon N. Ray (London: Hart-Davis 1958) 165–8. Wells was, for a time, sufficiently in agreement with James occasionally to turn out some decidedly James-like phrases, for example: 'I want nothing so much as to know how people feel, to get to the red living thing beneath what they have learnt and beneath their instinctive defences' (George Meek, *George Meek: Bath Chair-Man*, intr. H.G. Wells [London: Constable 1910] xiii).

23 H.G. Wells, 'The Depressed School,' review of *Eve's Ransom* by George Gissing, *The Saturday Review* (27 April 1895) 531. Cf. *Experiment in Autobiography* 581.

24 James, in a letter to Wells of 3 March 1911. Reprinted in Edel and Ray, *James and Wells* 126–9.

25 For a discussion of Wells and the 'condition of England' novel, see David Lodge, *Language of Fiction: Essays in Criticism and Verbal Analysis of the English Novel* (London: Routledge and Kegan Paul, and New York: Columbia University Press 1966) 214–42.

26 Pelling, *Modern Britain* 39.

27 Schultze, *H.G. Wells* 18. See also 12–17.

28 G.M. Trevelyan, *Illustrated English Social History* (London, New York, Toronto: Longman's, Green 1952), vol. 4, 123.

29 Schultze, *H.G. Wells* 3. The development of invasion literature is traced by Hynes, *The Edwardian Turn of Mind* 34ff.

30 Quoted by MacKenzie, *The Time Traveller* 298. Wells's reaction, which he knew to be typical, is of major importance to *Mr Britling*.

31 Quoted by Samuel Hynes in *Edwardian Occasions: Essays on English Writing in the Early Twentieth Century* (London: Routledge and Kegan Paul 1972) 22.

32 Bergonzi, *The Early Wells* 9.

33 *Promise of Greatness: The War of 1914–1918*, ed. George A. Panichas (London: Cassell 1968) 323.

34 *Experiment in Autobiography* 667.

35 'The War of the Mind,' reprinted in *The War That Will End War* (London: Palmer 1914) 90.

36 'The Sword of Peace,' reprinted in ibid. 15. Wells's warm regard for the older Germany will have owed not a little to his reading 'my old friend' Humboldt's *Cosmos (sic)* at an impressionable age (see *Experiment in Autobiography*, 98, 173). Wells's affection for the 'ordinary' German was quickened by a family holiday · in July 1910 in the Odenwald, details of which are incorporated in *Mr Britling*, esp. 275–7 (cf. M.M. Meyer, *H.G. Wells and His Family [as I have known them]* [Edinburgh: International Publishing 1956] 66–8). These governess's reminiscences also identify the original of Herr Heinrich: 'He was a young Pomeranian – Karl Bütow by name – a student of philology, serious, methodical, polite and typically German' [129]).

37 'The War of the Mind,' 77.

38 'Why Britain Went to War: A Clear Exposition of What We Are Fighting For,' reprinted in *The War That Will End War* 8.

39 'The War of the Mind,' 93.

40 'The Opportunity of Liberalism,' reprinted in *The War That Will End War* 62.

41 'Why Britain Went to War,' 12.

42 *The Passionate Friends* (1913). Quoted Müllenbrock, *Literatur und Zeitgeschichte* 184.

43 'Why Britain Went to War,' 13.

44 Schultze, *H.G. Wells* 51. The immediate reference is to *Boon* (1915).

45 Ibid. 67.

46 Quoted by Schultze, *H.G. Wells* 52.

47 Wells's unexpected religious phase, while controversial, was treated with all the seriousness that a time of great uncertainty brings forth. See, for example, what would otherwise be a baffling literary oddity: F.W. Worsley, MA, BD, chaplain to the forces in France, *Letters to Mr Britling: A Reply to Mr H.G. Wells* (A series of letters addressed to one of the most notable characters in modern fiction, in which the author – himself a Chaplain with the troops in France and therefore in touch with what men are thinking about Christ and His Church – takes up the challenge thrown down by Mr H.G. Wells in 'Mr Britling Sees it Through') (London: Scott 1917).

48 It is worth pointing out that while most of *Mr Britling* draws freely on Wells himself and his household, Hugh is a fictional addition (*Experiment in Autobiography* 670) whose death was nevertheless 'real' enough to prompt 'many letters of condolence for his [Wells's] loss' (MacKenzie, *The Time Traveller* 311).

49 The by-now notorious zeal of many prominent European intellectuals for the First World War is well analysed by Roland N. Stromberg in 'The Intellectuals and the Coming of War in 1914,' *Journal of European Studies* 3 (1973) 109–22.

50 International languages were an old interest of Wells himself. Roger Chickering points out (*Imperial Germany and a World without War: The Peace Movement and German Society, 1892–1914* [Princeton, NJ: Princeton University Press 1975] 129–30) that since Esperanto was felt by German nationalists to be a threat to the German language and culture, its being taught in German schools was not publicly advocated. Chickering, of course, is concerned specifically with the espousal of Esperanto by German pacifists.

51 Schultze, *H.G. Wells* 19.

52 Ibid. 24.

53 Cf. David Lodge ('Utopia and Criticism: The Radical Longing for Paradise,' *Encounter* [April 1969] 65–75): 'Wells' Utopia is a class society in which the classes are distinguished not by breeding or by cash, but by intelligence and vocational aptitude, with a decent middle-class standard of living available to all. In a sense it was a generous attempt on Wells' part to imagine a social structure which would make available to everyone the kind of success and happiness he had personally achieved in the teeth of great disadvantages. Or more cynically, you could call it the paradise of little fat men.' This may usefully be contrasted with Hans Kohn's discussion of 'Staatsräson' in *The Mind of Germany: The Education of a Nation* (New York: Scribner's Sons 1960), which rests its case on such asseverations as this by Friedrich Naumann: 'In our political activity we do not wish to imagine that we shall thereby enhance the happiness of individuals ... our concern is not happiness but the duty we have to fulfil to the nation in which we were born.'

54 At once some of the sharpest and most sympathetic criticism of Wells's utopianism is to be found in George Orwell, 'Wells, Hitler and the World State,' *Horizon* (August 1941), reprinted in *The Collected Essays: Journalism and Letters of George Orwell*, ed. Sonia Orwell and Joan Angus (London: Secker and Warburg 1968), vol. 2, *My Country Right or Left: 1940–1943* 139–45.

55 W.W. Wagar, *H.G. Wells and the World State* (New Haven: Yale University Press 1961) 31.

HERMANN BOESCHENSTEIN

The First World War in German Prose after 1945: Some Samples – Some Observations

Not surprisingly, the First World War continues to make its thematic appearance in German literature after 1945. People who personally experienced the years from 1914 to 1918, either as soldiers or as civilians, are still with us. Anyone born before 1898 was liable to be conscripted; and, if still alive, he may retain vivid recollections of those fateful times and use them for literary purposes. Others who were children or adolescents during the war may, nevertheless, have felt its impact during their formative years. Autobiographical writing dealing with that period can hardly bypass the First World War. And while the time is coming when personal memories will have vanished, there will always be novelists with a preference for historical subjects who may go back to 1914. As yet no particular bias for the historical novel is needed to conjure up the First World War; any generation or family novel with a grandfather in it must, of necessity, reverberate to the shots of Sarajevo.

The reappearance of the First World War – so many years after its enactment on the fields of Flanders, before Verdun, on the eastern plains, in the Isonzo valley, and on the oceans of the globe – tempts one to make some a priori assumptions. Is it not to be expected that the distance in time, even if it has not dimmed the vividness of the grim scenes on the battlefields, will at any rate mute or silence the optimistic ideological and emotional overtones, the pacifistic fervour we find in some of the earlier war novels? Writing after the Second World War, the faith in peace that prevailed at the time can still be mentioned in order to complete the record; but it can no longer be the basis of a passionate appeal to reshape the world, as it was after 1918. Subsequent developments have belied the expressionistic promise of reborn man; they have even revealed it to be an excessive and unwarranted expectation. Was not warfare between 1914 and 1918 still governed by standards of chivalry and humanity? It is an often-repeated observation in our texts that, compared with the ferocity of the Second World War, the first was fought by civilized nations adhering to international tenets of morality.

Hans Marchwitza's autobiographical work *Meine Jugend* was first published in 1947 and reprinted in 1976. Among the war books appearing after 1945 it is the one that recaptures life in the war zone – in the trenches and behind the lines – with the immediacy of Barbusse and Remarque. Yet, on his tour through the grisly details of the battle scenes, Marchwitza retains a firm grip on his ideological thread: only organized labour, that is, the socialists, will be able to put an end to this cataclysm and prevent its recurrence.

A victim of brutal exploitation and a witness to the callousness of the ruling class since his childhood, Marchwitza comes to the conviction that social improvements have to await the proclamation of a socialist régime. The story of his youth ranks as one of the most merciless exposures of the plight of the miners in Upper Silesia yet written. Poverty, illness, child labour, anxiety, and frustration hold the masses in thrall to misery on both sides of the Polish-German border, with, if anything, even greater cruelty on the Polish side, because the Poles as foreigners can be used to hold wages down and working hours up. To escape the clutches of hopelessness Marchwitza and some of his friends move to the Ruhr district, only to find that working conditions are no better there than back home. By way of compensation, the rays of socialistic enlightenment fall on some of the youths. They are encouraged by a few defiantly idealistic agitators to emerge from their apathy, to stay away from the pubs, and to read Marx, Zola, and Dostoevsky. They have just barely established contact with these intellectual, uplifting forces when war breaks out. These Silesian proletarians, held together by Marchwitza for obvious narrative reasons, are not, to be sure, swept off their feet by patriotic enthusiasm. For them the war is a welcome shelter from hunger. They were rejected by the army in peace-time because their emaciated bodies were not fit for service; they now go wild with joy when they are handed their uniforms. But their sweethearts and wives have a clearer premonition of what is in store for the men marching to the station under a shower of martial music and flowers than do the soldiers themselves.

Writing probably a good twenty years after the events and as a seasoned author with a number of novels to his credit – all of which deal with the concerns of the working class – Marchwitza has no problem with style. In *Meine Jugend*, he writes with his customary bent for realistic description, a style that bears close resemblance to that of Remarque. And like this famous predecessor, he organizes a welter of material by trying to keep his group of buddies together, physically and socially. Duty in the trenches and rest periods provide an alternating pattern, and a short spell on the Russian front makes for an interesting diversion. Marchwitza's men, of course, cannot warm up to any display of patriotism. Already as boys they have learned that the Kaiser regards ordinary people merely as cannon fodder and that the monarchy serves only the fortunes of the rich. The horrors, deprivations, and chicaneries they are now subjected to form a natural by-product of the system. To them, Verdun and all the other battlefields are sausage-grinders that crush friend and foe alike. A flicker of hope for a drastic change after the war is all that can give meaning to their existence. Survival and preservation of their camaraderie are uppermost in their minds, and they dread the possibility of a rift in their group more than the French machine-guns. The greatest strain in this respect comes when the *chef de bande* is promoted to lance-corporal. How can he avoid, now that he is forced to issue commands, either souring relationships with his friends or arousing the displeasure of his superiors? There is no end to the slyness, deceit, and wit needed to skirt around a thousand pitfalls. Desertion, as an *ultima ratio*, is also considered and, on occasion, seriously initiated. But the would-be deserters, instead of gaining their relative freedom, chance upon a group of Russian deserters whom they have to march back to the German line as prisoners of war, there to be hailed as heroes and rewarded for their bravery.

Finally, however, Marchwitza's alter ego in uniform succeeds, with one of his friends, in being taken prisoner by a French soldier. The latter, noticing the tattooed arm of the German, asks him: 'Vous mineur?' Enemies in war, colleagues in their peace-time occupation and misery, they now march into captivity. They can hear, from somewhere, the singing of the 'Marseillaise.' Marchwitza remembers his father humming the same tune; another song comes to his mind and, quoting from it, he concludes the story of his war experiences: 'Aux armes, citoyens! Formez vos bataillons! Marchons – marchons.' A sentimental flourish? No; rather the appropriate clarion call for one who so ardently believes in the saviour-mission of European socialism.

Marchwitza rushed to the barracks as if to a Salvation Army soup-kitchen. He must have felt regrets about the consequences, but not about his motivation. Carl Zuckmayer, on the other hand, freely confesses to having shared the popular frenzy of 1914, not so much for nationalistic reasons but because, with many older, mature people, he sensed the

breeze of a *ver sacrum* blowing into the land, a return of the spiritual uplift
of 1848; he was naïve enough to take seriously Emperor William's declaration that division among the political parties was a thing of the past and
that the era of collective unity and harmony had arrived. Like Max Brod
and Werner Kraft, he needed some time to realize that he, along with
millions of others, had been duped and was merely a puppet dangling on
the strings of political manipulators. It was only much later that he heard
of a few, such as Alfred Lichtenstein, who had kept their cool and protested the shameless demagogy. Zuckmayer had his first misgivings about
the system when he noticed that the Alsatian soldiers had been allotted to
various regiments from other provinces, instead of being allowed to stay
together. Their dialect made them the butt of unfriendly jokes and drew
down on them the suspicion of being lukewarm patriots.

In his autobiography, *Als wär's ein Stück von mir* (1966), Zuckmayer
raises and answers the question of why he had never written a war book
nor kept a diary from 1914 to 1918, and why afterwards he had never
dreamt of his war experiences, except immediately following his release
from the army. All this, he thinks, resulted from his subconscious wish
(was it perhaps prompted by the embarrassment of his erstwhile surrender to mass emotion?) not to comment on the war before he could reflect
on it with the advantage of greater maturity. The war for him was too
much a crucial phase in modern history to be left to subjective musing –
unless an individual felt confident and competent to speak for his whole
generation, a generation that, he hoped, would want to hear the voice of a
good European.

As such he now speaks, with none of the intellectual gyrations of Ernst
Jünger, who explained the war as a pattern and prefiguration of a radically industrialized society, a 'total mobilization' of bodies and souls for the
purpose of serving a hard-core élite of leaders who would, in turn, impose
on mankind a new style of life, heroic nihilism. Zuckmayer's insights stem
from the opposite concern, concern for the restoration of freedom and
individualism. To him war is an abominable dereliction of our civilization
that must be outlawed in the future. Those who were caught in it – let us
assume, for the last time in history – had to try as best they could to
extricate some values from these otherwise wasted years. Earlier war
novels by Remarque, Beumelburg, Döblin, and others found these values
in the friendship that grew up among the soldiers; Marchwitza, as we have
seen, also extols the bond of camaraderie as the one redeeming feature of
army life. Zuckmayer, the poet, is, if anything, even more sensitive to and
receptive of such emotional currents; they constitute for him in civilian

life an almost forgotten experience by no means easy to come by. He considers himself fortunate in having gone up to the front line as a private with no authority over others. He had to earn the respect and affection of his fellow soldiers the hard way, accommodating himself to their individualities, taking his share in common responsibilities, learning, in short, how to live with other human beings. He can say of this lesson that it stood him in good stead when, as an exile in the United States, he again had to adjust to an entirely new environment.

Zuckmayer's book exudes the warmth and humanity that we encounter in all his writings. The chapter on the war years epitomizes this faculty of his to generate mutual sympathy: no mere make-believe of good intentions would do; a soldier had to prove his solidarity, often at the risk of his life. Again, as in Marchwitza's account, the danger of becoming alienated from the group through promotion looms up. Zuckmayer ended the war as a lieutenant and artillery observer, but neither rank nor medals could separate him from his men. He needed these close contacts with the soldiers for his own emotional development and intellectual maturation. Understandably he can say that the four years in the army – time he would normally have spent at university – enriched him with an inestimable insight into people from all walks of life and with all sorts of attitudes. But, of course, he sought and gained more than mere knowledge about others; there was, as well, the activation of mind and soul and the clarification of certain burning issues and dilemmas.

One of the latter deserves mention for its all-too-human implications. When he enlisted, Zuckmayer had pledged himself to remain faithful to the girl he left behind, but later, he found himself yielding to the temptations offered by friendly women in French and Belgian towns. To explain and endure this strain on his conscience he resorts in the book to the mysticism of a double existence, which is both compatible with and an integral part of his one and only love. The affairs are with women who themselves either yearn for tenderness and affection or take pity on the young men, who might be dead in a few short days. They will, when hostilities cease, be punished for their 'betrayal,' will have their heads shaved and be driven naked through the streets, themselves victims of the war. In their embrace Zuckmayer feels not remorse but the inebriating rapture of being in tune with cosmic forces, carried away by passion and pity, and cleansed, in the proximity to Eros-Thanatos, of fear and loneliness, thereby restored to his true self and his longing for the undying love of the girl back home. How his fiancée accepted this Dionysian variety of faithfulness we are not told.

Zuckmayer's political awakening came late in the war, during the battle in Flanders in the summer of 1917. With the force of a revelation, it occurred to him that this internecine strife was not the inevitable manifestation of some mysterious national destiny, but rather the result of colossal political blundering, the fruit of over a century of blind nationalism, a suicidal explosion of brutal urges that might well mark the end of European civilization. Many others arrived at similar conclusions between 1914 and 1918. In this connection, Zuckmayer brings some interesting facts to light. Imbued with the desire for more information, he became an avid reader, soon to be nicknamed 'the reading lieutenant.' The army had its own mobile bookstores and, much to his surprise, Zuckmayer discovered that the prevailing rigid military surveillance tolerated an astounding measure of liberal writing and reading. The manager of the bookstore in his section, a poet and confessed anarchist, carried – in addition to the patriotic fiction of the day, supplied by Walter Bloem, Ludwig Ganghofer, Rudolf Herzog, and many more – a stock of leftist literature: René Schickele, Karl Kraus, and Franz Pfemfert. At a time when mutinous sailors were being executed in Kiel, the army was selling the literary dynamite of the *Aktion*. (Other writers have attested to this intellectual free trade enjoying protection from high above, a startling contrast to the hare-brained intolerance of the Hitler period.) Zuckmayer wrote to Pfemfert, commending him on his stand, and submitted a few poems of his own. The letter passed the censors, and so did the issue of the *Aktion* containing Zuckmayer's poems. He had made his literary début and found his political bearings. A last assignment, which in all likelihood would have killed him, was called off, and thus a progressive author was saved and able to throw in his lot with the emerging German Republic.

No one can speak for his entire generation; representation of a segment of it is all we can expect. Zuckmayer succeeded in speaking for those who had come to hate war and who endeavoured to prevent its recurrence. In this regard he is in complete agreement with the communist or socialist Marchwitza. But while the latter can end his recollections on a strong note of European solidarity, we seem to detect in Zuckmayer's last pages a trace of apprehension. Marchwitza marches into French captivity to the tune of the 'Marseillaise.' Zuckmayer, when leading his battered men homeward, hears them singing: 'wie zu Kriegsbeginn: "In der Heimat – in der Heimat."' This makes him reflect on a striking difference; at the *Chemin des Dames*, the *poilus*, he remembers, used to sing the 'Internationale' when climbing out of the trenches to be relieved. His own men fall back on nostalgic, pseudo-romantic words and melodies. The reader wonders how long it took them to switch from sentimentality to the brutality of the 'Horst-Wessel-Lied.'

One has the impression that the accounts of Marchwitza and Zuckmayer could have been written much earlier in exactly the same vein. It is, on the other hand, most unlikely that Erwin Blumenfeld's *Durch tausendjährige Zeit* (1976) could have been written before 1945. The nightmarish interlude of National Socialism was prerequisite to his style of writing, as well as to his thinking and reactions to life. He himself was lucky enough to elude the tentacles of inhumanity, but the thought of what had happened to so many others and what might have happened to him bears heavily on his imagination. He survived physically, but to regain his peace of mind he obviously had to write this book, in order to take the Third Reich apart and show it as the mixture of pomposity and lunacy that it was. The hatred that has built up in him against the crimes perpetrated by the system, the laughter prompted by its stultifying ineptitude, and the sadness of man's inability to cage the monsters before they were let loose, all combine to release a Rabelaisian power of expression and a riot of castigation, ridicule, and negation. Blumenfeld's verbal broadside is aimed at the eruption of national madness as well as at its antecedents in the Wilhelminian period. He takes on the whole century to the extent that he has lived in it, which is a good deal of it – he was born in 1898.

When war broke out, he turned a deaf ear to the shouting, celebrating crowds. What he observes is an upsurge of mass hysteria, from which not even Thomas Mann could distance himself. His own foolishness is of a more pardonable nature, thinking as he did that by joining the ambulance corps he would be sheltered by international law and universal regard for a humanitarian assignment. He soon learns that it is a short step from the 'Lausoleum' to the 'Mausoleum,' as he puts it in a typically excessive pun.

There are passages where gallows humour is replaced by a more subtle kind that reminds us of Hašek and his soldier Šveik. True enough, Blumenfeld, like Šveik, deploys all his cunning to make himself inconspicuous as a military daredevil. He is as much afraid of his German compatriots as he is of the French. But generally Blumenfeld is much more vociferous in his opposition to the establishment than is Šveik; his massive blasts at it have no counterpart in Hašek's work. The very texture of the two war books emphasizes the differences between them: a quiet epic flow in Hašek, a succession of dramatic scenes in Blumenfeld, now burlesque, now sad, mostly effervescent with simultaneous horror and humour, always staged with a keen sense for effect – sometimes too overtly so. Some episodes are grossly mawkish – for instance, when he is assisting a surgeon who is really not a medical doctor but a veterinarian; another depicts the macabre trade in human bodies. For relief we have tales of frolicsome hilarity, such as Blumenfeld's appointment as a book-keeper to a military brothel or his involvement in the flourishing sale of army provisions, and, not to be forgotten, his way of securing for himself a safe spell behind the lines by teaching French – which he doesn't know – to a sergeant who wants to become a customs officer after the war. All the while our soldier has one eye on the immediate need to stay alive and the other on Holland, the country to which he plans to desert. He will ultimately go there, but only after the war, with his commander-in-chief, Kaiser Wilhelm, arriving there before him.

A girl is waiting for him in Holland, and the glow of love is strong enough to brighten even these terrible years. There is a place, however small, for a flower in this Brueghelian world. More space for such amenities of existence will be available to Blumenfeld once he has finished dismantling the epoch from 1914 to 1945 and tossed the shreds into the furnace of his scorn and disgust (he moved to New York and became a famous photographer).

Max Brod in *Streitbares Leben* (1960) and Werner Kraft in *Spiegelung der Jugend* (1973) have written autobiographically about the First World War. Brod just barely mentions his brief service in the army. His overriding concern is the liberation of Bohemia and the founding of an independent Czechoslovakia. With Masaryk as their hope and leader, he and his friends try hard to inject into the political movement a conviction that the new republic, if it is to become a viable state, must adhere to a humanita-rian code and work out a constitution in accordance with the highest ethical standards. The dream of a 'Nationalhumanismus' that would safeguard individual freedom and the exercise of individual conscience was not realized; disenchanted, yet doggedly defending the religious components of his political credo and his confidence in the teleological nature of the historical process, Brod saw all of his efforts coming to naught with Hitler's conquest of Czechoslovakia. He had to transfer his idealism to Israel, which seemed more willing to facilitate its practical application.

Werner Kraft, another early emigrant to Palestine and a leading intel-lectual like Brod, was, during the First World War, in a position to observe some of the more intimate cultural aspects of the time, such as the activities of prominent philosophers, writers, and artists in and around Berlin. The enlightenment that Lieutenant Zuckmayer had to glean from a military bookstore Kraft was able to get from direct sources. He moved

in circles in which minds were battling for the future of German culture –
some asserting Germany's spiritual hegemony, such as Stefan George and
Rudolf Borchardt, an outright panegyrist on the salutory influence of
war, others, such as Ernst Lessing, abhorring war and pleading for
pacifism. Contacts with these men were made possible by Kraft's service in
hospitals around Berlin and by a sergeant who obstinately claimed that
Kraft was an essential part of his outfit and so prevented his being sent to
the fighting lines. But if Kraft enjoyed physical safety, mentally he was
exposed to great stress, confused and torn as he was by the conflicting
views of his philosopher friends. The influence of Borchardt must have
proved particularly irksome, emanating from a man who fitted all of the
popular conceptions of genius and yet one who was totally blind to the
needs of the people, and who outlined in the field of culture the same
élitist and expansionist goals that the military brass entered on the map
of Europe. The tensions that young Kraft endured were, of course, a
prefiguration of those that, a few years later, tore asunder the German
Republic.

We noted earlier that men born after 1898 are unlikely to have done
active service, but they may have childhood memories of the First World
War. Julius Hay, born in 1900, and Manès Sperber and Elias Canetti, both
born in 1905, published autobiographies in the seventh decade of their
lives. The three of them happen to have spent their youth within the orbit
of the Austro-Hungarian monarchy, Sperber in Galicia and Vienna, Hay
in Hungary, and Canetti in Vienna from 1913 to 1916. All three express
the feeling that their lives were moulded by impressions received in early
years. Hay playfully yet insistently hypostatizes the twentieth century,
with which he entered the world, into a sort of mystic companion and
demonic force whose grip he could not shake off, much as it bothered
him. The gods in which he earnestly believed – an idealistically tempered
Hungarian socialism or communism – failed him, and he spent years in
constant fear of incarceration by friend and foe. Although he was of
military age in 1917, the war did not interfere with his first schooling. He
was not drafted, thanks to an unexpectedly sensible Austrian decision to
spare the younger generation and have it available for the tasks of victory
and peace.

As he relates in his autobiography *Geboren 1900* (1971), Hay saw himself
inexorably drawn to the side of progressive thinking and social reforming. Having joined the forces of Bela Kuhn, he had to flee after the
take-over by Admiral Horthy, first to Austria, then to Germany. A successful dramatist in Berlin, he was imprudent enough to go to Russia;

here his uncouth companion, the twentieth century, served him with what was probably the worst experience of his life – Hay calls it the 'Unending St Batholomew's Night of Josef Stalin.' The dreaded knock at his door, anticipated every night, never came; but prosecution and imprisonment awaited him later in Hungary, where his national and humanitarian brand of communism aroused the displeasure of the home-grown Stalinists.

The gods that failed Hay also deserted Sperber – unless it was the other way around. Sperber has informed us in a number of books – most notably in *Wie eine Träne im Ozean* (1961) – of his intellectual odyssey and defection from dogmatic Marxism to a conscientious, honest search for truth, and of an endeavour to ameliorate the conditions of men in a climate of reason, patience, and tolerance. In 1974 he published a more directly autobiographical account of his childhood: *Die Wasserträger Gottes. All das Vergangene*. The title refers to a most decisive turn in his inner life that redirected his whole existence. Sperber tells us of growing up in the small town of Zablotow, in the plains between the Pruth and the Danube, a place rich in Jewish folklore and religious observances. It dawns on him one day how great the gulf is that separates the well-to-do families like his own from the poor waterbearers who supply the households from the village fountain. Insight and resolution come to him with the suddenness of a pietistic conversion: no matter what station he might attain in life, he would always stay on the side of the 'Wasserträger' and become, if not one of them, then at any rate their spokesman. He had found his ethical bearings and his social obligation, and before long he had occasion to test the strength of his pledge under the pressure of more adverse circumstances. Having tasted the dangers of war when Zablotow was alternately occupied by Russians and Austrians, the family moved to Vienna, where it soon became embroiled in the constraints of a city that was overrun by fugitives from the war zone, whom it could ill afford to feed and shelter. Such first-hand knowledge of large-scale poverty made the boy only more determined to eradicate the roots from which it springs.

Sperber was experiencing, in his own words, 'die nackte Menschlichkeit,' a realization that he considers inherent to true humanity and that entails the impossibility of remaining unconcerned with and unmoved by the fate of our suffering fellow-men. For one so young the question was, of course, to find ways and means of implementing such good will within the prevailing dire reality. Made aware by other exiles of the contrast between a worsening situation and a patriotic propaganda that still fanned the expectation of an imminent victory and subsequent prosperity, he becomes first of all a convinced pacifist. But what is he to do? When Friedrich Adler shoots and kills the prime minister, Count Stürghk, Sperber both identifies with the assassin and abhors him. Adler's later acquittal comes as a great relief, but it does not answer the question that is to haunt Sperber for a long time: whether or not force is a legitimate weapon against political adversaries.

Sperber's autobiography covers the first sixteen years of his life; far from suggesting a solution to the dilemma he describes, the author prepares us for much more upsetting future predicaments. The lad gets into serious trouble by running messages for an odd assortment of would-be revolutionaries; but, for once, mercy is shown. His mother warns him to stay away from political dissidents until he has gathered more experience. He naturally pays no heed to her good advice, because he is convinced that the time of waiting is over and that one has to join the fray if one wishes to have some say in the better world to come. Sperber was wrong, and he paid dearly for his mistakes. But this is not what his autobiography talks about. Its raison d'être is to record a boy's archetypal awakening to human responsibility for the underprivileged, to human sympathy, as it were.

Elias Canetti spent the years from 1913 to 1916 in the Austrian capital. The milieu in which he existed differed vastly from that of Sperber and was located somewhere between the upper-middle class and the jet set of our day. His mother, a rich widow, fastidious in her tastes, highly intellectual, and ambitiously furthering the education of her three sons – the other two had been sent to a private school in Switzerland – kept Elias away from contamination by common people and ordinary concerns. The Canettis cannot, of course, live fully oblivious to the dark clouds of an Austrian defeat, but for a long time they refuse to be intimidated; we hear of a journey made to Bulgaria in 1915, but not a word is said of what they saw while travelling through the war-torn countryside. The boy's mind, like that of his mother, feeds on fantasy and literature; the tribulations of Ulysses and the obsession of Medea are of greater interest to him than are the fortunes and misfortunes of the contemporary world. One day, however, he happens to witness the arrival of Galician refugees from the war zone, herded into freight cars 'like cattle.' Shaken to the bones as he is, the sight does not stir up his conscience as had that of the waterbearers in Sperber's case. Canetti's conversion was to occur later. For the time being, a domineering mother and her insistence on the incessant intellectual training of her first born – Canetti makes no secret of his brilliant mind – keep him secluded from the outside world.

Canetti's autobiography, *Die gerettete Zunge* (1977), leads up to the year

1921, when he was sixteen. The book does little to take the pulse of a disintegrating nation; rather, it shocks us with the portrait of a frivolous society that refuses to take notice of reality. Knowing Canetti's later development, we feel that destiny is standing in the wings and waiting for the day when he will be expelled from this fool's paradise; we have a strong premonition that difficult days lie ahead for this adolescent who gives every promise of becoming an outstanding Jewish intellectual.

In 1916 his mother took him to Zurich, where he was to have completed his secondary schooling. What more could he have wished for than to be set down on this island of peace that was cultivating and saving for better times the heritage of European humanitas? But what an ironic turn of events: true enough, he is spared the inconveniences of a country at war, yet he cannot be saved from a first encounter with an even greater threat to culture and humanity, anti-Semitism and the perverted mentality from which it originates. This happens, of all places, at a high school in cosmopolitan Zurich, where some thoughtless students display racial arrogance and animosity. The teachers do not fail to drive the ugly symptom underground, but the reader has an ominous feeling that Elias will have to cope with it again somewhere else. His mother, with the blindness of a well-meaning character in a tragedy of fate, does her best to deliver him to his enemies.

In one of her whimsical, erratic moods she decides, in 1921, to send him to Germany, to a country that, as she sees it, is about to mobilize all of its ingenuity and energy to recover from defeat. Elias protests his mother's plan but, as always, has to obey. Fate, we know, was kind to him and enabled him to get out of Germany before it was too late, so Canetti can conclude his account with a sigh of relief and even with a word of gratitude for his mother's decision. 'Es ist wahr, dass ich, wie der früheste Mensch, durch die Vertreibung aus dem Paradies erst entstanden bin.'

Anna Seghers and Heinrich Böll, intrigued by the problem of historical continuity, have detected and drawn the unbroken line that runs from the First World War to the second and, in Böll's case, beyond. The instability of the Weimar Republic made it possible for survivors of the old military caste to go into hiding and to re-emerge at an auspicious moment. Anna Seghers, in *Die Toten bleiben jung* (1949), has illustrated the arc – and its connecting links – of the German military establishment that swings from one decade to the next, never relenting its brutal power for long. In 1919 an officer orders the shooting, without trial, of a young man suspected of belonging to the Spartacus rebels; in 1944 the same officer, now under the aegis of Hitler, has, on the Russian front, a group of soldiers executed for disobeying nonsensical, suicidal commands. One of them is the son of the man whom he had shot in 1919. Father and son are both victims of an incorrigible upper class, a clear enough indictment of an antiquated social structure that, for Seghers, is now finally destroyed in East Germany.

Heinrich Böll, in *Billard um halb zehn* (1959), tries to set up a less simplistic and more detailed model of historical causality from the time of the 'Imperial Fool' – his characterization of Wilhelm II – to the present. He is less certain than Seghers, at any rate as far as West Germany is concerned, that the 'buffalo' type of man (Hindenburg is one of the prototypes) has disappeared and that the 'lambs' have gained the upper hand. Could it be that he has himself to blame for this pessimistic diagnosis? The reduction of men to either buffaloes or lambs is too crude to do justice to the mass of people who fall between the two animal extremes and exhibit in their lives a vast range of patterns of behaviour that defies rigid classification. Böll's tendency away from realism to symbolism is apt to throw man on to a Procrustean bed.

The optimistic outlook at the conclusion of Anna Seghers's novel recurs in Wolfgang Joho's *Der Weg aus der Einsamkeit* (1953). The central character, Heinrich Ramuz, a medical doctor, has his misgivings about a Germany chanting its way to the front lines in 1914, but he must keep them to himself, seeing that even his socialist acquaintances are wildly waving their flags. Returning from the war, he is resolved to do his share in restoring national reason and thinks he can best do that by joining the Democratic party. He soon realizes, however, that his fellow-members are more interested in promoting their electoral chances or in discussing financial measures than in stamping out the threat of war that haunts him with indelible memories. With the coming of Hitler's storm troopers his life is doomed to frustration and inactivity; his medical licence is annulled because he criticized the practice of euthanasia. In the last days of the Second World War he is shot by a Hitler zealot for attempting to negotiate the surrender of his home town.

The lesson Ramuz had learnt in the First World War but had been unable to translate into reality, is carried forward by his son, also a medical doctor and, like his father, a thorn in the flesh of National Socialism. After the war he makes his way into East Germany, which, he hopes, will give him the opportunity to work in a progressive society. He is under no illusions about the arduous task of establishing true socialism, yet he is strong enough to take disappointment in his stride and to preserve his faith. It would be hard to find another East German novel that carries out the process of adjustment to a socialist régime with such a demonstration of fearless critical reservations on the one hand, yet with, on the other, so much quiet steadfastness of purpose to overcome the mistakes and stupidities committed by the government.

A subtle link between an individual's life and the First World War appears in Peter Härtling's novel, *Eine Frau* (1974). To be sure, Katharina Wüllner is only fourteen in 1914, and though her two brothers serve in the army, little is said about it. The family takes scant notice of the war, except for its repercussions on its business. Much of the atmosphere is determined by a Jewish uncle who has premonitions of the world changing, most likely for the worse. It is immediately after the war that Kathy comes under the strong influences of its aftermath in the artists' colony at Hellerau, where a number of young people are playing with visions of socialism, emancipation, and free thought. The general drift towards conservative and then totalitarian politics dispels these nebulous ideals and turns Kathy, sensuous, attractive, and zealous for life and pleasure as she is, into a pragmatist; she marries a German who is a thriving manufacturer in Bohemia, a character cut out to embrace National Socialism, whose loss of business and life causes the reader no great regret.

Kathy returns as an expellee to Germany, still full of joie de vivre and ready to adapt herself to the hand-to-mouth existence after 1945. The permissive spirit of Hellerau is spreading over the whole of the country, and it keeps her alert, resilient, and mildly cynical. Her uncle, who committed suicide during the Hitler régime, would have rejoiced over Kathy's vitality and her skill at mastering life without the bondage of principles or ideologies. If she occasionally complains that she has never lived but has had her life lived for her, pushed around by others, she humorously understates the case: she has always given tit for tat, adultery for infidelity. Outside of our theme, yet closely related to it, Härtling's excellent novel is of great interest in that it continues the history of Czechoslovakia where Roderich Menzel (whose work this discussion will also treat) leaves off, after 1918. Events from then on to Kathy's expulsion are masterfully mirrored in her experiences in Bohemia. This novel repeats the singular achievement of Fontane: to make individuals transparent mediums for the portrayal of society, and society for the portrayal of the undulations of historical events.

It could be expected that the First World War as a theme would be frequently woven into the tapestry of such semi-historical novels as those of Böll, Seghers, Joho, and Härtling, or into any novel of panoramic dimensions. The great surprise comes with Roderich Menzel's *Als Böhmen noch bei Oesterreich war. Die Tannhoffs. Roman einer Familie* (1974), and

Walter Kempowski's *Aus grosser Zeit* (1978), works that deal to a very considerable extent with the First World War – they could, with some slight exaggeration, be called war novels. Menzel's novel belongs among the series of fictional accounts depicting and explaining the collapse of the Hapsburg monarchy rendered by Karl Kraus, Felix Braun, and Joseph Roth. Its resemblance to *Radetzkymarsch* is obvious, though the history of the three generations of Tannhoffs is not spread over as wide a time as that of the Trottas but largely telescoped into the war years. The theme, an antiquated class system relying heavily on military power and now shaking on its foundations, is struck early in the book. Years before, one of the Tannhoffs, a family prominent in textile manufacturing in Bohemia, had had to leave the country because he had dared to spurn a sacrosanct custom by refusing a duel with a fellow officer: 'A drunken man cannot insult me.' Thousands before him must have felt the same way, but few had mustered the courage to act in accordance with their conviction. Moreover, Tannhoff can point out that, as a Catholic, he is forbidden to engage in duels. He is told that he should have taken this into consideration before becoming an officer. A court of honour sentences him to demotion, and the Emperor nods his approval. Tannhoff emigrates to Australia and becomes a legendary figure in the family as a successful prospector.

This strand of independence reappears among his descendants, notably in Franz Joseph Tannhoff. When war breaks out, we see him and his cousin Rainer at odds in their views on the future, one skeptical, the other optimistic, like most others in August 1914. For the sake of ideological balance or fictional impartiality, Menzel places two more figures on the side of reason and apprehension. Dominik Tannhoff, a great-uncle to the younger generation, is an avid student of history and philosophy, proudly aware of Austrian cultural achievements; to the list from Haydn to Grillparzer he adds Freud, Alfred Adler, and Schönberg. But he is not blind to the cracks and blemishes in his society, anti-Semitism being one of the worst. He keeps his cool after the shots at Sarajevo and ventures to say that war would heap a burden of misery on the nation out of proportion to the loss of an archduke and his wife. Professor Hojer, a history teacher at the local gymnasium, is even more outspoken against the encroachment of the national frenzy on individual judgment. He places the halo of the so-called makers of history – Alexander, Caesar, Frederick the Great – against the background of their crimes and tries to acquaint his students with truly heroic characters.

Such and similar warnings are, of course, cried into the wind. The Austrians go to war, and the Germans hold them to the letter of their political alliance, infusing in them the conviction of Teutonic invincibility. Even when defeat is evident, one of the Austrian superpatriots who has swallowed German propaganda hook, line, and sinker and who fights for them on the home front, addresses a gathering of veterans, old ladies, and boys to tell them what Germany will request at the peace-conference table: Luxemburg will be incorporated in the German state; the iron-ore deposits of Brie-Longwy must be handed over to the Germans, who will also demand permission to use the Belgian coast for military goals; the annexation of Liège and Verviers by Prussia is a foregone conclusion, with Lithuania and Eastland thrown in for good measure. The kingdom of Poland will become a close ally, while the Ukraine will be granted independence. On top of it all, Germany is to receive a compact colonial empire and a war indemnity of one hundred billion marks. 'And Austria?' a heckler asks. He is told that Venice and Milan will be returned to the Austrians, who, if they wish, may also gobble up Montenegro and take their revenge on the Rumanians. To complete the picture, Austria and Germany will in due time become one nation, and hegemony must, as a matter of course, be placed in the hands of the Germans, in recognition of their superior exploits in the war.

Such details fall into line with Menzel's soberly realistic presentation. If his novel encompasses a broader range of details than any other work dealing with the Austrian situation – except *Die letzten Tage der Menschheit* – it also stands out by virtue of its objectivity. This becomes pleasantly patent in Menzel's treatment of his sub-plot, the independence movement of the Czechs. Hewing close to the grim reality of war does not, as in so many war novels written in the twenties and thirties, impair the translucence of the underlying historical evolution, and the mutinous Czechs form part of this clarity of historical movement. Menzel portrays the Czechs with highly individual strokes that prevent their becoming stolid symbolic figures or political puppets. His characters may not exhale the lyrical moods of Joseph Roth's men and women, who seem to feel the approaching end as much in their bones as in their minds. Roth re-creates the emotional climate of the times; Menzel discusses and illumines the workings of history, here the dissolution of the Danubian Empire. When Roth dismisses the reader with a strong premonition of impending doom, Menzel recounts its unfolding. The two Tannhoffs meet for the last time on the Isonzo line; predictably, Rainer, the more aggressive of the two, refuses to surrender and marches home a free man, while cousin Franz Joseph, long distrustful of Austrian politics and military ambitions, is taken prisoner.

Menzel has no quarrel with the outcome of the conflict. He abhors war and the fact that statesmen employ it to solve their problems. As to the separation of Bohemia and Moravia from Austria, he feels that it was inevitable, and he gives it his blessing in a touching expression of well-wishing addressed to Beneš in Paris in 1917: 'May you show yourself worthy of the gift of an independent Czechoslovakia if, as now seems likely, the Allies should win the war.'

Odd enough, this reprise of the First World War so many years after 1918! But stranger still is the fact that the same should happen again, four years later. 'Great Times' is the term Kempowski applies to the Wilhelminian period as a whole, but his novel is very partial to the years 1914–18, devoting 250 pages to them out of a total of 500. Kempowski was born in 1929, so the time described, far from being experienced by him, is as it was for Menzel a fictional evocation.

Kempowsky won immediate acclaim – and has sustained it – with a number of autobiographical accounts that are distinguished by a highly personal and original approach to reality, dryly bitter when he writes of his lengthy prison term in East Germany but characterized by a happy mixture of moods when he deals with more propitious situations. One of his favoured devices is to conjure up nostalgic reminiscences of his bourgeois childhood and then to move them into the light of humour, irony, and sarcasm. The Wilhelminian epoch, a storehouse of quaint antiques, must have proved an irresistible attraction for his special treatment, his seemingly affectionate, though basically irreverent and derisive eye. Stepping outside the range of autobiography, however, he appears to do less well in transforming reality into entertainment or even hilarity, and the war years in particular resist his whimsical bias. He does not have Blumenfeld's temperament nor his artistic power.

While he cannot spare his protagonist Karl, a soldier from 1915 to 1918, some unnerving experiences, he tries his best to assign him relatively safe tasks. It is the author rather than the soldier who has to be on guard against danger – against the danger of turning the war zone into a playground for the humorist. Karl and the group he is with march light-heartedly up to the trenches in France, still believing that the French grenades are filled with sawdust. It will be some time before we hear the first shells burst, for the author interrupts his story by taking us back to Rostock, where Karl is from and where he has relatives. When we return to the battlefield, we do so via the reminiscences of one of Karl's friends, who informs the narrator, sixty years after the event, of Karl's performance – or lack of it – in the war. Distance of time and a selective memory see to it that the emphasis rests on the lighter side.

Continuing his direct narration, Kempowski finally arranges for the baptism of fire. Karl emerges from it unscathed. He has now graduated into a real, fighting soldier, and deserves to be taken out of harm's way to become involved in amorous adventures at Bruges. Further to deflect our eyes from the squalour of trench warfare, Kempowski invites us to the sumptuous quarters of an air-force squadron, where a friend of Karl is stationed and where, except for an occasional, cavalierly fought duel in the sky, all is peaceful as in civilian life. Next Karl is posted to light duties behind the lines, thanks to some influential people back home. The author has by now rendered him all but bullet-proof, and Karl returns from a serious engagement with nothing worse than a mild form of gas-poisoning, which earns him a rest period in dreamlike surroundings with books to read, horses to ride, pipes to smoke, and home-leave to boot. When he returns, it is October 1918. To make certain that nothing untoward will happen to him, the author arranges for an enclave of reason and mutual aid between the fighting lines: no shooting, but rather friendly intercourse between English and German combatants. When the commander hears of it, he has the English bombarded; the latter retaliate, and Karl gets his last taste of real war. He survives, and the First World War and *Aus grosser Zeit* come to an end. Kempowski is a past master in stringing together amusing episodes. His humour is entertaining but has no moral function comparable to the humour in *Šveik*, where it serves as protective armour and as a means to attack, and where it helps to reconstruct continuously in our minds the world of true civilization as fast or faster than the cannon can destroy it.

There must be many more instances of German fiction written after 1945 that deals at some length with the First World War. If a more ambitious investigation were attempted in order to include the more casual references to the years from 1914 to 1918, the amount of material would become immense. A few samples must suffice to indicate some of the narrative purposes that brief allusions to the First World War are made to serve. The simplest is that of using the war as a chronological indicator. A passing remark that such and such a man lost a leg near Verdun may help us to see 'erzählte Zeit' in its context; this timekeeping device is particularly helpful in novels that are parsimonious in revealing chronology.

But there are more important narrative services that the war of 1914–18 can render. Delineation of character is one of them. When, for example, in *Muckefuck* (1967) by Georg Lentz, a group of veterans exchange their caustic views on the First World War, we can bet that they must loathe the coming of National Socialism and its glorification of military heroes. Conversely, where a narrator needs a bully of a man to play the eager aspirant to the SA, he will easily find one among some unreformed sergeants of the First World War. Heinrich Böll, in *Gruppenbild mit Dame* (1971), explaining the business-sense of the wreath-manufacturer Pelzer, makes him a soldier in the maintenance corps. As such, he has to search the debris left after battle for still usable material; this provides him with the opportunity to pilfer the pockets of dead soldiers and collect all sorts of currencies, German, French, Belgian, English, and American. After 1918 he has enough cash to set himself up in business and to succeed with his accustomed ruthlessness. R.J. Humm, in his novel *Der Wicht* (1976), describes the strange mutation of a man from total indifference to public life to active participation. His protagonist, a respected Zürich high-school teacher, was twenty-one years old when the war broke out. He ignored it as best he could, pursued his historical studies, and worked on a dissertation on the crowning of medieval kings. What free time was left he spent in the company of women of easy virtue. Incredible as it sounds, he has not read a newspaper for many years. The outbreak of the Second World War changes all of this, mainly because he comes into contact with a family of refugees from Germany waiting for passports to leave Europe. His help is needed, and he proffers it tactfully and generously.

There is, furthermore, the anecdotal or episodic use of war material. Arnold Kübler's *Oeppi und Eva* (1951) comes to mind in this connection. Oeppi, studying in Zürich to become an actor, falls in love with the wife of a German who serves on the western front and is taken prisoner by the French. Though deeply in love with each other, they can and will, however, not forget the husband. Eva sincerely wishes to join him again after the war. The two lovers experience an amalgam of conflicting emotions that could easily erupt in some uncontrollable outburst of jealousy, impatience, remorse, or cynicism. They can bear the stress only because they realize its humanizing power, learning from it to consider their passion as an event and episode that must be handled with reason and respect for the husband's rights. If Oeppi stands to lose most, he is also the one who has gained most from Eva, who has taught him to be considerate of others, to avoid hurting them, not to judge them harshly, and, most significantly, better to understand women in their difficult role as guardians of reason, love, and agape. Years later, Eva gets a divorce from her husband and marries Oeppi.

For similar instances of episodic use, one would naturally turn to the panoramic novels in recent German literature. My own limited forays in this direction have proved rather unfruitful, or else revealing in an unforeseen way. Günter Grass, Martin Walser, Uwe Johnson, and Siegfried Lenz make very few references to the First World War and, when they do, it is mainly to fill in biographical detail or to indicate the time of some event. There is no explanation for the war nor significance attached to it; the writer's privilege to take his material from wherever he wishes is assumed.

In some cases, however, omission seems to be deliberate. We wonder why Heimito von Doderer has, in his wide-arched novels *Die Strudlhofstiege* (1951) and *Die Dämonen* (1957), none of the many military ranks populating the scene tell us much about the years from 1914 to 1918, although they served in the field. Was it because in *Das Geheimnis des Reichs* (1930) Doderer had given a full account of the horrors he had witnessed as a prisoner of war in Russia during the civil war? Or did he feel that the society drawing rooms so often frequented by his causeurs were not the place, considering all the sensitive ladies present, to relate battlefield stories? The one exception occurs in *Die Dämonen*, when the former sergeant Gach tells of a cavalry attack in the early days of the war; the Austrian and Cossack squadron leaders meet half-way between the troops and exchange, with crossed swords, some ritual salute, like ships on the ocean. After this the battle starts in earnest. (Menzel, by the way, tells the same story.) But it is to be noted that Gach's listeners are two young men who are fascinated more by Gach's racy idiom than by his tale. The sergeant leaves no doubt about the fact that hostilities did not continue on this quaint note of military decorum; the hussars soon had to dismount from their horses and fight along with the foot soldiers. But no one asks him to tell us more about it. It turns out that Gach has been brought into the picture to assist in solving the tangled case of a last will left by his former commander and now contested by relatives. The sergeant and the First World War have been recalled for narrative reasons, serving a purely episodic function.

Günter Grass remains similarly silent where one would expect him to speak out against the insanity of 1914 to 1918. In *Der Butt* (1977), an over-extended survey of happenings in and around Danzig going back to prehistoric times and coming up to 1945 and beyond, one would have welcomed a few vignettes from the First World War, if only to provide relief from the repetitiveness of the earlier chapters. Our hopes run high when we are taken to Zurich, in the company of Rosa Luxemburg and Ernst Michels, to attend August Bebel's funeral. We stand on the threshold of 1914, but the war is skipped over with a few remarks.

It has been mentioned that, during the war, some writers underwent the process of maturing to political and social manhood. Others briefly touch on the impact of this period on the mind, none more forcefully than Hans Albrecht Moser in *Vineta* (1955). Saremo, the principal character in this 'Gegenwartsroman aus künftiger Sicht,' as the subtitle has it, is a young Austrian who develops his own independent view of life and volunteers for service in 1914. However, because of his non-military bearing, he is advised to help out on the farms and to re-apply later, should the army ever need him. The day never comes, and Saremo can quietly go on, finding confirmation in the war for his aversion to present-day moral and cultural standards, and preparing himself for a life with a radically different set of values. He will avoid, as much as possible, participation in the hustle and bustle of our civilization, disregard the superficial aims of our leaders in art, philosophy, and politics, and withdraw into a frugal existence, there to try to attain a truly humane or sincere level of being.

Some of Moser's reflections on war – as expressed in *Vineta* (Zurich: Artemis 1955), pages 460–3 – represent the conclusions reached by a majority of the German authors who have written about the First World War since 1945:

Völker wollen nicht den Krieg, aber was sie tun, führt zum Kriege.

Unter allen Lebewesen ist das furchtbarste der Mensch: denn bei ihm kommt zur Bestie noch die Intelligenz hinzu.

Es hilft nichts, den Krieg zwischen den Staaten abschaffen zu wollen, solange nicht der Kampf zwischen den Menschen abgeschafft ist.

Die Dummheit der Menschen war von jeher die beste Stütze der Mächtigen dieser Welt.

Publications of George Wallis Field

BOOKS

A Heine Verse Selection (ed.) London: Macmillan 1965. Pp. xxxv, 145
Fontane: Irrungen, Wirrungen (ed.) London: Macmillan 1967. Pp. xliii, 233
Hermann Hesse. New York: Twayne, 1970; reprinted New York: Hippocrene Books 1972. Pp. 198
A Literary History of Germany in the Nineteenth Century 1830–1890. London: Ernest Benn; New York: Barnes and Noble 1975. Pp. xvi, 214
Hermann Hesse: Kommentar zu sämtlichen Werken. Stuttgarter Arbeiten zur Germanistik 24. Stuttgart: Heinz 1977. Pp. 245. Reprinted, new, expanded edition 1979. Pp. 270

ARTICLES

'"Basic French" in Japan,' *The School*, secondary edition, vol. 28, no. 1 (October 1939) 127–9
'Schiller's Theory of the Idyl and *Wilhelm Tell*,' *Monatshefte* 42 (January 1950) 13–20
'The Past Speaks for Germany,' *University of Toronto Quarterly* 20 (July 1951) 357–68
'Again the Hungarian Hero Dies,' *The Globe and Mail* (15 December 1956) 21
'Hermann Hesses Mahnung an die Menschheit' and 'Ein kanadischer Professor besucht Hermann Hesse,' in *Fünfter Archiv-Sonderdruck des Westdeutschen Hermann Hesse-Archivs* (July 1957). Pp. 16
'Hermann Hesse: A Neglected Nobel Prize Novelist,' *Queen's Quarterly* 45 (1958) 514–20

'German Literature of the Nineteenth Century, 1830–1880' (ed., et al.), *Germanic Review* 35 (1960) 83–117

'Schiller's *Maria Stuart*,' *University of Toronto Quarterly* 29 (April 1960) 326–40

'Hermann Hesse as Critic of English and American Literature,' *Monatshefte* 53 (April–May 1961) 147–58

'Hermann Hesse's Last Poem,' *The German Quarterly* 37 (January 1964) 100–1

'The War in Waziristan, *The Canadian Intelligence Quarterly* 4, no. 3 (July 1966) 4–7

'On the Genesis of the Glasperlenspiel,' *The German Quarterly* 41 (November 1968) 673–88. Reprinted in *Materialien zu Hermann Hesse 'Das Glasperlenspiel,'* ed. Volker Michels (Frankfurt: Suhrkamp 1974) 175–93

'Goethe and *Das Glasperlenspiel*: Reflections on "Alterswerke,"' *German Life and Letters* 23 (1969) 93–101

'*Das Glasperlenspiel*: Concerning the Date of Its "Einleitung,"' *The German Quarterly* 43, no. 3 (May 1970) 538–9

'Credits – Methods – Standards,' *The Canadian Modern Language Review* 28 (January 1972), no. 2, 39–42

'Music and Morality in Thomas Mann and Hermann Hesse,' in *Hermann Hesse: A Collection of Critical Essays*, ed. Theodore Ziolkowski (Englewood Cliffs, NJ: Prentice-Hall, 1973); reprinted from *University of Toronto Quarterly* 24 (1955) 175–90

'Polarities and Symbols of Synthesis in the Works of Hermann Hesse,' *Queen's Quarterly* 71 (Spring 1974) 87–101

'Kanada,' in *Hermann Hesses weltweite Wirkung. Internationale Rezeptionsgeschichte,* ed. Martin Pfeifer. (Frankfurt: Suhrkamp 1977) 172–90

'Silver and Oranges: Notes on Mörike's Mozart-*Novelle*,' *Seminar. A Journal of Germanic Studies* 14, no. 4 (November 1978) 243–54

'The Idiosyncrasies of Dubslav von Stechlin: A Fontane "Original,"' in *Formen realistischer Erzählkunst*, Festschrift für Charlotte Jolles, ed. E. Sagarra and J. Thunecke (Nottingham: Sherwood Press 1979)

'The Case for Käthe in Fontane's *Irrungen, Wirrungen*,' in *Analecta Helvetica et Germanica*, Festschrift zur Ehre Hermann Boeschensteins, ed. A. Arnold, H. Eichner, E. Heier, S. Hoefert (Bonn: Bouvier 1979) 266–75

'Hermann Hesses moderne Märchen,' in *Hermann Hesse Heute*, ed. Adrian Hsia (Bonn: Bouvier 1980) 204–32

'Ludwig Börne,' 'Alfred Döblin,' 'Annette von Droste-Hülshoff,' 'Heinrich Heine,' 'Hermann Hesse,' 'Nikolaus Lenau,' 'Heinrich Mann,' 'Eduard Mörike,' 'Erich Maria Remarque,' 'Anna Seghers,' 'Arnold Zweig,' in *The Academic American Encylopedia*, 21 vols. (Princeton, NJ: Aretê 1980)

REVIEWS

The Canadian Forum 33 (July 1953) 95–6; 33 (February 1954) 260–1

Queen's Quarterly 63, no. 4 (Autumn 1956) 466–8; 64, no. 2 (Summer 1957) 297–8;
65, no. 2 (Summer 1958) 356–7; 64, no. 4 (Winter 1959) 713–14; 70, no. 3
(Autumn 1963) 461–2; 80, no. 2 (Summer 1973) 291–2

German Life and Letters 13, no. 4 (July 1960) 313–14

The German Quarterly 36, no. 4 (November 1963) 474–6; 37, no. 2 (March 1964)
165–7, 187; 38, no. 1 (January 1965) 76–7; 39, no. 3 (May 1966) 382–6; 51, no. 2
(March 1978) 219–20

Monatshefte 56, no. 6 (November 1964) 315–16

Seminar 5, no. 1 (Spring 1969) 65–7; 7, no. 2 (June 1971) 156–7; 9, no. 2 (June
1973) 161–2; 10, no. 2 (May 1974) 151–3, 158; 11, no. 4 (November 1975)
244–6; 12, no. 2 (May 1976) 121–2

The Canadian Modern Language Review 24, no. 4 (June 1968) 88–90

Die Unterrichts-Praxis 9, no. 1 (Spring 1976) 134–5

Germano-Slavica 2, no. 5 (Spring 1978) 374–5

Contributors

CHARLES N. GENNO
Victoria College, University of Toronto

AUGUSTINUS P. DIERICK
Victoria College, University of Toronto

DAVID JOHN
University of Waterloo

HEINZ WETZEL
University College, University of Toronto

MANFRED KUXDORF
University of Waterloo

ANTHONY W. RILEY
Queen's University

COLIN BUTLER
University College, University of Toronto

HERMANN BOESCHENSTEIN
Professor Emeritus, University College, University of Toronto

Index

166 Index

Ehrenstein, Albert 17, 32; 'Tubutsch,' 17
Emerson, Ralph Waldo 5; 'Self-reliance,' 5
Engelke, Gerrit 30
Eykman, Christoph 110

Field, G.W. 41
Flake, Otto 72
Flechtheim, Ossip 94
Fontana, Oskar Maurus 8–9, 14
Fontane, Theodor 57
Forster, J.G. 97
Frank, Leonhard 16–33; 'Die Kriegskrüppel,' 31; 'Die Kriegswitwe,' 28–9, 30; 'Das Liebespaar,' 29–30; *Der Mensch ist gut* 17, 26; 'Die Mutter,' 29; *Die Ursache* 17; 'Der Vater,' 27–8, 29, 30
Friedlaender, Salomo 71–92; *Anti-Remarque* 76; 'Friedensberichterstattung,' 80; 'Geist und Krieg,' 79; *Hat Erich Maria Remarque wirklich gelebt?* 71, 73, 84; *Der Holzweg zurück oder Knackes Umgang mit Flöhen* 72–5 passim, 85, 87; 'Ich-Autobiographische Skizze. 1871–1936,' 72; 'In welchem Jahrhundert und in welcher Form möchten Sie gelebt haben?' 75; *Kant für Kinder. Fragelehrbuch zum sittlichen Unterricht* 73, 76; 'Der nachträgliche Heldentod,' 80; 'Neues Kinderspielzeug,' 80; *Reflex der Groteske* 78; *Schöpferische Indifferenz* 83; *Schwarz-Weiss-Rot* 81; 'Schwarz-Weiss-Rot oder Deutschlands Sieg über England unter Goethes Farben,' 81; 'Weltfriedenswettbewerb,' 79
Frisé, Adolf 3

Galsworthy, John 118
Ganghofer, Ludwig 143
George, Henry 120; *Progress and Poverty* 120
George, Stefan 108, 146
Gesner, Konrad 39; *Tierbuch* 39
Goethe, J.W. von 77, 81, 83; 'Farbenlehre,' 81; *Faust* 13; *Götter, Helden und Wieland* 77
Goeze, Johann Melchior 72
Goldberg, Mark 105
Gorky, Maxim 118
Grass, Günter 93, 157; *Der Butt* 157
Grimmelshausen, H.J.C. von 82; *Simplicissimus* 82

Härtling, Peter 151; *Eine Frau* 151
Hašek, Jaroslav 144
Hasenclever, Walter 17; *Der Sohn* 17
Hauptmann, Gerhart 75
Haussmann, Conrad 43
Hay, Julius 146–7; *Geboren 1900* 146–7
Hegel, G.W.F. 19
Heine, Heinrich 80, 97, 98; 'Die beiden Grenadiere,' 80
Herrmann-Neisse, Max 16; *Hilflose Augen* 16
Herzog, Rudolf 143
Hesse, Hermann 34–49; *Demian* 34–49; 'Merkwürdige Nachricht von einem Stern,' 40; 'Vogel,' 40–1
Heym, Georg 16, 17, 27, 32; 'Der fünfte Oktober,' 27; 'Der Irre,' 17; 'Die Sektion,' 17
Hölderlin, Friedrich 36, 47; 'Patmos,' 36
Höxter, John 76
Humboldt, Wilhelm von 136n
Humm, R.J. 156; *Der Wicht* 156